CAMDEN COUNTY GEORGIA

Inferior Court Minutes

- 1794-1815 -

(Volume #1)

Compiled by:
Michael A. Ports

Southern Historical Press
Greenville, South Carolina

Copyright 2018
By: Michael A. Ports

All rights reserved. No part of this publication may be reproduced, stored in a retrieval system, transmitted in any form, posted on to the web in any form or by any means without the prior written permission of the publisher.

Please direct all correspondence and orders to:

www.southernhistoricalpress.com
or
SOUTHERN HISTORICAL PRESS, Inc.
PO BOX 1267
375 West Broad Street
Greenville, SC   29601
southernhistoricalpress@gmail.com

ISBN #0-89308-981-8

Printed in the United States of America

Introduction

The Georgia General Assembly created Camden County February 5, 1777, from St. Mary's and St. Thomas' Parishes, one of the original eight counties established by the first state constitution. The Town of St. Mary's was the first seat of County government until 1800, when the state legislature designated Jefferson as the new county seat. However, during the period covered by the court minutes, the justices held court at both Jefferson and St. Mary's. Portions of modern Brantley, Charlton, and Wayne counties once were part of Camden County.

The Inferior Court, made up of five elected justices of the peace for the county, tried any civil case, except those involving title to land. The Inferior Court had jurisdiction over all county business matters, such as care for the poor, building and maintaining the courthouse and jail, building and maintaining public roads, bridges, and ferries, issuing licenses to sell liquor, nominating justices of the peace, performing naturalizations, appointing guardians, authorizing apprenticeships and indentures, and administering county funds.

The following transcriptions are taken from the microfilm at the Georgia State Archives of the first two volumes of extant Inferior Court Minutes. Desciptions of the microfilm appear in the appropriate sections that follow. John Jamieson served as court clerk for the years 1794 and 1795, R. M. D. J. Elliott served as clerk for the years 1796 and 1797, and Isaac Crews served from 1798 into 1815. In addition, Thomas Rudulph and Augt. F. Penkie served as deputy or temporary clerks. For the most part, the handwriting of all five gentlemen is legible, making the transcription reasonably straightforward and not too difficult. The occasional ink smear or other imperfection is noted in brackets, for example [smear] or [illegible]. The transcription follows Sperry's recommended guidelines for reading early American handwriting.[1] Generally, the transcription maintains the overall format of the minutes, but presents the case citations, jury panels, lists of witnesses, signatures, and other court proceedings in a standard and consistent format. No grammar or spelling errors are corrected in the transcription, although a few commas, semicolons, apostrophes, and periods are added for clarity. The clerks entered a vertical squiggly line to delineate case citations, affidavit and petition headings, and signature citations, replicated by the symbol } in the transcription.

The original signatures of the three clerks, as well as the various justices, appear numerous times thoughout the minutes, most often at the end of each day's session, attesting to the accuracy of the minutes. The minutes contain many other original signatures, mostly of attorneys filing various motions, petitions, and affidavits as well as those parties filing bonds for appeals and stays of execution and those subscribing to oaths.

Sometimes the clerk formed the letters "a" and "o" in a very similar manner, making abbreviations like Jas. and Jos. and surnames Bagg and Bogg or Shannan and Shannon difficult to distinguish. At other times, the letters "a" and "u" are too similar to differentiate such names as Burton and Barton or Barnett and Burnett, or Barns and

---

[1] Sperry, Kip, *Reading Early American Handwriting*. Genealogical Publishing Company, Baltimore, Maryland, Sixth Printing, 2008.

Introduction

Burns. In a similar manner, the names Edmond and Edmund can be difficult to distinguish. The formation of the letters "n" and "r" at the end of surnames sometimes appear to be the same. Inavariably, the formation of the capital letters "I" and "J" are identical. Determining which letter usually not difficult when the first letter of a name, but almost entirely a guess when a lone middle initial. The clerk often crossed the letter "t" by extending the horizontal line across the entire word, making it difficult to distinguish between such surnames as Walters and Watters. Compounding the problem, he sometimes neglected to cross any "t" in a word, making a "t" appear to be an "l," confusing such names as Motes and Moles as well as Prevatt and Prevall. Moreover, the names Hall and Hale can be difficult to distinguish when the clerk made the second "l" smaller than the first. Careful researchers will consult the original record or the microfilm copy to either confirm the transcription of formulate an alternative interpretation of the clerk's handwriting.

Neither of the two original record volumes contains an index. However, a complete full-name index follows the transcriptions. The symbol ___ in the index indicates that the name or part of the name is covered by an ink smear or is otherwise obscured. Surnames appearing in the index without a first name or initials indicates entries like Mr. Smith, Captain Jones, or Johnson's Ferry. People of Color are listed in the index under the heading Slaves or Free People of Color. The pages of neither of the two original record volumes are numbered. However, three successive underscores (___) indicate the bottom of each original page. By first determining the date of a particular entry in the court minutes, locating that entry in the original record volume or microfilm copy should not be too difficult.

The book is dedicated to the memory of the author's many Georgia ancestors, most of whom migrated down the Great Wagon Road, settling on the Georgia frontier in the decade following the Revolutionary War. Many thanks are offered the kind, patient, and generous staff of the Georgia Archives for their assistance and suggestions, not only in locating the original records, but in understanding their historical context. Thanks also are offered LaBruce Lucas of the Southern Historical Press for his sage professional advice and counsel. Special thanks are offered to Marcia Tremonti for her patience and encouragement throughout the entire process of transcription and publication.

Inferior Court Minutes Book 1

The heading on the microfilm reads

Camden County
State of Georgia
Superior Court
Inferior Court Minutes
1794 - 1801

The Genealogical Society of Salt Lake City, Utah, in cooperation with the Georgia State Archives in Morrow, Georgia, produced the microfilm at the Camden County Courthouse in Woodbine, Georgia on July 16, 1958, the microfilm is widely available.

On the spine of the original record volume is printed

Camden County Inferior Court Minutes 1794 – 1801

At the top of the inside cover, someone wrote

Laminated 1952 by the Ga. Dept. of Archives and History

The minutes begin on Saturday, January 4, 1794 and continue through January 6, 1801.

Inferior Court Minutes Book 1

Minute Book Inferior Court County of Camden

Provided for S^d Court at the Expence of [blot]

John Jamieson

Chambers in St Mary's Town, Camden County, before Thomas King, Esquire one of the Justices of the Inferior Court of said County.

Saturday, January 4th 1794

The Clerk chosen at the late Election, who being duly sworn and having on the day after the Election taken the Oath of Office prescribed by the Judiciary act before his Honor John King, Esquire, one of the Justices of the said Court, appeared and produced a list of those liable to pay Taxes in this County, certified by Alexander Young, Esquire, Collector, a Jury list was formed and regulated in the presence of Said Justice Thos King, Esquire by the Clerk agreeable to the present Judiciary act (and as will hereafter appear) and their names amounting in all to One hundred and Thirty Eight, being written on separate pieces of paper, which being placed in Box N° 1, out of which were drawn for the ensuing Courts as follows & placed in Box N° 2.

Turn Over

Jurors drawn

1. John Beazely
2. Langley Bryan
3. John Coleman
4. Michael Styers
5. James Woodland, Junr
6. Eleazer Waterman
7. And^w Fitch
8. Hugh Lee
9. John Godfrey
10. Jacob Mickler
11. George March
12. Richard Gascoigne
13. William Eason
14. William King
15. William Elliott
16. Stephen Blackmer
17. Thos McClean
18. John Craford
19. Philip Goodbread
20. John Gray
21. Richd Kennedy
22. Philip Guilder
23. William Niblack
24. Timothy Powers
25. Robert Stafford
26. John Hatcher
27. John Paris
28. William Wright
29. Alex^r McMillian
30. Bens Oscar
31. James Bennett
32. Mich^l Rudolph
33. Jeh^d Bulkley
34. William Johnston
35. John Jamieson
36. Daniel Bacon

Ordered Venires do issue Accordingly.

Inferior Court Minutes Book 1

The whole of the Inhabitants being as follows.

1. William Reddy
2. Saml Meers
3. Rand^f McGillies
4. John Dilworth
5. Christ^n Garman
6. John Jamieson
7. John Mason
8. Talmage Hall
9. James Holmes
10. [blank] Hackett
11. Thos Harris
12. Steph^n Freeman
13. Joseph Archer
14. Elihu Hebbard
15. Jacob Cunns
16. Saml Smith
17. Simeon Dillingham
18. Allen Keggan
19. Wm Mills, Senr
20. William Mills, Junr
21. David Bristow
22. Thos McClean
23. Allanning Tinker
24. Thos Carr
25. Robert Seagrove
26. Thomas Lamb
27. William Oliver
28. Thos King
29. James Woodland, Senr
30. William Moubray
31. Philip Goodbread
32. Ja^s Seagrove
33. Wm Simpson
34. John King
35. Richd Carnes
36. Richd Elliott
37. William Johnston
38. Allen Thomas
39. Thos Wright
40. Langley Bryan
41. Robt Stafford
42. Thos Stafford
43. John Jones
44. [blank] Jones
45. John Craford
46. John Gray
47. Wilson Williams
48. Drury Fort
49. John Eason
50. Abner Hammond
51. John Fowler
52. John F. Randolph
53. James Moore
54. William Cryer
55. J. W. Hunter
56. Wm Taylor
57. Wm Niblack
58. Henry Wright
59. Alexander Young
60. Thos Rudolph
61. Mich^l Rudolph
62. James Gray
63. Isham Spalding
64. Jacob Clark
65. Ezekiel Smith
66. Thos Norris
67. Danl Miller
68. James Vincent
69. Nathl Palmer
70. Ben Johnston
71. Laurence O'Kelly
72. John Godfrey
73. John Bingham
74. Wm T. Stillwell
75. Joseph Washburn
76. James Neilson
78. Joseph Judson
79. James Wright
80. Robert B. Lewis
81. Richd Stevens
82. Wiley J. Belvin

Turnover

Continued

83. Ja^s Anderson
84. Jno Woodland, Junr
85. Wm Wright
86. Hugh Brown
87. Jno Beazley
88. Wm Howard
89. Wm Eason
90. Wm Cartmell
91. Jno Coleman
92. Jno Follard
93. Francis Oliver
111. Mich^l Styers
112. Jeh^d Finch
113. Peter Mickler
114. Timo. Powers
115. Zach Haddock
116. George Cornelious
117. Jere. Tate
118. Jeh^d Bulkley
119. Jno Hampton
120. Richd Gascoigne
121. Hugh Lee

Inferior Court Minutes Book 1

94. Isaac Clayton
95. Robt Brown
96. Jno McCleery
97. Jno Taylor
98. Antony Suaris
99. James Beazly
100. Jacob Mickler
101. Robt Harris
102. And^w Douglass
103. Ge^o March
104. E. B. Hopkins
105. John Young
106. Jno Parker
107. Eleazer Waterman
108. Wm King
109. James Bennett
110. Elkan^h Briggs

122. Ja^s Hudson
123. Wm Reddick
124. Ben^a Briar
125. Stephen Blackmer
126. Richd Kennedy
127. Philip Guilder
128. John Paris
129. Danl Bacon
130. John German
131. William Elliot
132. Samuel Dorrel
133. Alex^r McMillian
134. Philip Jinkins
135. Danl Mathers
136. And^w Fitch
137. John Hatcher
138. William Dawson

Examined

Thos King, J. P.

Test. John Jamieson, C. I. C. C. C.

At an Inferior Court begun & held for the County of Camden in the Town of St Mary's Tuesday March 11th 1794.

Present, Richard Carnes, John King, Thos King, & William Montbray, Esquires

The ~~attending~~ Jury being called, the following persons appeared, viz.

1. Wm Johnston
2. George March
3. Willm King
4. Alex^r McMillian
5. Jacob Mickler
6. John Coleman
7. ~~Alex^r McMillian~~ Ric^d Gascoigne
8. Jno McClary
9. Jeh^d Bulkely
10. E^u Hebbard
11. Wm Mills, Senr
12. Robert Brown

Allen Keggan in room of Wm Johnston.

N° 2

Johnston & Langstaff }
     vs   } Attach^t
James Allen   }

Verdict. We, the Jury, find that it appears that Four hundred & Forty pounds, five shillings, & Eight pence is due to the Plaintiffs, with Cost of Suit.

Inferior Court Minutes Book 1

Court adjourned untill to Morrow morning to meet at 9 o'Clock.

Wednesday morning March 14th 1794. The ~~Court~~ Court met agreeable to Adjournment. Justices Present as Yesterday.

Antonia Suaris }
     vs   } Debt on Note
William Howard }

Verdict of the Jury, find for the Plaintiff Eight pounds Sterling, with Cost of Suit.

Jurors present

    1. George March   7. Allen Keggan
    2. Wm King   8. Wm Youngblood
    3. Th^o Norris   9. Ja^s Jordan
    4. Jacob Mickler   10. Wm Mills
    5. Jeh^d Buckely   11. Richd Gascoigne
    6. James Woodland, Senr 12. John [faint]rowes

John Crews }
     vs   } Debt on Note
Hugh Lee   }

Verdict for the Plaintiff six pounds, with Interest & costs of suit.

Jury as before.

Thos Skrine }
     vs   } Eject^t
Wm Mills, Senr }
& John Mason }

Verdict. We, the Jury, find for the Defend., with cost of suit.

Jurors

    1. Ge^o March   7. Wm Youngblood
    2. Ja^s Woodland, Senr 8. James Jordan
    3. Wm King   9. John Crewes
    4. Jacob Mickler   10. Nathl Palmer
    5. Jeh^d Bulkely   11. Alex^r Young
    6. Allen Keggan   12. Richd Gascoigne

Inferior Court Minutes Book 1

Robert Harris }
     vs   } Debt on Note
Ralph Thompson }

Verdict. We, the Jury, find for the Plaintiff the sum of Forty nine pounds, nine shillings, & Two pence, with Int^r & Cost of suit.

Jury as in preceding action.

Wm Cartmell & Co }
     vs   } Attats
Thos McClain   }

Verdict. The Jury find for the Plaintiffs Judgement for the sum of Seven pounds, Eleven shillings, & five pence farthing, with costs of suit.

Jury as in the Two actions above.

The Court adjourned untill 9 o'Clock to morrow morning.

Thursday Morning, March 13th 1794, the Court met agreable to adjournment. Justices present as Yesterday.

Thos Norris }
     vs   } Case
James Allen }

Dismissed for want of Evidence.

Crocker & Sturgis }
     vs   } Debt
Wm Oliver   }

Continued by the Consent of Parties.

———

Ordered. That M^r Jno McClary be appointed overseer of the poor for this County and that the Collector of Taxes be authorised to collect from each person liable to pay Tax in this County a sum Equal to one fourteenth part of the General Tax for the relief of the poor agreable to Law.

Ordered. That the Oathes of Allegiance to the United States of George March & Antonia Suaris on Naturalization be filed of record.

Ordered. Antonia Suaris have Licence to Keep a Taveren in the Town of St Mary's, he conforming to the Law in That Case made & provided.

Inferior Court Minutes Book 1

Ordered. That, on the petition of John Jamieson praying leave to prove his being addmitted a Citizen, that the deposition of Wm Parker be filed of Record.

Ordered. That Wm Parker be appointed to serve as ~~Constable~~ one of the Constables in this County.

Ordered. That Abner Mitchell, Jacob Cunns, & Richd M. J. Elliott be appointed to serve as Constables in said County.

Court adjourned untill Court in Course.

Attest. John Jamieson, C. I. C. C. C.   John King
                                                R. Carnes
                                                Thos King
                                                Will Mottbray

---

Chambers in St Mary's Town, ~~before~~ Camden county, before his honour Richard Carnes, Esqr, One of Justices of the Inferior Court of said County, the Clerk appeared with the Jury box of said Inferior Court, out of which were drawn, agreable to the Judiciary act in that Case made and provided, for the ensuing September term. July 10th 1794

1. Alex^r Young
2. Danil Miller
3. John Mason
4. James Moore
5. John Young
6. Laurence O'Kelly
7. Wm Reddick
8. Samuel Smith
9. Ja^s Vincent
10. James Seagrove
11. Saml Dorrel
12. Richd Stevens
13. Henry Wright
14. Thos Lamb
15. Peter Mickler
16. And^w Douglass
17. John Dilworth
18. John Randolph
19. Zachariah Haddock
20. Jacob Cunns
21. Drury Fort
22. James Anderson
23. Ja^s Gray
24. Ja^s Holmes
25. Wm Mills, Senr
26. Allen Keggan
27. John Hampton
28. Jno Parker
29. E^u Briggs
30. Wm Moubray
31. Wm Simpson
32. Wilson Williams
33. Wm Mills, Junr
34. Joseph Washburn
35. Jno Bingham
36. Simeon Dillingham

Ordered a Venire issued accordingly.

Examined.   R. Carnes, J. P.

Attest. John Jamieson, Clerk

At an Inferior Court begun and held for the County of Camden, Tuesday, September the Ninth One thousand seven hundred & ninety four, the Clerk at Ten o'Clock in the

Inferior Court Minutes Book 1

forenoon called the Court & no Justices being present, it was adjourned by proclamation untill three o'Clock in the afternoon.

Attest. John Jamieson

Present Tho[s] Rudulph, D. I. C. C.

The Court was called agreable to adjournment and was adjourned untill Court in Course.

Attest. John Jamieson, C. I. C. C. C.

Georgia }
County of Camden } Tuesday March 10th 1795. The Inferior Court was called at Ten o'Clock and there being Only two Justices in Tow, it was adjourned untill Wednesday Ten o'Clock.

Attest. John Jamieson, Clerk I. C. C. C.

Wednesday. The Court was called agreable to adjournment & adjourned untill Thursday Ten o'Clock.

Attest. John Jamieson, Ck

Thursday. The Court was called & adjourned untill Friday ten o'Clock.

Attest. John Jamieson, Clk

Friday. The Court met agreable to adjournment. Present, Rich[d] Carnes. The Court was Ordered to be adjourned untill to morrow ten o'Clock.

Attest. John Jamieson, Clk

Saturday. The Court was called, present as Yesterday and was adjourned untill Saturday ten o'Clock the 28th Instant.

Attest. John Jamieson, Clk

On the Twenty Eight, only Two Justices attending, viz. R. Carnes & Tho[s] King, who Ordered the Court to be adjourned without Day.

Attest. John Jamieson

Georgia }
Camden County } Tuesday, Sept[r] 8th 1795, being the Day pointed out by the Judiciary act of said State for holding an Inferior Court in said County. The Court accordingly met. Justices present John King, R. Carnes, Tho[s] King, & John Burrowes, Esq[rs].

Inferior Court Minutes Book 1

The Sheriff returned the Venire & called the Jury duly summoned.

1. James Moore	9. John F. Randolph
2. Laurence O'Kelly	10. Zachariah Haddock
3. Wm R. Reddick	11. Drury Fort
4. Saml Smith	12. William Mills, Senr
5. James Vincent	13. Jno Hampton
6. Richd Stevens	14. Wm Simpson
7. Henry Wright	15. Wilson Williams &
8. John Dilworth	16. William Mills, Junr

Wilson Williams only appeared.

The Court was then adjourned untill to morrow ten o'Clock.

Attest. John Jamieson, Clk

———

Wednesday Septr 9th 1795

The Court met agreable to adjournment, present John King, Thos King, R. Carnes, & Jno Burrowes, Esquires.

Ordered. That John Jamieson have a License to retail Liquors in the Town of St Mary's, he having given a satisfactory Bond.

Constables for this present year

For the 1st District,   John Brown & Jeremiah Tate.

" " 2nd "   Math^w Simpson, James Wright, & Joseph Judson

For the 3rd district,   Wm Wright & David Bailey and

For the 4th district,   Stephen Hubanks

Ordered. That Mrs Eve Wright have a License to keep a Tavern in the Town of St Mary's, on her complying with the Law in Giving Bond and paying into the Office accordingly.

James Seagrove }
    vs   } Debt
Samuel Smith   }

Ordered. That the Sheriff take sufficient Bail for appearance at next Court.

Inferior Court Minutes Book 1

The Court then adjourned untill Court in Course.

Attest. John Jamieson, Clk   Thos King, J. P.
　　　　　　　　　　　　　　　 R. Carnes, J. P.

Georgia　　　　　　}
Camden County　} Wednesday the first of June ~~being~~ one Thousand seven hundred & ninety six, being the day pointed out by the Late Judiciary act for holding a Court in the County afors^d. The Sheriff opened the Court by proclamation and none of the Justices attending, it was accordinly adjourned till Thursday ten o'Clock.

attest. R. M. D. J. Elliott, C. I. C. C. C.

Thursday Ten o'Clock. The Court was called & adjourned for want of the Justices' attendance agreable to Law By me.

R. M. D. J. Elliott, Clk

Friday the Court was called & adjourned agreable to Law, none of the Justices attending, untill Saturday Ten o'Clock.

Attest. R. M. D. J. Elliott, C. I. C. C. C.

Satur^d Ten O'clock The Court was Called agreeable to adjournment. Justices present John King, Thos King, & Richd Carnes, Esq^{rs} & the Majority ware of opinion they ware Disqualified by the State Judiciary; and Doubted the Authenticity of the Judiciary, then brought into

Turn over

Court and would not Proceed to Business. The Court was adjourned untill Court in Course.

Attest. R. M. D. J. Elliott, C. I. C. C. C.

Chambers in St Mary's 8th July 1796 Before Thos King & John Burrows, Esq^{rs} of said County, the Clerk appeared with the Jury Box of said Inferior Court, out of which was drawn (agreeable to the Judiciary Act made & provided in that Case) the following persons to Serve as Jurors at the next succeeding Term. (Towit)

1. Wm King	13. Jeh^d Bulkley	25. Isham Spalding
2. Ja^s Macoom	14. Richd Stephens	26. Jno M. Fowler
3. Jno F. Randolph	15. Zac^h Haddock	27. Ja^s N. Wright
4. Alex^r Elliott	16. Jno Hampton	28. Ja^s Vincent
5. Alvin Thomas	17. Wm Johnston	29. Bnj. Criar

Inferior Court Minutes Book 1

6. Jerry Helverston
7. Jn° Edwards
8. Tho[s] Bryson
9. Charles Smith
10. Jn° Parris
11. Ja[s] Bennet
12. Phil[p] Goodbread
18. Hugh Brown
19. W[m] Mills, Sen[r]
20. Lang T. Bryant
21. Ben J. Johnston
22. Jn° Jones
23. Jeramy Tate
24. Henry Hart
30. Drury Fort
31. Ja[s] Woodland
32. W[m] Simpson
33. Peter Mickler
34. Ja[s] Moore
35. Francis Oliver
36. Ja[s] Seagrove

Ordered that a Venire Issue.

The whole of the Inhabitants being as follows.

1. Ja[s] Wright
2. Jn° Gorman
3. W[m] Simson
4. Francis Oliver
5. Rich[d] Stephens
6. Isham Spalding
7. Ja[s] Woodland, Sen[r]
8. Jn° Jones
9. W[m] Johnston
10. Langley Bryant
11. Zac[h] Haddock
12. Hugh Brown

13. Jn° King
14. Rich[d] Carnes
15. Ja[s] Macoomb
16. Jn° Paris
17. Ja[s] Bennit
18. Tho[s] Bryson
19. R. McGillis
20. Jeh[d] Bulkley
21. Jn° Hampton
22. Henry Heart
23. Philip Goodbread
24. Alvin Thomas
25. Ja[s] Seagrove
26. Jerry Helverston
27. Jn° Edwards
28. Char[l] Smith
29. Jn° F. Randolph
30. Ben[j] Criar
67. Sam[l] Smith
70. W[m] Reddy
72. Jn° Jamieson
31. Ja[s] Nix
32. Peter Mickler
33. Jerem[h] Tate
34. Jn° M. Fowler
35. Ja[s] Moore
36. Rich[d] Elliott
37. Ben Johnston
38. W[m] Mills, Sen[r]
39. Drury Fort
40. W[m] Moubray
41. Alex[r] Elliott
42. W[m] King
43. Joseph Judson
44. Wilson Williams
45. Tho[s] Wright
46. Jn° Crawford
47. Ja[s] Helverston
48. Ge° March
68. Wiley J. Belvin
71. Jn° Helverston
73. Laurence O'Kelly
49. Ja[s] M. Holmes
50. Jn° Beasley
51. Jn° Taylor
52. Rich[d] Gascoigne
53. Dan[l] Mather
54. Jacob Clark
55. Jacob Clayton
56. Jacob Mickler
57. Ja[s] Armstrong
58. Tho[s] Randolph
59. Antonia Suares
60. Rob[t] Stafford
61. W[m] Cryer
62. Rob[t] Brown
63. W[m] Niblack
64. Jn° Dilworth
65. Abner Hammond
66. W[m] Mills, Jun[r]
69. W[m] Elliott
E[u] Hebbard
74. Ezekiel Smith

Examined.

Tho[s] King, J. P.
J. Burrows, J. P.

~~Chambers in S[t] Mary's 21st March 1797 Before their Honours Jn° Burrows, Rich[d] Carnes, & Tho[s] King, Esq[rs], Justices of the Inferior of Said County, the Clerk appeared with the Jury Box of Said Inferior Court, of which~~

Inferior Court Minutes Book 1

St Mary's. At an Inferior Court on Tuesday Novr 1st 1796 to be held in & for the County of Camden. Present, their Honours John King, Thos King, Richd Carnes, Esq^{rs}.

The Panal Jury List being Called, the f following appeared.

    1. Philip Goodbread   6. William King
    2. Richd Stephens   7. Alex^r Elliott
    3. Drury Fort   8. Wm Johnston
    4. Wm Simpson   9. John Helverston
    5. John Edwards

There not being a Sufficient number of Jurors appearing, the following ware drawn out of the Talesman.

    10. John Jamieson   11. A. Hammond
    12. Joseph Judson

The Court was adjourned untill tomorrow morning 9 o'clock.

Wednesday 2nd. The Court met agreeable to adjournment. Justices as yesterday.

The Jury Sworn as follows.

    1. Philip Goodbread   6. Wm King   11. Thos Gardner
    2. Richd Stephens   7. John Jamieson   12. Ja^s Woodland, Senr
    3. Drury Fort   8. A. Hammond
    4. Wm Simpson   9. Joseph Juson
    5. Jno Edwards   10. A. S. Bullock

Wm Jones   }
    vs   } Attach
Francis Goodwin }

Witness Sworn, Wm Jones, Junr

Verdict, we find for the plaintiff Forty three Dollars & 62½ Cents, with Costs of Suit.

Signed   John Jamieson, Foreman

Antonia Suares }
    vs   } Attach^t
Citizen Ferrea }

Witness sworn, Wm Plowden.

Interpretor Wm Gibson.

Inferior Court Minutes Book 1

Verdict, we find for the plaintiff one hundred & twenty two Dollars & 98 Cents, & Costs.

Signed   John Jamieson, foreman

On the Petion of Drury Fort.

Ordered, that on his producing the necessary vouchers to be filed in the Clerk's office of this Court, for Establishing the Claims which he has now produced to the Court, that an order Issue for the Sale of the Real Estate of Robert Bolton, Deceased to him said fort, as administrator of Said Estate.

Ordered, that A Tax be Levied on the present inhabitents of this County Equal to one Sixth part of the Genl Tax for the year Seventeen hundred & Ninety four.

Ordered, that James Seagrove, William Johnston, & John F. Randolph, Esq^{rs} be appointed Commissioners to Mark, Lay out, & keep in Repair a Road Leading from the Town of St Mary's to Coleram, & also a Road

---

from the Aforesaid Town to prince's Bluff on Crooked River, & further that all persons Liable to work on the Roads agreeable to the Road Law Between Crooked River & St Mary's are hereby made Liable to work on said Roads.

It is further ordered, that Drury fort, Habakuk Wright, & John Bailey be appointed Commissioners to mark, Lay out & keep in repair a Road Leading from prince's Bluff on Crooked River, the Nearest & best way, to the old Town Bluff on Great Satilla River, & to make return thereof to the next Inferior Court.

The Court then adjourned untill 10 o'clock tomorrow morning.

Thursday, the Court was Called agreeable to Adjournment & adjourned untill tomorrow ten O'clock by order of Messrs King & Carnes.

Friday, no other Business appearing before the Court, the same was adjourned untill Court in Course.

Attest. R. M. D. J. Elliott, C. I. C. C. C.

Examined   Thos King
                                            John King, J. P.
                                            R. Carnes, J. P.

Chambers in St Mary's 21st March 1797, before Jno Burrows, Richd Carnes, & Thos King, Esq^{rs}, Judes of the Inferior Court, the Clerk appeared with the Jury Box, out of

Inferior Court Minutes Book 1

which was drawn (agreeable to the judiciary act in that Case made and provided) the following persons to serve as Jurors to Serve at the Next Succeeding Term.

(To wit)

1. Antonia Suares	13. Jacob Clark	25. Wm Mills
2. Jno Helverston	14. Joseph Judson	26. Wm Mills, Junr
3. Wm Elliott	15. Wm Ready	27. Richd Stephens
4. Danl Mather	16. Isaac Clayton	28. Ja^s Moore
5. Wm Niblack	17. John Crawford	29. Peter Mickler
6. E. Hebberd	18. Robt Stafford	30. Jerm. Tate
7. Wm Cryer	19. Thos Wright	31. Jno Hampton
8. Wiley J. Belvin	20. Wilson Williams	32. Ja^s N. Wright
9. L. O'Kelly	21. Richd Gascoigne	33. Ben^j Oscar
10. Robt Brown	22. Ja^s Helverston	34. Ja^s Woodland
11. Thos Rudulph	23. Jno Jamieson	35. Alen Thomas
12. Jno Beesley	24. Jacob Mickler	36. Zach Haddock

Ordered, that Randolph McGillis ~~and~~ be and is hereby appointed Collector of Tax for the County of Camden for the Years One Thousand Seven Hundred and Ninety Six and Ninety Seven, and R. M. D. J. Elliott be and is hereby appointed Receiver of Tax Returns for the Same years.

R. M. D. J. Elliott, C. I. C. C. C.   J. Burrows, J. P.
                                      Thos King, J. P.
                                      R. Carnes, J. P.

At an Inferior Court in and for the County of Camden on Thursday the first day of June 1797. Present, their Honours John King, Thos King, William Moubray, Richd Carnes, & John Burrows, Esq^{rs}, Justise of Said Court.

The Venire being Called, the Following appeared.

1. Antonia Suares	6. Richd Gascoigne
2. Wm Niblack	7. Jno Jamieson
3. E^u Hebbard	8. Richd Stephens
4. Wm Cryer	9. Benjamin Oscar
5. Joseph Judson	10. Wm Elliott, who was

Excused from Indisposition

Ja^s Seagrove }
    vs   } Deb^t
Saml Smith }

Judgment by default having been taken, an Inquiry was ordered.

Inferior Court Minutes Book 1

Antonia Suares }
    vs   } Attach^t
Thos Reily }

Witness sworn, J. Burrows.

We find for the Plaintiff Fifty One Dollars & forty two Cents, with Costs of Suit.

Signed   Alex^r Elliott, Foreman

Jury Panneld & sworn in the above Cause.

1. Wm Niblack
2. Eu. Hebbard
3. Wm Cryer
4. Joseph Judson
5. Richd Gascoigne
6. Jno Jamieson
7. Richd Stephens
8. Ben^j Oscar
9. Jno Jones
10. Wm Simpson
11. Alex^r Elliott
12. Wm Clark

John King }
    vs   } Attach^t
Abner Hammond }

Judgment by default.

Richd Stephens }
    vs   } Case
Joseph Judson }

Cont^d by the pltf's affidavit.

There being no more Jury Causes, they were thanked by the Court & dismissed.

Personally appeared Claude Borel, formerly a Citizen & Subject of France, who on application to become a Citizen of the United States, Hath Taken & subscribed the Following Oath, agreeable to the Law of Congress passed the twenty Ninth day of January one Thousand Seven hundred and Ninety five.

I, Claude Borel, do Solemnly Swear that I have Resided two years within the Jurisdiction of the United States & one year in the County of Camden, that I will Support the Constitution of the United States, & that I do absolutely & Entirely renounce abjure All Allegiance & fidelity to any foreign Prince, Potentate, State, or Sovereignty whatever, & particularly whereof I was before a Citizen or Louis, King of France, or his Successors, & also to the State & republic of France

Inferior Court Minutes Book 1

France. So help me God.

Signed   C. Borel

Sworn In open Court

& he was accordingly admitted to the rights of Citizenship.

Ordered, that a Tax be levied on the present Inhabitants of this County Equal to one Sixth part of their General Tax for the year One Thousand Seven Hundred & Ninety Seven.

The Court then adjourned untill tomorrow Ten O'clock in the Morning.

R. M. D. J. Elliott, C. I. C. C. C.   John King, J. P.
                                                 R. Carnes, J. P.
                                                 Will Moubray, J. P.

Friday, the Second, the court met agreeable to adjournment. Present, their Honours Jno King, Richd Carnes, & William Moubray, Esq^{rs}.

On the Petition of Mr Laurance, applying for Licence to Retail Spirituous Liquours.

Ordered, that Licence Issue by the Clerk, on his giveing Bond and Security as the Law directs, Antonie Suares, Security.

———

On the ~~Petition~~ application of Joseph Judson for Licence to Retail Spirituous Liquours.

Ordered, that the Clerk take order accordingly, James M. Lindsay, Security.

On the Application of James M. Lindsay for the same.

Ordered, that the Clerk take order accordingly for the same, Joseph Judson, Security.

On application of William Gibson for the Same.

Ordered, that the Clerk take Order accordingly, Jno Jamieson, Secu.

On application of Mrs Eave Wright for the same.

Ordered, that the Clerk take Order Accordingly, John Jamieson, Security.

On application of Richd Gascoige for the same.

Ordered, that the Clerk take order accordingly, & William Gibson, Security.

———

Inferior Court Minutes Book 1

On the Communication of Habakkuk Wright to the Court, Stating that A Certain White Boy had Kidnapped by Nathan Atkinson and Isaac Clayton and Sold by them to a Certain Capt Church. Ordered, that the necessary process Issue against the said Atkinson and Clayton to bring them to Justice, and it Recommended to Mr John King to Issue the same.

The Jury Box was Brought into Court & the Following were drawn to Serve as Jurors at the Next Succeeding Term.

~~The Court than adjourned untill Court in Course.~~

1. Jerm. Helverston
2. Phil^p Goodbread
3. Will King
4. R. McGillis
5. Wm Moubray
6. Drury Fort
7. Richd Carnes
8. Will Johnston
9. Jno Gorman
10. Jno F. Randolph
11. Ja^s Bennet
12. Ja^s Vincent
13. Ja^s Seagrove
14. John Jones
15. Ja^s McComb
16. Isom Spalding
17. Will Simpson
18. Hugh Brown
19. Charles Smith
20. Langley Bryant
21. Alex^r Elliott
22. Henry Hart
23. Will Ready
24. Will Mills
25. Thos Rudulph
26. Danl Mather
27. Robt Stafford
28. Richd Stephens
29. Will Mills, Junr
30. Zac. Haddock
31. Jno Beesley
32. Will Cryer
33. R. Gascoigne
34. P. Mickler
35. L. O'Kelly
36. Jacob Clark

The Court then adjourned untill Court in Course.

Examined
R. M. D. J. Elliott

Will Moubray, J. P.
Thos King, J. P.
J. Burrows, J. P.
R. Carnes, J. P.
John King, J. P.

At an Inferior Court held in & for the County of Camden on Wednesday the first day of November 1797. Present, their Honours Thos King, Will Moubray, Jno Burrows, & Richd Carnes, Esq^{rs}.

The Venire Being Called, the following appeared.

1. R. McGillis
2. Will Moubray
3. Richd Gascoigne
4. Thos Rudulph
5. Isom Spalding

There not being a Sufficient Number of Jurors, the following were Sumoned out of the Bystanders.

1. Wm Clark
2. Wm Simpson
5. Alex^r Elliott
6. Ja^s Woodland

Inferior Court Minutes Book 1

    3. A. Suares   7. Joseph Judson
    4. Wm Jones   8. Jno Jamieson
                                               9. Ja^s N. Wright

Ja^s Seagrove }
    vs   } Debt
Saml Smith }

The Defendant failing to appear, Ordered on Motion of Mr Ja^s Jordan

———

Jordan, Att^y in fact for the Plf, that the Original & additional Bail Bonds be Assigned.

There being no Jury Business, they were dismissed untill tomorrow Ten O'clock & the Court adjourned untill Same time.

R. M. D. J. Elliott   Thos King, J. P.
                                            J. Burrows, J. P.
                                            Will Moubray, J. P.
                                            R. Carnes, J. P.

Thursday, the Second, the Court Met Agreeable to Adjournment, Justises present as yesterday.

Jury Sworn.

      1. Richd Gascoigne   5. Antonie Suares   9. Jno Jamieson
      2. Thos Rudulph   6. Ja^s Jordan   10. J. N. Wright
      3. Wm Clark   7. Alex^r Elliott   11. Robt Brown
      4. Wm Simpson   8. Jo^s Judson   12. Wm Ashley

John King   }
    vs   } Attach^t
Abn^r Hammond }

Verdict for Plaintiff Four Hundred & Twenty Eight Dollars & fifty Seven Cents, & Interest Since the twenty fourth of Decr One Thousand Seven hundred & Eighty three on Said Sum, & Costs of Suit.

Signed   John Jamieson, foreman

———

There being no more Jury Business, they were thanked by the Court & Dismissed.

Richd Stephens }
    vs   } Case
Joseph Judson }

Inferior Court Minutes Book 1

This being the third Term, & the Caus having been Called from the Commencement to the adjournment of this Term, & the Plf being three times Called to Prosicute his Suit, & failing to appeared, & no person Stating any objection, the Same is Dismissed.

The Court having taken into Consideration the Petition & account of Ja^s Woodland, Coroner, are of opinion that the Charges are Justly Due him, but the County Not Liable for them.

The Same on John Jamieson, amounting to Eleven D^{rs} & 50 Cents. Admitted.

The Same on R. McGillis, Sheriff, for Guardin & Dieting Prisoners, Amounting to Three hundred & Eighteen D^{rs} & 77½ Cents. Admitted.

Ordered. That the above admitted accounts be paid by Anuel Installments, not Exceeding two thirds of the County Tax.

Ordered. That part of the Order of this Court Novr Term Last be Repealed sofar as Directs the Road Leding from the Town

---

of St Mary's to Old Town Bluff on Great Satilla River, Cossing at Prince's Bluff on Crooked River, & be Left to the Commissioners then appointed, "& that Hugh Brown is hereby appointed a Commissioner in Addition to the former," & that they are hereby authorized to Lay out the said Road the Nearest, Best, & Most Convenient way across s^d Crooked River.

The Court then adjourned untill Court in Course.

Attest. R. M. D. J. Elliott, C. I. C. C. C.   Thos King, J. P.
　　　　　　　　　　　　　　　　　　　　　　Will Moubray, J. P.
　　　　　　　　　　　　　　　　　　　　　　R. Carnes, J. P.

St Mary's May 2nd 1798

At the Clerk's office, Before Richard Carnes, Thos Carnes, & William Moubray, Esq^{rs}, Judges of the Inferior Court, the following persons Were drawn to Serve as Jurors for the Said Court at the Next Succeeding Term.

  1. William Elliott   3. Wilson Williams
  2. Allen Thomas   4. Ja^s Woodland, Senr

---

   5. Jacob Mickler   20. Ja^s Bennet
   6. Robt Brown   21. Wm Johnston
   7. Jno Crofford   22. Wm Simpson
   8. Jo^s More   23. L. O'Kelly
   9. Thomas Wright   24. Thos Rudolph

Inferior Court Minutes Book 1

10. Jn⁰ Helverston
11. Jaˢ Wright
12. Jn⁰ Hampton
13. Isaac Cleaton
14. Joseph Judson
15. Wᵐ Niblack
16. Jn⁰ Jamieson
17. Jeremiah Helvison
18. Antoine Suares
19. Elihu Hebbard

25. Charles Smith
26. Daniel Mathers
27. Robᵗ Stafford
28. R. McGillis
29. Henry Hart
30. Jn⁰ Beesley
31. Alexʳ Elliott
32. Jn⁰ Brown
33. Habᵏ Wright
34. Stepen Eubank
35. Jaˢ Woodland, Junʳ
36. Wᵐ Gormon

Attest.
Isaac Crews, C. I. C. C. C.

R. Carnes, J. P.
Will Moubray, J. P.

Sᵗ Mary's, May 16ᵗʰ 1798

Ordered, that Randolph McGillis be and is hereby Appointed Collector of Taxes for the County of Camden for the Year One Thousand Seven hundred & Ninety Eight and Isaac Crews be and is hereby appointed Receiver of Tax Returns for the Same Year.

Attest.
Isaac Crews, C. I. C. C. C.

R. Carnes, J. P.
Will Moubray, J. P.
J. Burrows, J. P.

At an Inferior Court in & for the County of Camden, in the Town of Sᵗ Mary's, on Friday the first day of June One Thousand Seven Hundred & Ninety Eight. Present, Their Honours Thoˢ King, William Moubray, & John Burrows, Esqʳˢ, Justices of Said Court.

The Venire being Called, the Following Jurors Answered.

1. Wilson Williams
2. Jacob Mickler
3. Joˢ More
4. Jaˢ N. Wright
5. Jn⁰ Jamieson
6. Antoine Suares

7. Elihu Hebbard
8. William Johnston
9. R. McGillis
10. Alexʳ Elliott
11. Wiliam Simpson
12. Thoˢ Wright

There Not Being a Sufficient Number of Jurors present, the following by Standers were paneled.

William King & Alexʳ Candlesh

Inferior Court Minutes Book 1

Wm Simpson }
    vs   } Case
Judson   }

Witness Sworn, William Cryer.

Verdict for plaintiff.

We, the Jurors, find for plaintiff, the Def^{dt} Not Considered as a public Officer, but an Individual, Eighty Seven Dollars & twenty five Cents, and Cost.

[blot] Sign^d Wm Johnston, Foreman

Jurors Sworn in the Above Cause.

---

1. Wilson Williams	5. Ja^s N. Wright (struck through)	9. R. McGillis
2. Jacob Mickler	5. Jno Jamieson	10. Alex^r Elliott
3. James Moore	6. Antoin Suares	11. Wm King
4. Ja^s N. Wright	7. Elihu Hebbard	12. Alex^r Cardlish
	8. Wm Johnston	

Reddin Blunt   }   Walter Drummond }
    vs   }Assault & Bat   vs   } Assault
Walter Drummond & Wife }   Reddin Blunt &   }
                                                     Charlton Mizels   }

The Above Causes being Examined by the Court, are of Opinion that Said Suits are not Recognizable before them and are Dismissed.

Court Was adjourned Untill tomorrow Ten o'clock.

Attest.   Thos King, J. P.
Isaac Crews, C. I. C. C. C.   J. Burrows, J. P.

Saturday, the Second day of June, the Court met According to Adjournment, present their honours Thos King, Jno Burrowes, & Richd Carnes, Esq^{rs}, Justices of the Said Court.

Antoine Suares }
    vs   } Attacht
Arch^d Randall }

Debt on Notes & the Signature proved by the Oath of John Patterson in Open Court.

Inferior Court Minutes Book 1

On the Application of Joseph Judson for Tavern Licence. Ordered, the Cleark Issue the License, he Complying with the Law.

Ordered, that a County Tax be levied on the present Inhabitance of this County Equal to One Sixth part of the General Tax for the Year Seventeen Hundred and Ninety Eight.

Ordered, that the Accompt of William Johnston ~~be paid~~ for One hundred and Seventeen Dollars & thery Cents, Admitted be paid by Installments, One third Annually.

Ordered, that Thos Cryer, Ja^s M. Lindsay, & Jacob Mickler be appointed Commissioners of a Road to be Laid out the Best & Nearest Direct Way from the Town of Saint Mary's to Join a Road from Huckleberry Bluff on Great Satilla River. And, they are hereby appointed Overseers of the sd Road & Authorized to Call out the Inhabitance of the first, Second, & ~~Fourth~~ Fourth District of Said County Agreeable to the Road law of this State.

Ordered. That Jno Baily, John Campbell, & Hugh Brown be Appointed Commissioners to [blot] Mark and lay out a Road, from a Crossing place on Crooked River pointed out by the aforesaid Baily, the Nearest & Best way to huckleberry Bluff on Great Satilla River. Likewise, the affore Mentioned Gentle^s Are Appointed Overseers of Said Road and Are Authorized to Call out the Inhabitens of the Second and third Districts Agreeable to the Road Law of this State to Cear the Same at Least fifteen feet Wide.

Ordered. That Elihu Hebbard & Wm Gibson, Esq^{rs} be and is hereby Appointed Overseers of the Poor for the first District; for the Second District, Thos Cryer; for the Third, John Campbell; for the fourth, Thos King & William Johnston, Esq^{rs}; for the fifth, Hugh Brown.

The Court the Adjourned Untill Court in Course.

Attest.	Thos King, J. P.
Isaac Crews, Clk	R. Carnes, J. P.

St Mary's Saturday September 1st 1798 at the Clerk's Office

Before their Honours William Moubray & John Burrows, Esq^{rs}, Judges of the Inferior Court, the following persons were Drawn to Serve as Jurors for the Next Succeeding Term of Said Court.

1. Langley Bryant	14. Ja^s Vincent	25. Wm Simpson
2. Jacob Clark	15. Wm King	26. Thos Rudulph
3. Ja^s Seagrove	16. Wm Moubray	27. Ja^s Bennet
4. Ja^s MaComb	17. Jeremiah Helverston	28. R. McGillis
5. Jno Jones	18. Richd Carnes	29. Wm Johnston
6. Richd Stephens	19. Drury Fort	30. Ja^s Helverston

Inferior Court Minutes Book 1

7. Hugh Brown	20. Jn° Gorman	31. Danl Mather
8. Zachariah Haddock	21. Wm Cryer	32. Ja^s Moore
9. Isham Spaulding	22. Wilson Williams	33. Thos Wright
10. Richd Gascoigne	23. John Hampton	34. Wm Niblack
11. Philip Goodbread	24. Ja^s Wright	35. John Busby
12. Peter Mickler	25. Alex^r Elliott	36. Stephen Eubanks

Ordered the Venire to Issue.

Attest. Isaac Crews, Clk

At an inferior Court held in and for the County of Camden at St Mary's, On Thursday the first Day of November 1798. Present, their Honours John King, Thos King, & R. Carnes, Esq^{rs}, Judges of Said Court.

Cadwallader Evens }
    vs   } Attach^t
Robert Morris }

Judgment by Default.

Joseph Rain, a Young man, a Native of the State of Georgia, & wished he left the Said State with his father, Returned to the County of Camden before he was Twenty One Years of Age.

Where fore it is Ordered, that the Said Joseph Rain do take the Said Oath in Open Court, which he did Accordingly.

Mr Jamieson, Att^y fore Mrs Patty Bemiss, Administratrix of the Estate of Captain Eleazer Bemiss, Deceased, petitioned the Court for leave to sell two Lots of Land in the Town of Brunswick, in the County of Glyn, Stating that such sale would be of Benefit to the Heirs & Creditors of Said Estate.

Ordered, that Notice hereof be Given

---

in One of the Gazettes of this State for Nine Months Before an Order Absolute Can be Made Agreeable to Law.

Court then Adjourned till tomorrow Morning Nine O'clock.

Attest.   John King, J. P.
Isaac Crews, Clk   R. Carnes, J. P.
                                            Thos King, J. P.

Inferior Court Minutes Book 1

Friday, the Second, the Court met According to Adjournment. Judges present as Yesterday.

On the petition of Neddy Rogers.

Ordered, that the Indentures be Cansiled in presence of the Clerk.

~~William Mickler~~ }
   ~~vs~~   } ~~Debt~~
~~John Gorman~~   }

The Above Suit being Called, and mad Default. Where fore it is Ordered, that the Sheriff Assign Over the bail Bond to the plaintiff.

William Mickler }
   vs   } Debt
John Gorman   }

It appearing by the return of the Sheriff, That the defendant in the Above Cause has Given Bail for his

———

Appearance at this Term, and being three times Called, and his Securities being also three times Called to produce him, or to enter Special bail, they made Default. Where upon it is Ordered, that the Bail Bond be Assigned to the use of the Plaintiff, in terms of the Act in such cases, on Motion of Mr Jamieson, Att^y for the Plaintiff.

Ordered, that so much of the Order made on the first of June Last, as respects the Road being laid out from the Crossing place on Crooked River to Huckleberry bluff of Satilla River, be Repealed and that the Said Road be Laid out the Nearest Convenien way to Inkechee Bluff on Satilla River, and that William Ashley be Appointed a Commissioner & Overseer of Said Road in Lue of Mr Hugh Brown, who Refused to Serve.

James N. Wright }
   vs   } Attach^t
Samuel Smith   }

It appearing by the Return of the Sheriff in the Above Cause, that a horse Saddle & Bridle has been Attached as the property of the Defendant. On Motion of

———

of Mr Jamieson, Att^y for the plaintiff. It is Ordered, that the Said Horse Saddle and Bridle by Sold by the Sheriff of the County, and that the Money Arising from such sale shall be lodged in the Clerk's office of this County, in the Terms of the Act of Assembly in such cases made and provided.

Inferior Court Minutes Book 1

On the petition of John Bailey, praying to be admitted a Citizen of the United States. It is Ordered, that the following Oath be administered to him. I, John Bailey, in presence of Almighty God, Solemnly Swear that I have Resided five years in the United States and One in this State and that I will support the Constitution of the United States and that I do absolutely and entirely renounce and abjure all allegiance and

---

and fidelity to any foreign prince, potentate, State, or Sovereignty Whatever, and particularly the King of Spain whereof I was before a Citizen & subject.

Sworn to in open }	
Court Novr 2nd 1798 }	John Bailey
Isaac Crews, C. I. C. C. C. }	

Ordered, that a road be Laid out from Old Town Bluff on Great Satilla River to the Glynn County line, that is the post Road the Nearest & best way to Said Glynn County Line, & that John Dudley, John Brown, & Wm Talley be Appointed Commissioners & Overseers of said Road.

On the petition of Elizabeth Rudulph, Thomas Wright, Joseph Dove, Eve Wright, S. Caulkins & C°, John Mellaine, ~~Hugh~~ Hays & Vickary, & Richard Gascoigne, & Harmen Courter, for Tavern Licence. Ordered, that their Petitions be Granted, on their Complying with the Law in Such Cases & that the Clerk take Security.

On the Petition of John Hopkins, praying Assistance as an Infirm poor man, , Ordered, that the Overseer of the poor furnish hime with One Dollar in provisions ~~for which~~ per week untill the Next term of the Inferior Court and the Collector of the County Tax is hereby required to furnish the Overseer Accordingly.

Ordered, that the Account of James M. Lindsay be Admitted for Twelve Dollars, & ~~paid~~.

The Court then Adjourned till tomorrow Eleven O'lock.

Attest.	John King, J. P.
Isaac Crews, Clk	Thos King, J. P.
	R. Carnes, J. P.

Saturday, the third day of November 1798, the Court Met According to Adjournment. Justices present as Yesterday.

Ordered, that a Poor Tax be Laid on the Inhabitants of this County, which shall be Equal to One fourteenth of the General Tax for the present Year.

Inferior Court Minutes Book 1

On the petition of Wm Holsrighter & Philip Warner, praying to become Citizens of the United States. It is ordered, that the following Oath be administered to them. We, Wm Holsrighter & Philip Warner, do solemnly swear that we have Resided five years within the Jurisdiction of the United States & One year in this State, and that we will support the Constitution of the United States, and that we do absolutely and entirely renounce and abjure all allegiance and fidelity to any foreign prince or potentate or Sovereignty Whatever and particularly the Emperor of Germany, whereof we were before Citizens & Subjects.

Sworn to in Open   }
Court Novr 3rd 1798 }

Willm Holsroeghter
Philip Werner

Isaac Crews, C. I. C. C. C.

———

Court then Adjourned Untill Court in Course.

Attest. Isaac Crews, C. I. C. C. C.

St Mary's 20th March 1799, at the Clerk's office.

The Honb^{le} John King & James Seagrove, Esq^{rs}, Judges of the Inferior Court, Corrected the Jury list and Drew the following persons to Serve as Jurors for the Next term of Said Court. (Viz)

1. Franes Young
2. Charlton Miszells
3. Wm Gorman
4. Hob^k Wright
5. Joseph Morgan
6. Ja^s Vincent
7. John Travank
8. [blank] Colder
9. Courtes Higingbotham
10. John Jones
11. Zahariah Haddock
12. Wm Smith
13. William Motes
14. James Hayes
15. Langley Bryant
16. John Haller
17. Richd Lang
18. James MaComb
19. Mathew Motes, Junr
20. Silas Lusby
21. Joseph Bains
22. John Hampton
23. William King
24. Danl Mather

Attest. Isaac Crews, C. I. C. C. C.   Ja^s Seagrove, J. P.

———

St Mary's March 23rd 1799

At a Meeting of the Justices of the Inferior Court to Appoint a Receiver and Collector of Taxes for the present Year, the following persons were appointed & Qualified

Inferior Court Minutes Book 1

According to Law, Viz, James M. Lindsay, Receiver of Returns of Taxable property, & Randolph McGillis, Collector of Taxes for said Year.

Attest.
Isaac Crews, C. I. C. C. C.

Ja^s Seagrove, J. P.
R. Carnes, J. P.
John King, J. P.
Thos King, J. P.

State of Georgia }
Camden County } At a Meeting of the Justices of the Inferior Court, at the Court House in the Town of St Mary's, on Monday the first day of April 1799. Present, the Honourable John King, James Seagrove, Richard Carnes, & Thomas King, Esquires. They Proceeded to Nominate two Justices in Each Captain's District in Said County, in Conformity to the 3rd Article and 5th Section of the

———

Constitution, and the following Concerned Resolution of the Legislature of Said State, dated at Louis Ville 16th Feby 1799.

On Motion.

Resolved, that the Justices of the Inferior Courts of the Several Countys Shall on the first Monday in April Next at the Court House in the Respective County's and [blot] Nominate two Justices of the Piece in Each Captain's District Agreeable to the 5th Section of [blot] the 3rd Article of the Constitution & Certify and Transmit the Same to his Excellency the Governor Within twenty days thereafter.

Nomination for the first District, Harmen Courter & James Jordan.

for 2nd District, John Hampton & Richard Lang.

3rd Ditto, John Eaton & Adam Cooper.

4th d^o, Thos Stafford & William Johnston.

5th d^o, John Crews & John Brown.

       Ja^s Seagrove, J. P.   Thos King, J. P.
Attest. John King, J. P.   R. Carnes, J. P.

Isaac Crews, C. I. C. C. C.

———

Inferior Court Minutes Book 1

St Mary's Satturday June the first 1799, the Inferior Court for the County of Camden was Opened According to Adjournment, there being No Jury Attending the Court, was Adjourned Untill Monday ten O'Clock.

Attest. Isaac Crews, C. I. C. C. C.

Monday, June the 3rd, the Court Met According to Adjournment. Present, the Honb^{le} John King, Ja^s Seagrove, Richard Carnes, & Thos King, Esquires, Justices of Said Court.

The Venire being Called, the following Jurors Appeared, Viz.

1. Francis Young }
2. Courtes Higingbotham }
3. Richard Lang }

There Not being a Sufficient Number of Jurors present, the following by Standers Were Summoned as a talesman to Attend for the present Term, Viz.

1. R. McGillis	4. James Woodland, Senr	7. Benjamin Hart
2. James Jordan	5. John How	8. Joab Dyer
3. John Cheevlear	6. David Garvin	9. Joseph Doer

Cadwalader Evans }
    vs   } Attached
Robert Morris }

Jury Pannelled & Sworn.

1. Francis Young	7. James Woodland, Senr
2. Courtis Higingbotham	8. John How
3. Richard Lang	9. David Garvin
4. Randolph McGillis	10. Joseph Doer
5. James Jordan	11. Joab Dyer
6. John Cheavlear	12. Benjamin Hart

We find for the Plaintiff three thousand four hundred & twelve Dollars & fifty Cents, and Interest from the twenty Eighth day of May One thousand Seven Hundred & Ninety Six, with Costs of Suit.

                                        David Garvin, foreman

James Seagrove }
    vs   } Debt
Samuel Smith & }
James N. Wright }

Inferior Court Minutes Book 1

Jury panneld & Sworn.

   1. Francis Young   7. James Vincent
   2. Courtis Higingbotham   8. John How
   3. Richd Lang   9. David Garvin
   4. R. McGillis   10. Joseph Doer
   5. Richd Elliott   11. Joab Dyer
   6. John Cheavelear   12. Benjamin Hart

We find for the Plaintiff three hundred and forty Seven Dollars twenty Six & a half Cents, And Interest from The twentieth day of May One Thousand Seven Hundred & Ninety four & Costs.

                David Garvin, Foreman

this Court then adjourned untill tomorrow ten o'clock.

Attest.   John King, J. P.
Isaac Crews, C. I. C. C. C.   R. Carnes, J. P.
                Thos King, J. P.
                Ja^s Seagrove, J. P.

Tuesday, June the fourth, the Court Met According to Adjournment, Justices Present as Yesterday.

James N. Wright }
  vs   } Attach^t
Samuel Smith }

Jury Panneld & Sworn.

   1. David Garvin 5. John How   9. Henry Hart
   2. R. McGillis   6. Ben^j Hart   10. Richd Lang
   3. F. Young   7. John Colder 11. John Chevlear
   4. Joseph Doer   8. James Vincent 12. Courtis Higingbotham

---

We find for the Plaintiff Sixty Nine Dollars, & Interest from the fourth day of June One thousand Seven Hundred & Ninety Six, & forty Dollars for two Journies to Savannah, and Costs of Suit.

                David Garvin, Foreman

James Smith & John How this day Came in to Court & Made Application to Become Citizens of the United States.

Inferior Court Minutes Book 1

Upon the Petition of Patrick Kernan, Praying to become a Citizen of the United States, the following Oath was Administered to him and he Admitted Accordingly.

I, Patrick Kernan, do Solemnly Swear in the Presence of Almighty God, that I have Resided Within the Limits & Under the Jurisdiction of the United States Ever since the twenty Eighth day of August in the Year of our Lord One Thousand Seven Hundred & Ninety four, and that I will Suppoart the Constitution of the United States, and that I do Solemnly and entirely Renounce & Abjure all Allegiance

---

and fidelity to Any foreign prince, Potentate, State, or Sovereignty Whatsoever, and particularly the King of Great Britain and the Government thereof, so Help me God.

Sworn in Open Court Patrick Kernan
Attest. Isaac Crews, C. I. C. C. C.

Pierce Butler }
    vs   } Attach^t
Robert Morris }

Jury Pannelled & Sworn, viz.

1. David Garvin
2. Courtis Higingbotham
3. Joseph Doer
4. James Vincent
5. John How
6. John Colder
7. R. McGillis
8. Henry Hart
9. Benjamin Hart
10. John Whitgrove
11. Richard Lang
12. John Gorman

We find for the Plaintiff Eight thousand Dollars, with Interest from the twenty Second day of May Seventeen Hundred & Ninety Seven, & Costs of Suit.

David Garvin, Foreman

Upon the Petition of Joseph Judson, Thos D. Garvin, & Mrs Luuise Bishop, praying to Obtain Tavern

---

Licences to Retail Spirituous Liquors.

It is Ordered, their petitions be Granted on their Complying with the Law.

Upon the Petition of John Travant, Setting fourth that he had bound his daughter Elizabeth to Joseph Judson by Indenture & that of Late She has Been Very Illey treated by Mrs Judson, Which Charge was Sufficiently Substantiated by the Evidence of Mss^{rs} William Gibson, Joseph Doer, David Garvin, James M. Lindsay, & Hugh Vickery, to the Satisfaction of the Court.

Inferior Court Minutes Book 1

It is Ordered, that Joseph Judson Shall deliver up to John Travant his Said Daughter, with her Indentures & Cloathing.

Court then Adjourned Untill Ten O'Clock to morrow.

Attest.	John King, J. P.
Isaac Crews, C. I. C. C. C.	Ja^s Seagrove, J. P.
	Thos King, J. P.

Wednesday, June the fifth, the Court Met According to Adjournment. Present, John King, James Seagrove, Thos King, & R. Carnes, Esquires, Justices of Said Court.

Up on the Petition of Stephen Waterman for a Writ of Habeas Corpus, the Same being Granted, & he Accordingly Brought in to Court.

It is Ordered, that he be Admitted to Bail, which was taken in Court as follows.

Stephen Waterman, Harman Courter, & James Seagrove Appeared in Court and Acknowledged themselves Indebted to the Governor, for the time Being, in the Sum of three thousand Dollars, that is to Say, Stephen Waterman in the Sum of One thousand five hundred Dollars & Harman Courter & James Seagrove in the Sum of Seven Hundred & fifty Dollars Each, Conditioned that, if the Said Stephen Waterman do Appear at the Next Superior Court to be held in & for the County of Camden on the first Monday in October Next & there to Stand to & Abide by the Determination of the [blot] Court in a

---

Charge of Murder, & not Depart without Leave, then the Obligation to be Void, & if Otherwise to Remain in full force & Virtue.

Up on the Petition of Levy Sparksman for a Writ of Habeas Corpus, the Same Being Granted & the prisoner being ~~boug~~ brought in to Court.

It is Ordered, that the Sheriff take Bail in the Sum of One Thousand Dollars, viz, the Principle in the Sum five hundred Dollars, Securities in five hundred Dollars.

Upon the Petition of John Sparkman for a Writ of Habeas Corpus, the Same Being Granted, & the Prisoner being Brought in to Court.

It is Ordered, that the Sheriff take Security in the Sum of One thousand Dollars. The Principle in 500 Dollars, Securities in the Sum of 500 Dollars.

Upon the Petition of Levy Sparkman for a Writ of Habeas Corpus, the Same Being Granted, & the prisoner being Brought in to Court.

Inferior Court Minutes Book 1

It is Ordered, that the Sheriff take Security in the Sum of One thousand Dollars. The Principle in 500 Dollars, Securities in the Sum of 500 Dollars.

It is Ordered, that the Justices of the Piece of the Different Districts in this County do Appoint two Constables in Each District, According to Law in that Case Made & provided.

It is Ordered, that the Account of James M. Lindsay, Amounting to Twenty One Dollars Eighty Seven & a half Cents, for Repairs done on the Jail be Admitted.

It is Ordered, that ~~the Justices~~ James M. Lindsay, Sheriff, do discharge his Account for Repairs of the prison, the Same Being $21.87½ Cents, out of Any Money of this Court in his Hands.

It is Ordered, that Thomas Rudulph, Goalor, do Sell Any property he Can find belonging to the following persons Confined in the Goil of St Mary's, viz, Levy Sparkman, Senr, Levy Sparksman, Junr, & John Sparkman, in Order to defray their prison

———

Expences and boarding or so much thereof as Shall be Equal to the discharge of Said Account.

It is Ordered, that James Jordan, Esquire be Appointed an Overseer of the Poor in the Room of William Gibson, Esquire, Resigned, for the first District in this County.

Upon the Petition of John Hopkins, Praying Some Assistance.

It is Ordered, that the Overseer of the Poor furnish him with One Dollar & a half p^r Week Untill the Next Meeting of this Court, & the Collector of the County Tax is hereby Requested to furnish the Overseer Accordingly.

The Court then Adjourned Untill the first Monday in July Next.

Attest.	John King, J. P.
Isaac Crews, C. I. C. C. C.	Ja^s Seagrove, J. P.
	R. Carnes, J. P.
	Thos King, J. P.

———

St Mary's July 1st 1799. The Court Met According to Adjournment, present James Seagrove, Thos King, & John H. McIntosh, Esquires, Justices of the Said Court.

Inferior Court Minutes Book 1

The Officers who hath Accounts to Setle Not Present, the Court was Adjourned Untill Monday the Eighth Inst Nine O'clock.

Attest.	Ja^s Seagrove, J. P.
Isaac Crews, C. I. C. C. C.	John H. McIntosh, J. P.
	Thos King, J. P.

Monday July 8th 1799. The Court Met According to Adjournment. Present, James Seagrove, Richard Carnes, Thos King, & John H. McIntosh, Esq^{rs}, Justices of Said Court.

James Jordan, Esquire Appointed Clerk of the Court of Ordinary.

the Account of James M. Lindsay, Sheriff, Ordered to be paid by the Prisoners, if the Prisoners are Not Able the County will pay the Same, Amting to twelve Dollars.

———

Ordered, that the Accounts be Settled According to the Statement by Randolph McGillis, Esr^e and filed in the Clerk's Office.

Upon the Application of Lewis Conrod Rhune, an Infurm Man.

Ordered, that he have twenty Dollars to provide him a passage to Charleston & his Subsistance while here & on his Passage & that the Money be deposited in the Hands of James Jordan, Esqr for the Above purposes.

Ordered, that the Order Made in favor of John Hopkins be Continued Untill the Next Meeting of this Court and that it be furnished in provisions.

James M. Lindsay, one of the Commissioners of the Road for this County, Came in to Court and Rendered his Account for Monies Arising for fines on defaulters, Amounting to 48.50.

Ordered, that Said Commissioner dispose of the Said Money in employing men to work on the Said Road on as Good terms as Possible.

———

Where as, Thos Stafford [blot] declined Serving as a Justice for the County of Camden in the fourth district Commanded by Capt Johnston, the Court Nominated Phenes Miller, Esqr in the Room of Said Stafford and that his Excellency the Governor be informed of the Same in Order that Said Miller be Commissioned.

Ordered, that a County Tax for the Year 1799 be Laid on the Inhabitance of the County Equal to One Sixth of the General Tax.

Inferior Court Minutes Book 1

Where as, William Ashley, who was Appointed a Commissioner of the Road for the Second district, Declines serving. The Court have Appointed William McKler, in the Room of Said Ashley.

The Court the Adjourned Untill Untill the Third Tuesday in October Next.

Attest.
Isaac Crews, C. I. C. C. C.

John H. McIntosh, J. P.
Thos King, J. P.
R. Carnes, J. P.

October 15th 1799, the Court Met According to Adjournment. Present, John King, James Seagrove, Richard Carnes, & Thos King, Esq^{rs}, Justices of Said Court.

This Being the day for Elletion for ~~for~~ County officers for this County, Court then was Adjourned Untill tomorrow Ten o'clock.

Attest.
Isaac Crews, C. I. C. C. C.

R. Carnes, J. P.
John King, J. P.
Ja^s Seagrove, J. P.

October 16th 1799. The Court Met According to Adjournment. Justices Present, John King, James Seagrove, & Richard Carnes, Esq^{rs}, Justices of Said Court.

List of Jurors drawn for Next Term.

1. James Hudson
2. Benjamin Turner
3. James Nix
4. John Burrows
5. John Burnet
6. Hugh Brown
7. Francis Sterling
8. Peter Mickler
9. Richd Lang
10. Ben^j Honker
11. Mat Motes, Junr
12. Samuel Sauls
13. James Jordan

---

14. Thomas Barhoff
15. William King
16. Ezekiah Tucker
17. William Talley
18. Ezekel Smith
19. John Dudley
20. Joseph Doer
21. John Oaks
22. John Busby
23. Antoine Suaris
24. John Barca
25. Stephen Eubank
32. John Hampton
33. John Bailey
34. Asa Hollon
35. Pierce Lane
36. Thos Tucker
37. Samuel Meers
38. James Woodland
39. James Doherty
40. Frances Settles
41. William Simpson
42. Courtis Higingbotham
43. Thos Wright

Inferior Court Minutes Book 1

26. William Dallas
27. Willm Ashley
28. Henry Jones
29. Willm Mickler
30. John Prevatt
31. Zachariah Haddock
32. Hab^k Wright
33. Nath^{nl} Wiles

44. Mathew B. Brazill
45. Isaac Clayton
46. James Williams
47. John Campbell
48. Eli Miller
49. Isaac Lang
50. Joseph Mills
51. William Gillit

Ordered. That the Order Made in favor of John Hopkins Continue Untill the Next Inferior Court.

A Letter was received from Capt Thomas Matin dated October the 15th 99.

The Court took the Contents Under consideration and directed the following Answer thereto, with the Marks for his Attention, Viz.

Sir. The Justices of the Inferior Court for the County of Camden have received Your Letter Dated yesterday & return you their thanks for your Marked Attention in laying before them Information of the Death of a Citizen Soldier in the army of the United States at Colerain on the River of St Mary's, an inquest has been Ordered by this Court to be held on the body of the Unfortunate person, and every other Measure will be taken by the Justices to have a full investigation of the Matter agreeable to Law & Justice.

We have the Honor to be with Highest ~~much~~ Consideration.

Court House
St Mary's, 16th Octr 1799

To Capt Thos Martin
Commander of the U. S. troops on St Mary's

Your Ob^t Humble Serv^{ts},
James Seagrove }
John King } Justices
R. Carnes }

Examined.

R. Carnes, J. P.
John King, J. I. C.
Ja^s Seagrove, J. I. C.

Court Adjourned Untill Court in Course.

Attest. Isaac Crews, C. I. C. C. C.

St Mary's, Monday Jany 6th 1800

Court Met According to Adjournment. Justices Present, John King, Ja^s Seagrove, & Thos King, Esquires, Justices of Said Court.

Inferior Court Minutes Book 1

Court Adjourned Untill Tomorrow at Ten O'Clock.

Attest.
Isaac Crews, Clk

John King, J. I. C.
Thos King, J. I. C.
Ja^s Seagrove, J. I. C.

St Mary's, Tuesday Jany 7th 1800

The Court met According to Adjournment. Justices Present, John King, James Seagrove, Thos King, & John H. McIntosh, Esquires, Justices of Said Court.

The Venire was Call^d.

Claude Borel   }
    vs   } Damage
Robert Cadman &   }
Richard Proctor   }

The parties came forward in Court & agreed to Come to Tryal.

Jury Pannelled & Sworn, Viz.

      1. Samuel Meers   5. William Dallas   9. William Clark
      2. Joseph Doer   6. Pierce Lane   10. William Simpson
      3. Thomas Wright   7. Elihu Hebbard   11. William King
      4. Thomas Bishop   8. Wilson Williams   12. Antoine Suares

Witnesses Sworn, Joab Dyer, Harmon Courtis, William Moubray, Henry Burah, & James M. Lindsay.

Verdict. We all Unaminously agree, That Cadman & Proctor have forfeited their Agreement, in the Sum of Two thousand Dollars & Costs.

                                        Samuel Meers, foreman

---

Court Adjourned Untill Tomorrow Nine O'Clock.

Attest.
Isaac Crews, C. I. C. C. C.

Ja^s Seagrove, J. I. C.
John King, J. I. C.
Thos King, J. I. C.
John H. McIntosh, J. I. C.

Inferior Court Minutes Book 1

Wednesday, Jany 8th 1800

The Court met According to Adjournment. Justices Present, James Seagrove, John King, Thomas King, & John H. McIntosh, Justices of Said Court.

John F. Randolph }
    vs   } Case
David Garvin   }

Dismiss't.

The Court proceeded to draw a Jury for the Next Term, as follows, Viz.

1. William Gibson
2. Walter Drummond
3. William Jones, Senr
4. William R. Reddock
5. John Hayse
6. Timothy Hopkins
7. Robt Taylor
8. William Motes
9. William Clubb
10. William Clubb
11. Allen Thomas
12. Joseph Musles
13. Ray Sands
14. Charlton Measles
15. Prentice Gallop
16. Thos Ellis
17. Richd Gascoigne
18. Jno King, Junr
19. Saml Higingbotham
20. Richd Barnard
21. Nath^n Atkinson
22. Danl Mather
23. Thos Horns
24. David Bailey
25. William Moubray

The Court proceeded to Appoint a Tax Receiver & Tax Collector for the Year Eighteen hundred, & Appointed Donald Thompkins Receiver of Tax Returns & Randolph McGillis Collector of Texas for said Year.

Ordered, that a County Tax be laid on the Inhabitance for the present Year Equal to One sixth part of the General Tax.

Up on the application of William Inus, the Court have rented to him, for the Term of One Year from the date hereof, Part of the Public square Adjoining Thomas Norrisis Lot, on which his dwelling House stands, being the North West part of said square, for which he agrees to pay Twenty five Dollars p^r Annum, & to Leave the said Lott in as good fence as he receives the same.

Up on the Petition of Thomas Rudulph, Thos Wright, & David Johnston, for Licence to Retail Spirituous Liquors.

Ordered, that their Petitions be granted & that the Clerk take security According to Law.

Thos Norris   }
    vs   }
William Jones }

Inferior Court Minutes Book 1

on the Petition of William Jones, setting forth that a distress Warrant has been served upon him at the Suit of Thomas Norris, for three Years & ten Months rent of a Certain lott in the Town of St Mary's at £16 Georgia Currency, and upon examination of the documents & prufts produced by William Jones, it appearing to the Court that the Said Jones having receipts in full from the Said Norris to the seventh of August in the year Seventeen Hundred & Ninety Nine. Ordered, that the Said Warrant be set a side and that the Said Norris Pay the Costs of suit.

The Court taking into Consideration the Present Unfinished state of the Court House, Ordered, that the Sheriff do Immediately procure Boards and other Materials and also workmen Necessary for putting the Said Court House in a Suitable Situation for the reception of the Courts. the Court therefore orders, that the Said Sheriff do draw from the Clerk of the Court the Sum of One hundred dollars, he to be Accountable for the disposal of the same.

Ordered, that the Clerk of this Court do without fail Collect all Money due and Make return of the same by Next Meeting of this Court.

Be it ordered, that a public Road be laid Out from the North to the south end of Cumberland Island, & that Phineas Miller, William Johnston, & John H. McIntosh, Esq^{rs} of said Island, be Commissioners for laying off and Appointing Overseers for working on the same, and that all Persons from the Age of Sixteen to forty five Years of age living on said Island, Agreeable to the Said Act of this State, shall be liable and Oblige to work on the Said road.

Examined.   Thos King, J. I. C.
                                           John King, J. I. C.
                                           John H. McIntosh, J. I. C.

Court Adjourned Untill Monday the seventeenth day of February Next, Ten O'clock.

Attest. Isaac Crews, C. I. C. C. C.

St Mary's, February 3rd 1800

Agreeable to an act of the General Assembly To impower & Require the Justices of the Inferior Court of the County of Camden, or a Majority of them, to Meet at the Court house in said County on the first Monday in February to Appoint an inspection of Cattle in Said County.

Inferior Court Minutes Book 1

John King & James Seagrove, Richard Carnes & Thomas King, Justices of Said Court, Met in compliance with the said Act, and proceeded to and Appointed Eleazar Bullard & William Ashley, Esquires Inspectors of Cattle for said County.

Attest.	Thos King, J. I. C.
Isaac Crews, C. I. C. C. C.	John King, J. I. C.
	R. Carnes, J. I. C.

St Mary's, Feby 17th 1800

The Court Was Called, there being No Justice Attending, Court was Adjourned Untill Tomorrow Ten o'clock.

Attest. Isaac Crews, C. I. C. C.

Tuesday Feby 18th 1800

The Court Met Agreeable to Adjournment. Present, John King, Richard Carnes, & Thomas King, Justices of said Court.

the Court adjourned from the Last Term, to this time, to settle the Accounts with the different County Offices, but Messrs Seagrove & McIntosh, Esq^{rs} being in Savannah at present and Could Not Attend, therefore, the Presiding Justices have thought proper to Adjourn Untill the second Monday in March, that all the Justices May be present.

John King, J. I. C.
R. Carnes, J. I. C.
Thos King, J. I. C.

Court Adjourned Untill the Second Monday in March. (Ten O'Clock)

Attest. Isaac Crews, C. I. C. C. C.

St Mary's, March 10, 1800

The Court was Called According to Adjournment & Adjourned Untill Tomorrow Nine o'clock.

Attest. Isaac Crews, C. I. C. C. C.

Tuesday March 11th 1800. The Court Met Agreeable to Adjournment. Justices present, John King, Richard Carnes, & Thomas King, Esq^{rs}, Justices of said County.

Inferior Court Minutes Book 1

The Court proceeded to & Settled the Accounts of the County with Clerk of the Court, whose acc^t Current was presented & Settled as Stated, & A Ballance due the County of thirty four Dollars & fifty two & three quarter Cents.

Randolph McGillis, Tax Collector, presented his Accts Current With the County for the Years 1798 & 99, & Settled as Stated, & Ballance due the County of Camden Seventy Eight Dollars & Seventy Nine & three quarter Cents.

The Court took the Accts of Mr William Jones, Late Goaler, Under Consideration, which admitted to The Amt Of one hundred & seventy two Dollars, the deducted his Note given to the Court & his fine in the Superior Court, which Note & fine Amts to Sixty seven dollars, Which then Leaves a ballance due to Mr Jones of One hundred & five dollars.

Ordered, that a further sum of two hundred Dollars be Appropriated to the Sheriff for Carrying on the work on the Court house.

To the Judges of the Inferior Court of Camden County,

The petition of Francis Gilmet Humbley Sheweth,

That, Your petitioner wishes to become a Citizen of the United States, having Resid for Six Years in Charleston and Upwards of Two Years in the County of Camden, and your Petitioner will ever pray &c.

Francis Guillemutte

We Recommend Francis Gilmate as a man of a Good Moral Character & well disposed towards the Government of the United States.

To the Judges of the Inferior Court }
Camden County }

Antoine Suares

William Gibson, Isaac Crews, William Jones, Senr, Churcer Homes, John Patterson, John Sleigh, James Smith, Harmen Courts, Joseph Dow, Hugh Vickorey, David Garvins, Willm Ashley, & R. M. D. J. Elliott

I, Francis Gilmet, do solemnly swear that I Have resided For two Years in the United States, that I will support the Constitution of the United States, and That I do Absolutely and Intirely Renounce and Abjure all Allegiance & fidelity to any Foreign prince,

Inferior Court Minutes Book 1

potentate, State, or Sovereignty whatsoever, & particularly to the late Kingdom, Now Republic of France, whereof I was before a Subject.

Sworn in Open Court   F. Guillemette

Attest. Isaac Crews, C. I. C. C. C.

                                          John King, J. I. C.
                                          R. Carnes, J. I. C.
                                          Thos King, J. I. C.

The Court then Adjourned Untill Court in Course.

Attest. Isaac Crews, C. I. C. C. C.

St Mary's, June 2nd 1800

At an inferior Court held in and for the County of Camden t the Court house in said County, present John King, Richard Carnes, & Thomas King, Esqr^s, Justices of said Court.

The Jury Venire wall Called and the following Jurors appeared and Answered to their Names, Viz.

      1. Francis Sterling   5. Samuel Meers   9. William Gillet
      2. Thos Bishop   6. Thos Wright   10. James Jordan
      3. Hab^k Wright   7. Isaac Clayton   11. Jno Burrows
      4. C. Higingbotham   8. Isaac Lang   12. Willm Simpson

There being No Jury tryals, they ware dismissed.

Ordered, that the defaultering Jurors be fined agreeable to Law, Except they do severally Make Sufficient Excuse on oath and file the same in the Clerk's office within thiry days.

The Court then proceeded to Lay of the Road Districts and appoint Overseers.

Ordered, that R. M. D. J. Elliott be appointed Overseer for the first district, from the Town of St Mary's to the Bridge on Crooked river.

And, that John Campbell be appointed for the 2nd district, Commencing at the Bridge on Crooked river and from thence to Brown's ferry on the Great Satilla river. & That John Brown, Esquire be appointed Overseer of the third district, Commencing at Brown's Ferry and from thence to the County line.

Inferior Court Minutes Book 1

and, it is further Ordered, that all the Inhabitance & Slaves liable to work in between the ~~mouth~~ head waters of Crooked river and St Mary's, together with all Inhabitants and Slaves liable to work residing on Cumberland Island south of the plum Orchard Spring Branch subject to work on the roads shall be under the Direction of the Overseer of the first 1st District to work on the said road.

and further, that all the Inhabitants and Slaves liable to work on the road in the second district, between the Crooked river, Great Satilla, including those on the Island of Cumberland north of the plum orchard spring branch, be under the direction of the Overseer of said District, to work on the road.

And, it is Also Ordered, thall the Inhabitants and Slaves liable to work on the roads

---

residing on the North side of Great Satilla river, to the Boundary line of this County, be Under the Direction of the Overseer of the 3rd (third) District to work on said Road.

Ordered, that the Clerk do make out a fair Coppy of all orders on petitions for Licences granted by this Court during this Year, Stating those that have been paid and given bond, & those that have Not, & Lay the same before the Grand Jury at the Next Superior Court.

It is Ordered, that the Justices of the Piece of the Different Districts of the County do Appoint two Constables in each district, according to Law in that Case Made & provided.

John King, J. I. C. C.
Thos King, J. I. C.
R. Carnes, J. I. C.

The Court then Adjourned Untill tomorrow ten O'Clock.

Isaac Crews, C. I. C. C. C.

Tuesday June 3rd. The Court Met Agreeable to Adjournment. Present As Yesterday.

The following Jurors, having been Summond to Attend this Court and Made default Yesterday in appearance, to wit, John Dudley, Ezekiah Tucker, Thomas Tucker, Benjamin Turner, & Antoine Suares, & Eli Miller, appeared and Made their ~~their~~ Excuses, Excused Accordingly.

Upon the Petition of Eve Wright, Larse Bishop, Joseph Dorr, & Joab Dyer, For Tavern Licence. It is Ordered, that their petitions be granted, and that the Clerk take Security and Issue Licence According to Law.

Inferior Court Minutes Book 1

Ordered, that William Jones, Junr be Appointed Receiver of Tax returns for the present Year, in Lue of Mr Donald Thompkins, who was Appointed at the Last term and refused to Act.

It is Ordered, the Clerk of this Court do preserve a Coppy of the List of Names of the free persons subject to work on the high roads, together with the Names of the Slaves & the persons to whom they belong, which shall be filed of Record, and it shall be the duty of the Overseers of the Road to Make a true Statement & return of the situation of the Roads and Bridges within their respective Districts on the first day of Each term of this Court, and shall likewise make a true return on the Same day of the Names

———

of the Inhabitants & Slaves Subject to work on the high roads within their Respective Districts Clearly ~~distinguishing~~ designating the day and parts of Day wherein eah have worked, and wherein they have failed to work, so that this Court May be inabled to Know the Situation of the Roads & the Names of Defaulters, and it shall be the duty of the Clerk to furnish each Overseer with a Certified Coppy of this Order.

Examined.   Thos King, J. I. C.

Court then Adjourned Untill Court in Course.

Attest. Isaac Crews, C. I. C. C. C.

Jury for Next Term.

1. James Smith
2. Joseph Mills
3. Joseph Dorr
4. David Mizele
5. John Hampton
6. Archibald Shields
7. William R. Reddick
8. Elihu Hebbard
9. John Monfort
10. John Patterson
11. James Jordan
12. Thomas Tucker
13. Clay Borne Wright
14. David Bailey
15. Samul Mirs
16. Mathew Motes

———

17. Francis Sterling
18. Langley Bryon
19. John Eaton
20. Francis Young
21. William Ashley
22. Pierce Lane
23. Silas Lasley
24. Jacob Clark

Attest. Isaac Crews, C. I. C. C. C.   Ja^s Seagrove, J. I. C.

St Mary's, Jany the fifth 1801

The Inferior Court Met Agreeable to Law, present James Seagrove, Thos King, and John H. McIntosh, Esquires, Justices of Said Court.

Inferior Court Minutes Book 1

The Jury Venire was Called and the following Jurors Answered their Names, Viz, Ja^s Jordan, Saml Meirs, Joseph Dorr, John Patterson, Francis Young, Ja^s Smith, & Mat Motes. There Not Being a sufficient Number of Jurors Attending, the following persons wars Summoned to serve at the present Term as Talesmen, Viz, Lewis Levy, Drury Fort, Harmen Courter, Willm Gibson, and David Reddick.

Ordered, that the Clerk Issue Executions Against all defaultering Jurors at the two last terms of this Court, Viz, Jan^y & June Terms 1800, for the sum of Ten Dollars Each.

Richd Carnes, Esqr, One of the Justices of said Court, took his seat.

Spuce Christopher }
    vs   }
Silvinus Church   }

Jury Pannelled & sworn.

1. James Jordan
2. James Smith
3. Saml Meirs
4. Joseph Dorr
5. John Patterson
6. Francis Young
7. Ma^t Motes
8. Lewis Levy
9. Drury Fort
10. Harmen Courter
11. Willm Gibson
12. David Reddock

Witness, Thos Rudulph & Robt Rudulph

Verdict, we find for the plaintiff Four hundred & sixty two Dollars, With Interest from the 8th August 1797, & Costs of Suit. St Mary's, Jany 5th 1801

Issued Jany 19 1801   Harmen Courter, Foreman

Court adjourned Untill Nine O'Clock tomorrow.

Attest.   Thos King, J. I. C.
Isaac Crews, C. I. C. C. C.   John H. McIntosh, J. I. C.
                                             Ja^s Seagrove, J. I. C.

St Marys, Jany 6, 1801

The Inferior Court met Agreeable to Adjournment. Justices present as Yesterday.

Robt Cadman & Co }
    vs   } Case
Claud Borel   }

Dismissed.

Inferior Court Minutes Book 1

George W. Lewis }
    vs   } Case
Ja^s N. Wright }

Dismissed.

John Bullen }
    vs   } Case
B. Hopkins }

Dismissed.

David Garvin }
    vs   } Attach^t
John Kanard }

Judgment By default.

Garvin & Miers }
    vs   } Attachment
William Carney }

Judgment by default.

George Tyson }
    vs   } Case
Christobal De Lehare }

Dismissed.

Upon the Petitions of Mrs Elizabeth Rudulph, Thomas Wright, Joseph Judson, & Messrs Goodbread & Hopkins for Tavern Licences.

The Court Ordered, that their petitions be granted & that the Clerk Security Agreeable to Law & Issue licence to the Above petitioners.

Ordered, that the Clerk of this Court do pay Doctor A. Y. Nicoll twenty One Dollars in full for his Services as Health Officer for the port of St Mary's & the County of Camden.

Ordered, that Thos McCall be and is hereby Appointed One of the Commissioners of the Road for Cumberland Island, in the room of William Johnston, to Set with Phineas Miller & John H. McIntosh on the said Island.

It is also ordered, that the several ~~Overseers~~ Overseers of the roads who ware Appointed by order of the Court of the 2nd of June last (The Overseers of the first District excepted) do file with the Clerk of this Court before the first day of the Next term, their Excuses or Excuse for Not Complying with the purport of the Said Order.

Inferior Court Minutes Book 1

Ordered, that a County Tax be laid on the Inhabitants of this County for the present Year Equal to One sixth part of the General Tax, and that Randolph McGillis be Appointed Collector of said Tax.

Ordered, that the defaultering Jurors at the present term be fined in the Sum of Ten Dollars Each, Unless they Make Sufficient Excuse Agreeable to Law.

Court then Adjourned Untill Court in Course.

Attest.
Isaac Crews, C. I. C. C. C.

Thos King, J. I. C.
Ja^s Seagrove, J. I. C.
R. Carnes, J. I. C.
John H. McIntosh, J. I. C.

Jury Drawn for Next term.

1. William Gibson
2. Allen Thomas
3. Isaac Clayton
4. Jacob Mickler
5. Harmen Courter
6. John Oaks
7. Joseph Thomas
8. John King, Junr
9. Benjamin Turner
10. William Dallas
11. Philip Hunt
12. Jeremiah McCarte
13. Ja^s Doherty
14. Timoth Hopkins
15. James Prevat

16. John Eaton
17. David Best
18. Charleton Meazels, Junr
19. James M. Holmes
20. Claborn Wright
21. John Prevatt
22. Eli Miller
23. Francis Settles
24. John Dudley
25. Wily J. Belvin
26. Robt Taylor
27. James Nix
28. John Jones
29. Saml Higingbotham
30. Willm Johnston
31. Edwd Hamilton
32. John Hampton
33. Ja^s Jordan
34. John Hogue
35. Hab^k Wright
36. A. Suares
37. David Bailey
38. Willm Ashley
39. Robt Stafford
40. John Campbell

Present
Isaac Crews, C. I. C. C. C.

Thos King, J. I. C.
Ja^s Seagrove, J. I. C.

Inferior Court Minutes Book 2

The heading on the microfilm reads

Camden County
State of Georgia
Superior Court
Inferior Court Minutes
1801 - 1815

The Genealogical Society of Salt Lake City, Utah, in cooperation with the Georgia State Archives in Morrow, Georgia, produced the microfilm at the Camden County Courthouse in Woodbine, Georgia on July 16, 1958, the microfilm is widely available.

On the spine of the original record volume is printed

Camden County Inferior Court Minutes 1801 – 1815

At the top of the inside cover, someone wrote

Laminated by the
Ga. Dept. of
Archives and History
1953

The court minutes begin on Monday, June 1, 1801 and continue through September 18, 1815. On the last page of the original record volume, the clerk enetered the schedule of court fees for various civil suits dated December 8, 1806.

Inferior Court Minutes Book 2

At an Inferior Court held in and for the County of Camden in the Town of St Mary's on Monday, the first day of June 1801.

Present, The Honorable John King, James Seagrove, Richard Carnes, Thomas King, and John H. McIntosh, Esquires, justices of Said Court. Continued from Book N° 1.

The Jury Venire was Caulled and the following Jurors Appeared, Viz.

1. William Gibson
2. Jacob Mickler
3. Harmon Courter
4. John King, Junr
5. John Prevatt
6. Samuel Higingbothom
7. James Jordan
8. Antoine Suares
9. Timothy Hopkins
10. John Eaton
11. James M. Holmes
12. Clabourn Wright
13. Eli Miller
14. William Johnston
15. John Hoge
16. John Campbell

Antoine Suares }
    vs   } Attachment
Archibald Randal }

Jury N° 1 Pannelled & Swon, Viz.

1. William Gibson
2. Jacob Mickler
3. Harmen Courter
4. John King, Junr
5. Ja^s M. Holmes
6. Claborn Wright
7. John Prevatt
8. William Johnston
9. Ja^s Jordan
10. John Hoge
11. Saml Higingbotham
12. Eli Miller

Verdict. We find for the Plaintiff thirty Six Dollars forty three Cents, With Interest from

___

from the twelfth of April 1794 and Costs of Suit. June 1st 1801

                                      William Johnston, Foreman

Garvin & Miers }
    vs   } Attachment
William Garvey }

Jury N° 1 Sworn.

Verdict, we find for the plaintiff Two hundred and forty Dollars, with Costs of Suit. June 1, 1801

                                        William Johnston, Foreman

Inferior Court Minutes Book 2

Thomas Bishop }
    vs   } Case
Edward Thompson }

Dismissed.

Court then adjourned Untill Nine O'Clock tomorrow.

Attest.   Thos King, J. I. C.
Isaac Crews, C. I. C. C. C.   John King, J. I. C.
                                     R. Carnes, J. I. C.
                                     John H. McIntosh, J. I. C.
                                   Ja^s Seagrove, J. I. C.

Tuesday June 2, 1801. The Court Met Agreeable to Adjournment. Present, John King, Richard Carnes, & Thomas King, Esquires, Justices of Said Court.

George Chadwick }
    vs   } Case
Benjamin Speers }

The Plaintiff being called

___

did Not appear, the Court therefore ordered a nonsuit, with Costs.

James Nelson }
    vs   } Trespass
Thomas Johnston }

The Plaintiff being Called, did Not Appear, the Court therefore ordered a Nonsuit, with Costs.

On the Petition of Woodford Maybry setting forth that his intermariage with Charlotte P. Taylor, relict of John Taylor, late of Chatham County, and that he has in his possession a property belonging to William J. Taylor, an Infant Under the Age of twenty one, & prays to be appointed Guardian to the Said Infant until he shall arrive at an age that Shall Authorize a choice of his own. The Petition having been read in open Court & Not Gainsayed, it is Ordered, that the Prayer of the said Petitioner be granted.

On the Petitions of Richard Gascoigne, Solomon Meers, Mrs Eve Wright, Jacob Mickler, & Walter Drummond, praying to Obtain Tavern Licence, it is ordered, that the prayers of the Said Petitioners be granted, and that the Clerk do take Security agreeable to Law.

___

Inferior Court Minutes Book 2

On the Petition of Jacob Mickler, Setting forth that he has a orphant Child Now living with him, by the Name of Sarah Clark, and praying that the Court would bind Said orphan, the Petition having been read in open Court & Not Gainsaid, it is Ordered, that the prayers of the Petitioner be Granted, that the Said orphan to be bound to the Petitioner Until she is fifteen Years of Age.

Ordered, that John Bailey, John Campbell, and William Mickler do pay all Moneys in their hands, Collected by them from persons in default in work on the roads, to the Clerk of this Court.

Ordered, that John Eaton, Esquire be appointed over Seer of the road in the Second district in the room of John Campbell, and that the Said John Campbell do deliver over the list of persons liable to work to Said John Eaton, and also that John Brown Continue as Overseer of the third district.

And Also, that Richard Elliott Continue as Overseer of the road in the first district.

The Court then adjourned Untill tomorrow Ten O'Clock.

Isaac Crews, Clk

———

                               R. Carnes, Thos King, John King, J. I. C.

Wednesday, 3rd June 1801. The Court Met agreeable to adjournment. Present, James Seagrove, John King, Richard Carnes, Thomas King, & John H. McIntosh, Esquires, Justices of Said Court.

On the Petitions of Terrel, & Dyer, & Thomas Bishop, praying the Court to Grant them licence to retail Liquors, it is Ordered, that the prayers of the Petitioners be granted, and that the Clerk do take Security agreeable to law.

Ordered, that the Clerk of this County do without delay make out a full Statement of the receipts and expenditures of all the funds of this County for the Years 1798 & 1799, and that a Copy of the Same be by him put up in each Captain's District for the examination of the Citizens.

The Court then Adjourned.

———

Untill Court in Course.

Attest.   Thos King
Isaac Crews, C. I. C. C. C.   Jas Seagrove
                                                 John King
                                                 John H. McIntosh
                                                 R. Carnes

Inferior Court Minutes Book 2

Clerk's Office Ap^r 20th 1802

The Jury list was corrected & the following persons drawn to serve at the Next Court, Viz.

1. Robt Rudulph
2. Jo^s Jackson
3. John Strother
4. William Gibson
5. Joseph Judson
6. John C. Nightingale
7. John Eaton
8. Willm R. Reddock
9. Willm Cook
10. Henry Sadler
11. Waller Drummond
12. Zachariah Haddock
13. John Silber
14. Matthew Motes, Junr
15. Joseph Thomas
16. Joseph Dorr
17. Charles Homer
18. Ezekel Smith
19. Matthw Simpson
20. Ja^s Williams

21. Joseph Rain
22. Ben^j Grubbs
23. David Williford
24. Jacob [blot] clark
25. Pierce Lane
26. John Hoge
27. Willm Lane
28. Silas Lasley
29. Ja^s Moore
30. Woodford Mabrey
31. William Jones
32. Peter Prevall
33. Jo^l Black
34. James Cammel
35. John Hampton
36. Francis Young
37. Donold Thompkins
38. Isaac Lang
39. John Floyd
40. John Enas
41. John Burnett
42. Harmon Courter
43. John Sleigh
44. Jordon Mabrey
45. John Mottes
46. Thos Tucker
47. Charles Floyd
48. Thos Prevall
49. John Hardy
50. Thos Bishop

Isaac Crews, Clk

At Capt John Eaton's, on Satilla, Monday the seventh day of June 1802, this being the day Appointed by Law for the Meeting of the Inferior Court for the County of Camden.

present, John King & Thomas King, Esq^{rs}, Justices of Said Court.

The Court was opened, and there Not being a Sufficient Number of Judges Attending, the Court was Adjourned Untill tomorrow Morning Nine O'Clock.

Isaac Crews, Clk

Inferior Court Minutes Book 2

Tuesday, June the 8th 1802. The Court Met Agreeable to Adjournment.

Present, their Honors John King, Richard Carnes, and John H. McIntosh, Esquires, Justices of Said Court.

The Venire was Called and the following persons Appeared and Answered to their Names (to Wit)

1. John Eaton
2. William Reddock

---

3. William Cook
4. Charles Homer
5. Matthew Simpson
6. Isaac Lang
7. Harmon Courter
8. John Sleigh
9. Woodford Mabrey
10. John Hoge
11. Ezekel Smith

There Not being a Sufficient Number of Jurors attending, the following was Summoned to attend as a tales Man (Viz) Nathan Atkinson.

David Garvin }
    vs   } Attachment
John Kanard }

Jury N° 1 pannelled & Sworn.

1. John Eaton
2. William Reddock
3. William Cook
4. Charles Homer
5. Matthew Simpson
6. Isaac Lang
7. Harmon Courter
8. John Sliegh
9. Woodford Mabrey
10. John Hoge
11. Ezekel Smith
12. Nathan Atkinson

We find the plaintiff the Neat Amount of the Within, Amounting to four hundred and Seventy two Dollars, with Costs of Suit.

                                            Charles Homer, foreman

---

William Gibson }
    vs   }
Thomas & Luerelia Bishop }

Dismissed.

Inferior Court Minutes Book 2

Antoine Suares }
    vs   } case
John Gojon   }

Dismissed.

George Cook   }
    vs   } Attachment
Abner Hammond }

Judgment by Default.

John Howel   }
    vs   } Attachment
Benjamin Speer }

Judgment by default.

Ordered, that a County Tax be laid on the Inhabitants equal to One sixth of the General Tax for the Year 1802, and that the Collector of the General Tax Collect the same.

Ordered, that a road be laid off, to run from Nodding's point by Mr Houston's plantation, then Near Hardy's, the Near hickory bluff, thence by Eubanks', then to and a Cross the Cross swamp at the Old Crossing place, and then into the public road J. Parrises, Agreeable the Petition of the Inhabitants,

---

but that the work be done by the Inhabitants Who reside in the little Satilla Neck, Who Shall Nevertheless be liable to Work as before on the Main public road, and that John Hardy, Nathan Atkinson, & George Morisson be Appointed as Commissioners for laying off and as Overseers for Working upon the said Road.

The Court then Adjourned Untill tomorrow Nine O'clock.

Isaac Crews, Clk   John H. McIntosh, J. I. C.
                                                       John King, J. I. C.
                                                       R. Carnes, J. I. C.

Wednesday, June 9, 1802

The Court Met Agreeable to Adjournment, present ther Honors John King, Richd Carnes, and John H. McIntosh, Esquires, Justices of Said Court.

Upon the petition of the following persons for Tavern licens, to wit, James Cammel, H. & D. Jones, Timothy Hopkins, Antoine Suares, Elizabeth Rudulph, Eve Wright, & King & Jones, and Also to Peter Mickler & Jacob Mickler.

Ordered,

Inferior Court Minutes Book 2

[In the lower left margin, the clerk wrote the following.]

those licence was Not taken out.

Ordered, that licences be Granted to the before Mentioned persons, on their Complying with the law, and that the Clerk take security & Issue the same.

Ordered, that the Overseers and Commissioners of the road, Severally, Make returns to the Clerk of this Court, within sixty days from this day, upon oath, of all Monies they have in their hands, Collected for fines, and that they pay the Money into the office at that time.

Ordered, that Mr Payton Skipwith be appointed Overseer of the road in the first District, John Eaton Overseer of Second District, and that James Williams be appointed overseer of the third District.

~~The Court then Adjourned Untill Court in Course.~~

The Court, after having taken up & finished the Business of the Court of Ordinary, Adjourned Untill Court in Course.

Isaac Crews, Clk

John King, J. I. C.
R. Carnes, J. I. C.
John H. McIntosh, J. I. C.

Jefferson, January 3rd 1803

The Inferior Court was opened Agreeable to to law, there Not being a Sufficient Number of Judges present, the Court was Adjourned Untill tomorrow Nine O'Clock.

Isaac Crews, Clk

Tuesday, January 4th 1803

The Court Met agreeable to adjournment, present James Seagrove, Richard Carnes, and John H. McIntosh, Esq^{rs}, Justices of Said Court.

Upon the Application of Jessey Lee, Jones & Son, and Lang & Eaton for Tavern licence.

Ordered, that the Clerk Issue licence to the Applicants on their Complying With the law.

The Court then Nominated Randolph McGillis a Justice of the peace in the first District, to fill the Vacancy of Ja^s Jordan, Esquire, Removed Out of the District.

Inferior Court Minutes Book 2

Whereas, an order was made by the last Court, that the Overseers and Commissioners of the Road Should Make returns to the Clerk of this Court of

---

the Monies in their hands Collected for fines, & though Notice has been Given them, Many of them have Neglected Making their return.

be Ordered, that the said Clerk Shall Again Give them Sixty days Notice of the Said Order, & that Should they Again Neglect Making their return, that he shall proceed against them as Law Directs.

The Court then Adjourned Untill Court in Course.

Attest.
Isaac Crews, Clk

Ja^s Seagrove, J. I. C.
R. Carnes, J. I. C.
John H. McIntosh, J. I. C.

Jurors drawn for Next term.

1. William Talley
2. Ja^s Hudson
3. Willm Johnston
4. Ezekel Parris
5. Philip Goodbread
6. A. Griffin
7. Joshua Meazell
8. Rufus Strother
9. William Simpson
10. Ge^o Haning
11. Willm Gormon
12. Garret Ludwith
13. John Prevatt
14. Henry Jones
15. John Walter
16. Edwd Rogers
17. Ephrim Brown
18. John Bailey
19. Mills Drury
20. Matthew Moles
21. Jno F. Garner
22. Hugh Brown

---

23. Timothy Cryer
24. Robt Burnett
25. Ray Sands
26. Edward Hamilton
27. James King
28. Ja^s Hutchinson
29. Thos King, Junr
30. John Beesley
31. Peter Mickler
32. Jno Thompkins
33. Francis Sterling
34. Solomon Meirs
35. John Meezeles

Attest. Isaac Crews, Clk

Jefferson, June 6th 1803

The Inferior Court was opened Agreeable to law. Present, their Honors James Seagrove, Thomas King, & Thomas Hutchinson, Esquires, Justices of Said Court.

Inferior Court Minutes Book 2

The Venire Was Called and the following persons Appeared, Viz.

Jo^s Judson
William Johnston
Ezekel Parris
Willm Simpson
William Gormon
Hugh Brown
Ja^s King

Willm Jones
Francis Sterling
John Prevatt
Ge^o Haning

There Not being a Sufficient Number of Jurors present, the following persons was Summoned as tales Men, John Garman, Richd Lang, & William Ashley.

George Cook }
    vs   } Attachment
Abner Hammond }

Jury N° 1 panneled & sworn.

1. Ja^s Hudson
2. William Johnston
3. Ezekel Parris
4. Willm Simpson
5. William Gormon
6. H. Brown
7. Ja^s King
8. Willm Jones
9. F. Sterling
10. John Gormon
11. Richd Lang
12. William Ashley

Verdict. We find for the plaintiff two hundred Dollars, with Interest & Costs of Suit.

                    Willm Johnston, Foreman

William Jones }
    vs   } Case
Richd Procter & }
George Evans }

Jury N° 1

John Prevatt was Sworn and paneled in Jury N° 1, in place of William Jones.

Verdict, we find for the plaintiff One hundred Dollars, with Interest and Costs of Suit.

                    William Johnston, Foreman

George Cook }
    vs   } Attachment
Teasdel & Kedal }

Dismissed.

Inferior Court Minutes Book 2

Isaac Wheeler }
    vs   } Debt
Thomas Norris }

Dismissed.

Thomas Johnston }
    vs   } Debt
William Jones & }
Richard Lang   }

Dismissed.

John Ross }
    vs   } Case
John Clark }

Dismissed.

Thomas Rudulph }
    vs   } Case
John McMurrey }

Nonsuit.

John George Schueltz }
    vs   } Debt
Charles Stheel   }

Settled.

Court Adjourned Untill tomorrow Nine O'Clock.

Isaac Crews, Clk   Thos King, J. I. C.
                                                       Ja^s Seagrove, J. I. C.
                                                       J. Hutchinson, J. I. C.

Tuesday, June 7th 1803. The Court Met Agreeable to Adjournment. Present, Their Honors, James Seagrove, John King, Thomas King, James Hutchinson, Esquires, Justices of Said Court.

The Court Drew the following for Next term.

      1. William E. Eddings   18. John Beesley
      2. Thomas Cryer   19. Charleton Mezele

Inferior Court Minutes Book 2

3. John Dickson
4. Richd Elliott
5. Ja^s Motes
6. Langley Bryant
7. Ja^s Smart
8. Burwell Atkinson
9. Isaac Tucker
10. John Howell
11. Phineas Miller
12. Ephrim Brown
13. Danl Mather
14. Antoine Suares
15. Payton Skipwith
16. Stephen Eubank
17. Henry Garvey

20. Darius Woodworth
21. West Sheftell
22. William McConnell
23. Charles Howell
24. James Jordan
25. Allen Thomas
26. John Oaks
27. Ja^s Prevall, Junr
28. Ja^s M. Holmes
29. Hab^k Wright
30. Thos Studstill
31. Richd Lang
32. William Gray
33. Richd Stephens
34. Saml Sauls
35. R. McGillis
36. [blot] John Brown

William Jones }
   vs }
Thomas Norris }

Discontinued.

Jurors attending.

1. William Johnston
2. Willm Simpson
3. Ge^o Haning
4. Willm Gorman
5. John Privall
6. Hugh Brown

7. Ja^s King
8. Willm Jones
9. Francis Sterling
Ge^o Cook }
Jno Hall } talesmen
Willm Ashley }

John Howell }
   vs } Attachment
Benjamin Speer }

Jury N^o [blank] Panneled & sworn.

1. Willm Johnston
2. Willm Simpson
3. George Haning
4. William Gormon
5. John Prevatt
6. Hugh Brown
7. James King
8. Willm Jones
9. Francis Sterling
10. Ge^o Cook
11. Jno Howell
12. Willm Ashley

Verdict. We find for the plaintiff Eighty Dollars, With Costs of Suit.

William Johnston, Foreman

Inferior Court Minutes Book 2

Domingo Fardy }
    vs   } Case
Harmon Courter }

Jury N° 1

Verdict. We find for the Plaintiff One hundred thirty three Dollars, With Costs of Suit.

                                    William Johnston, Foreman

---

Joseph Oswould, Junr }
    vs   } Assault & battery
Leon Devugneau   }

Jury N° 2

We find for the Defendant, Costs of Suit.

                                      Richd Lang, foreman

Jury N° 2 Pannelled & sworn on the Above Case.

    1. Lewis Levy   5. Willm Cook   9. Chas Homer
    2. Timothy Hopkins 6. Joseph Dorr   10. John Gormon
    3. Ja^s Campbell   7. Robt Brown   11. Nathan^l Wiles
    4. Ja^s Smith   8. Richd Lang   12. Lodwick Ashley

Robert Rudulph }
    vs   } Attachment
E. C. Terrel   }

Judgment by Default.

On Motion of Mr Clark, Attorney for the Heirs and representatives of the late James MaComb, that a Sale of the Real Estate of the Said James Should take place, and having produced to the Satisfaction of the Court the Certificate of due Notice having been Given.

It is Ordered, that the Order be made Absolute, there Appearing no persons to Gainsay the Same, and that a Sale do take place, first Giving 60 days Notice, agreeable to the terms of the law.

B. & J. Metcalf }
    vs   } attach^t
Patrick Reys }

Inferior Court Minutes Book 2

Dismiss^t.

Ja^s Jordan }
    vs   } Attachment
E. C. Terrel }

Dismiss^t.

Robt Rudulph }
    vs   } Attach^t
E. C. Terrel }

Judgment by default.

David Lewis }
    vs   } Attachment
E. C. Terrel }

Nonsuit.

Garret Ludwith }
    vs   } as above
E. C. Terrel }

Harmon Courter }
    vs   }
Ja^s Moore & }
Willm McConnel }

Dismiss^t.

Chas Homer }
    vs   } Attach^t
Richd Haymam }

Judgment by Default.

———

Chas Homer, Att^y in fact for }
Peter W. Greene   }
    vs   } Attach^t
William Norris   }

Judgement by Def^t.

Peter W. Greene }
    vs   } Attach^t
Eleazar Bullard }

Inferior Court Minutes Book 2

Judgement by Default.

John Ross }
    vs }
Isaac N. Meserve }

Jud. By Default.

The Court was adjourned Untill the first Monday in August Next.

Isaac Crews, Clk

Jefferson, Jany 2nd 1804

Court was opened & there Not being a Sufficient Number of Judges present, the Court was adjourned Untill tomorrow ten O'Clock.

Attest. Isaac Crews, Clk

Tuesday, January the 3rd 1804

The Court Met agreeable to ad Journment. Present, the Honb^{le} Ja^s Seagrove, Thomas King, William Johnston, & John Floyd, Esquires, Judges of Said Court.

The Jury Venire was Called and the following persons answered their Names.

Thomas Cryer excused.

    1. Richd Elliott   3. Henry Garvey
    2. Richard Lang   4. Thomas Studstill

The following persons ware Summoned as talesmen.

    5. John Crowford   8. David Lewis
    6. Timothy Hopkins   9. John May
    7. James Williams   10. Edward Hamilton
    11. West Shuffel, attending   12. Joshua Mazells

Thomas Rudulph }
    vs   } Case
George Haning }

Jury pannelled & Sworn N° 1.

    1. Richd Elliott   5. John Crowford   David Lewis
    2. Richd Lang   6. Timothy Hopkins   John May

Inferior Court Minutes Book 2

    3. Henrey Garvey   7. Ja^s Williams   E. Hamilton
    4. Thomas Studstile   8. West Sheftel   Joshua Measels

We find for the plaintiff One Hundred and Sixty

___

Sixty Dollars, With Costs of Suit.

                                          J. Williams, foreman

Robert Rudulph }
    vs   } attachment
E. C. Terrel   }

Dismissed.

Peter Madden }
    vs   } Case
George Haning }

Jury N° 1.

Habakkuh Wright appeared [blot] and was Sworn on the Jury in lue of David Lewis.

David Lewis sworn as a Witness.

We find for the plaintiff One Hundred and Seventy Eight Dollars 27¼ Ct^s, With Cost of Suit, and Interest on One hundred and fifty four Dollars 21 Ct^s, from the 21st October 1802.

                                          James Williams, foreman

Ge° H. Davidson }
    vs   } Case
Peter Madden   }

I confess Judgement for Two hundred and twenty Six $^{52}/_{100}$ Dollars, with Interest from 28th March 1802, With Costs of Suit.

                                            E. Atwater, Att^y for
                                            Peter Madden

Jany 3rd 1804

___

Inferior Court Minutes Book 2

William Jones }
    vs   } Case
John Strother }

Jury N° 1

Verdict. We find for the plaintiff Nineteen dollars and 83½ Ct^s, With Interest from the 12th Decr 1803, With Costs of Suit.

                                      J. Williams, foreman

Cook, Williford & C° }
    vs   } Debt
George Haning   }

Jury N° 1

We find for the plaintiff One hundred and Sixty one Dollars two & three quarter Ct^s, With Interest from the 14th July 1802, With Caust of Suit.

                                        J. Williams, foreman

Danl Sturges   }
    vs   } Case
George Hening }

Jury N° 1

We find for the plaintiff Fifty three Dollars 62½ Ct^s, With Costs of Suit.

                                        J. Williams, foreman

Williford & Cook}
    vs   } Case
Harmon Courter }

Settled.

Messrs Cooke, Williford & C° }
    vs   } Case
Francis Young, Junr }

Jury N° 1

Inferior Court Minutes Book 2

We find for the plaintiff Three Thousand Six Hundred and Ninety Nine doll^s 31 Ct^s, With Interest from the 22nd November 1802, With Caust of Sute.

              J. Williams, foreman

Messrs Richards & Cook }
  vs   } Case
Lewis Levy   }

Jury N° 1

We find for the plaintiff three hundred and forty Eight dollars & 61½ Cents, With Interest from the 7th May 1802, With Costs of Suit.

              J. Williams, foreman

Enoch Forbes   }
  vs   } Case
James Hutchinson   }

Jury N° 1

We find for the plaintiff Seventy five Dollars, With Costs of Suit.

              J. Williams, foreman

The Court adjourned Untill tomorrow Nine O'Clock.

Attest.   Thos King
I. Crews, Clk   Ja^s Seagrove, J. I. C.
               John Floyd, J. I. C.
               William Johnston, J. I. C.

Wednesday, January 4th 1804. The Court Met agreeable to adjournment. Judges present as Yesterday.

Daniel McNeal }
  vs   } Attachment
Peter Ancel   }

Discontinued.

Peter W. Green }
  vs   } Attachment
Patrick Rea   }

Jury N° 1 pannelled & Sworn.

Inferior Court Minutes Book 2

1. Richd Elliott	5. Thos Studstill	9. Jno Crowford
2. Richd Lang	6. Langley Bryant	10. West Sheffeld
3. Henry Garvey	7. Danl Mather	11. David Lewis
4. Hab^k Wright	8. John May	12. Ja^s Williams

The Jury are of oppinion that if the evidence adduced on the part of the plaintiff is Sufficient in law Whereon to found Our Verdict, Whereon to found our Verdict, then we are of the oppinion that the plaintiff have a Judgement for two hundred and Twelve dollars 48 Ct^s, but if the Court are of the Oppinion that the Evidence to the Jury on the part of the plaintiff

---

Plaintiff is Not of Sufficient Certainty to warrant a Verdict in favor of the plaintiff. Then we find for the Defendant, for Which we Crave the Oppinion of the Court.

R. M. D. J. Elliott, foreman

The foregoing Case is Continued, to be acted on at the Next Term of this Court.

Camden County

Cary Pratt & Eleazar Waterman

Submission to an award

Whereas, Cary Pratt and Eleazar Waterman have for the Speedy Amicable Settlement of divers Controversies and Suits, Which have lately Arisen between them Submitted them to the Award of James Seagrove & Thomas King, Esquires, Justices of the Said Court, and like Wise agreed that the Said Submission Should be Made a rule of the Above Mentioned Court. Whereupon, it is Ordered, upon the Motion of Mr Stevens, and producing the Affidavit of the Due Execution of the ~~said~~ Submission be that, that the Said Submission be maid a rule of the aforesaid Court, that Judgement be entered on the Award, and that execution issue at the instance of the party in Whose favor the Award is made, and it is further Ordered, that William Johnston, Esqr be added to the arbitrators. By the Court.

Peter W. Greene }
    vs   } Case
George Bullineau }

Jury N° 1

We find for the Plaintiff Seventy five Dollars, With Cost of Suit.

R. M. D. J. Elliott, Foreman

Inferior Court Minutes Book 2

Peter W. Greene }
    vs   } Case
George Bulleneau }

Jury Nº 1

Verdict. We find for the plaintiff Plaintiff Three Hundred and twelve Dollars & 40 Cents, With Cost of Suit.

                                      R. M. D. J. Elliott, Foreman

Jury drawn for the June Term 1804.

1. William Hazard
2. E. Grovenstine
3. Robert Stafford
4. Harmen Courter
5. John Silcock
6. Willm Eddings
7. James Williams
8. Robert Taylor
9. George Ker
10. John H. McIntosh
11. Rob McFarlane
12. Joshua Measels
13. James Smart
14. Stephens Eubank
15. Thos Prevatt
16. Wm Niblack
17. Charles Floyd
18. Wm Cook
19. James Moore
20. David Lewis
21. Allen Thomas
22. Wm Gibson
23. George Woodruff
24. John Bailey

---

25. Amos Higgenbotham
26. David Garvin
27. William Jones
28. Charleton Measels, Jr
29. Ray Sands
30. John Hall
31. Charlton Measels, Senr
32. William Lane
33. Joshua Measels
34. Nathan Atkinson
35. John Prevatt
36. Hamilton Jones

37. Thos McCall
38. Wm Markum
39. Wm Jones, Jr
40. Thos King, Jr

Francis Messault }
    vs   } Case
Francis Young }

Settled.

David Best }
    vs   } Case
Richard Carnes }

Inferior Court Minutes Book 2

Dismiss.

Cunninham & Townsend }
    vs   } Case
George Haning   }

Nonsuit.

Chas Homer, Att^y for }
P. W. Green   } attach^t
    vs   } Case
Willm Norris   }

dismisst.

Ja^s Seagrove }
    vs   } Attach^t
John Willm }

Judgement by Default.

———

Exors of Richd Gascoigne }
    vs   } Attach^t
Claud Borel   }

Judgement by Default.

Thos Johnston   }
    vs   } Case
Eleazer Waterman }

Jud^t by Default.

Willm & Ja^s Constable   }
    vs   } Case
Exor^s of Robt Seagrove }

Jud^t by Default.

George Hening }
    vs   } Attach^t
Richd Carnes   }

Jud^t by Default.

Inferior Court Minutes Book 2

Ja^s Burnet }
    vs   } Case
Strother & Evans }

Jud^t by Default.

The Court then adjourned Untill Tomorrow Nine O'Clock.

Attest.   Ja^s Seagrove, J. I. C.
Isaac Crews, Clk   William Johnston, J. I. C.
                                            Thos King, J. I. C.
                                            John Floyd, J. I. C.

Thursday, Jany 5th 1804

The Court Met agreeable to adjournment. Judges present as Yesterday.

Peter F. Mudy }
    vs   } Case
Willm Marcum }

Their Honors, the Justices of The Court.

On Motion of Elihu Atwater, Att^y for Peter F. Mudy, in the Case of Mudy vs Marcum, refered to arbitration.

Ordered, that the award of Isaac Crews and Timothy Hopkins, arbitrators in the Said Case, shall be a rule of the Said Court, provided Nevertheless that the Said arbitrators Make Out their Award and deliver the Same to either of Said parties, requiring the same before the first day of the Inferior Court to be held in June Next in and for the County aforesaid.

By the Court.

David G. Jones is Nominated receiver of Tax returns for the Year Eighteen Hundred and four for the County of Camden. & the Clerk of this Court is hereby directed to transmit the Nomination to the Executive as early as possible.

Resolved, that a Tax Not exceeding One Sixth of the General Tax Shall be levied and Collected for the Year 1804 & appropriated for County purposes.

Resolved. The first District of the rode is as follows. 1st From the river and Town St Mary's to Crooked river, and as high as Colerain Shall be Known as the first Road district and All persons liable to work on Said road Under the first road act residing Within the afore Mentioned limits Shall and hereby Made Liable to work on the road

Inferior Court Minutes Book 2

in Said District & that P. Skipwith, R. McGillis, and Willm Johnston, Esq^rs are hereby Appointed Commissioners for Said District.

2nd District. That from the North Side of Crooked River to the South Side of the river Satilla, and and as high on Said river as there are Settlements Shall be Known as the Second district, and all persons liable to work Shall and are hereby Made liable to work on the public road in Said District. That Woodford Mabrey, Isaac Crews, and John Floyd be and are hereby Appointed Commissioners for Said District.

3rd District. That from the North Side of Great

———

Grate Satilla River to the Derrion Line, Between the County of Camden and Glynn and to the Indian line to the Westward, be Known as the third district, and that all persons residing within Said District Shall and are hereby Made liable to work on Said District, and that John Brown, John Hardey, and James Williams are hereby Appointed Commissioners for Said District.

4th District, from the Shortest Ferry Between the Island of Cumberland and the Mane, to the Main public road leading from the town of St Mary's to Jefferson, Shall and is hereby declared to be the fourth District, and all persons residing on the Island of Cumberland Made liable by the road act Shall be liable to Work on Said District, & That Thomas W. Call, N. Greene, & Charles Floyd be and are hereby Appointed Commissioners for Said District.

The Commissioners for building a Court House in the Town of Jefferson, having laid before this Court a Contract of Willm Jones

———

Willm Jones, the Court is of Opinion that Mr Jones do build a proper Bench for the Judges, a Bar, two Sets of Seats each Side of the House for Jury, Arching a Cross the House, also a table for the lawyers.

ordered, that the Clerk Issue licence to Mr Isaac Lang, on his giving Security &C.

The Court then adjourned Untill the Second Monday in April Next.

Attest.	Ja^s Seagrove, J. I. C.
Isaac Crews	John Floyd, J. I. C.
	William Johnston, J. I. C.
	Thos King, J. I. C.

Jefferson, April 9th 1804

Court was opened Agreeable to adjournment, present their Honors Thomas King, Willm Johnston, and John Floyd, Esquires.

Inferior Court Minutes Book 2

The Court appointed the following persons as Overseers of the poor for the County, to wit, Robt McFarlin for first district, Payton Skipwith for the Second district, Woodford Mabrey for third, Thos King for the fourth, Hugh Brown for the fifth Dis^t.

The Inferior Court adjourned term

On Motion of Mr Townsend, Att^y for Mrs Suares, Executrix of the Estate of Antoine Suares, Deceased, that the dispute between the representatives of Antoine Suares and those of the Estate of Stephen Freeman, deceased, be left and refered to the arbitration of the following persons (Viz) On the part of the Estate of A. Suares, Willm Jones, Senr & Ja^s Townsend, and on the part of the Heirs and representatives, Saml Meers & R. M. D. J. Elliott.

On the petition of Elihu Hebbard, Stating that Isaac Flood, a Minor, bound at present to a Willm Harper, a Shoemaker, is Not treated as an apprentice of right Ought to be, and it Appearing to this Court that the Complaint Stated by the Said E. Hebbard is true, and Well Substantiated, it is therefore Ordered, that the Said Isaac Flood be taken from the Said William Harper, be No longer Considered his [blot] Apprentice, and further that he be bound Under the direction of Robert Rudulph, who at the request of the Said Isaac Flood is hereby appointed his Guardian.

On the petition of Heirs & Representatives of John Thompkins, deceased, to appoint refferies to Settle all Controversey between the parties.

Ordered, that Thomas King, William Gibson, and Randolph McGillis be Appointed refferies to Settle all Controverses that May arise between the parties.

The Court then adjourned Untill Court in Course.

Crews, Clk   William Johnston, J. I. C.
                                                                          John Floyd, J. I. C.
                                                                          Thos King, J. I. C.

Monday, June 2nd 1804

The Inferior Court Met & Was opened, present their Honors Ja^s Seagrove, Thos King, Willm Johnston, & John Floyd, Esq^{rs}, Justices of Saod Court.

The Jury Venire was Call'd And the following persons Appeared And Answered their Names, to wit.

       1. William Niblack   3. Chas Floyd
       2. Thos McCall   4. Ja^s Williams

Inferior Court Minutes Book 2

5. William Marcum
7. Robt McFarlin
9. Willm Gibson
11. John Balee
13. William Hazard excused

6. Christopher Grovenstine
8. Willm Cook
10. George Woodruff
12. Willm Jones, Junr

Payton Skipwith, Esqr Appeared in Court and was Sworn in as a Justice of the Inferior Court and took his Seat accordingly.

a letter was handed the Court from Mr William Jones, Senr, who was Summoned to appear as a Juror, Stating his reasons for Not being present, and he is excused accordingly.

Charles Homer }
    vs   } Attach^t
Richd Hayman }

Jury N° 1 pannelled & sworn.

1. Willm Niblack
2. Thos McCall
3. Chas Floyd
4. Ja^s Williams
5. Willm Marcum
6. C. Grovenstine
7. Robt McFarlin
8. Willm Cook
9. Willm Gibson
10. Ge^o Woodruff
11. John Balee
12. Willm Jones, Junr

Verdict. We find for the Plaintiff One hundred and twelve Dollars & fifty Cents, With Interest and Costs from Novr 19th 1801. 1801

                                Thos McCall, Foreman

Messrs Macleod & Miller }
    vs   } debt
Saml King   }

Jury N° 1 Sworn.

Verdict. We find for the Plaintiff and assess One Cent damages.

                                Thos McCall, foreman

The Court are of Opinion that the Verdict of Jury in the Case of P. W. Green vs Patrick Rea in January term 1804, Where they find for the Plaintiff two hundred & twelve Dollars $^{48}/_{100}$ be Now Confirmed.

John Ross   }
    vs   } Attachment
Isaac N. Meserve }

Inferior Court Minutes Book 2

Jury. This Suit Cont{}^d by plff's Att{}^y.

~~Ed~~ Ja{}^s Seagrove }
    vs   } Case
Edward Hamilton }

Jury N° 1 Sworn.

We find for the plaintiff two hundred and Nineteen dollars & 75 Cents, on his Making good and Sufficient titles According to Contract and allowing legal assets.

                                          Tho{}^s McCall, foreman

---

Tho{}^s King 3{}^{rd} }
    vs   } Attacht
Picket & Fabren }

Jury N° 1 Sworn.

We find for the Plaintiff One Hundred Dollars & Costs.

                                          Tho{}^s McCall, foreman

William & James Constable }
    vs   } Case
Ja{}^s Seagrove   }
Exo{}^r of Rob{}^t Seagrove   }

I Confess Judgement for three thousand five hundred & fifty dollars, with Costs of Suit. Jefferson, 4{}^{th} June 1804

                                        Ja{}^s Seagrove, Executor

Hunter & Minis }
    vs   } Case
Rob{}^t Rudulph }

I Confess Judgement for One hundred and fifty Six Dollars and twenty five Cents, With Costs of Suit.

                                        Ja{}^s Townsend, Att{}^y for Def{}^t

William Jackson }
    vs   } Attach{}^t
Cary Pratt   }

Jury N° 1 Sworn.

Inferior Court Minutes Book 2

We find for the Plaintiff One hundred and four Dollars and twenty five Cents, With Costs.

        Th⁰ McCall, foreman

Isaac Teasdel }
  vs   } Debt
John H. Harris }

Jury N° 1

Verdict. We find for the Plaintiff, With Interest & Costs.

        Th⁰ McCall, Foreman

Examined.   Ja^s Seagrove, J. I. C.
          John Floyd, J. I. C.
          Payton Skipwith, J. I. C.

The Court adjourned Untill tomorrow Nine O'Clock.

Attest. Isaac Crews, Clk

Tuesday, June 5th 1804, the Court Met agreeable to adjournment. Present, Their Honors Ja^s Seagrove, William Johnston, John Floyd, & Payton Skipwith, Esq^{rs}, Justices of said Court.

Peter W. Greene }
  vs   } Attach^t
Eleazar Bullard }

Jury N° 1 pannelled & Sworn.

1. Willm Niblack	5. Willm Marcum	9. Willm Gibson
2. Thos McCall	6. C. Grovenstine	10. George Woodruff
3. Chas Floyd	7. Robt McFarlin	11. John Balee
4. Ja^s Williams	8. Willm Cook	12. Willm Jones, Junr

We find for the Plaintiff two hundred and twenty five Dollars 25 Ct^s, With Interest from the 1st of August 1802 and Costs.

        Thos McCall, foreman

Inferior Court Minutes Book 2

Peter F. Mudy }
    vs   } Case
Willm Marcum }

I acknowledge Judgement for the Sum of four Dollars Eighty One & ¼ Cents, together With Costs of Suit. June 5th 1804

                                          Willm Marcum

Ja^s Williams }
    vs   } Case
George Cook }

Jury N° 1, Ja^s Williams left the Jury and Woodford Mabrey Sworn.

Verdict. We find for the Plaintiff Eighty Dollars, With Interest and Costs of Suit.

                                      Th° McCall, foreman

Exo^{rs} of Richd Gascoign }
    vs   }
Claud Borel, Senr }

Jury N° 2 pannelled & Sworn.

        1. R. M. D. J. Elliott   5. Ja^s Williams   9. Robt Rudulph
        2. Chas Homer   6. Moses Harrel   10. Oratio Lowe
        3. Willm King   7. Willm Cone   11. Timothy Hopkins
        4. Ja^s King   8. Ja^s Hudson   12. John May

Verdict. We find for the Plaintiff , with Interest & Costs, the Sum of three Hundred and forty One Dollars Seventy Seven Cents.

                                    R. M. D. J. Elliott, Foreman

---

Thomas Johnston }
    vs   } Case
Eleazar Waterman }

Jury N° 1

We find for the Plaintiff two hundred Dollars, with Interest from 1st Jany 1801 & Costs.

                                        Th° McCall, foreman

Inferior Court June Term 1804

Inferior Court Minutes Book 2

On Motion, it is ordered, that the Sheriff do deliver up the books of George Henning into the possession of Mess[rs] William Cook & James Townsend, Commissioners Appointed by this Court to Collect the debts for the advantage of the Creditors.

George Cook   }
    vs   }
Eleazer Waterman }

Dismiss[t].

Johnston & Elliott   }
Exo[rs] of Jo[s] Judson   }
    vs   } Case
Edward Hamilton   }

Jury N° 1

We find for the Plaintiff fifty One Dollars and Seventy five Cents and Costs.

                                                                      Th° McCall, foreman

---

Inferior Court June Term 1804

On Motion of Ja[s] Townsend, it is ordered, that Messe[rs] David Garvin & R. M. D. J. Elliott, Attornies for the Adminsitrator of, have full power and Authority to sell the real property of the Estate of Thomas Wright, late of this County, deceased, the requisitions of the law in that Case Made and provided, having been first duly Complied With.

Ordered, that M[r] William Deloney be Appointed Over seer of the poor in the fifth District, and Richard Lang for the Second District in Lue of Tho[s] King & Payton Skipwith, Esq[rs].

June Term

The Commissioners of the road for the first District of the Said County is ordered to pay to the Sheriff all Cost arising on process issued for the recovery of road fines, Ordered by the Court to be refunded.

Ordered, that public Notice be Given by Advertisement in the Most public places in the County, for all persons in default for Work to have been done on the road in the first District Under the direction of Payton Skipwith, Overseer of the road for said District, do appear before the Said Overseer and Shew Cause (if

---

if Any they have) On Oath, Why Warrants Should Not issue against their property, for the Amount due by them Severally.

Inferior Court Minutes Book 2

Tavern Rates for the County of Camden June Term 1804, to Continue One Year from this date.

For dinner 50 Ct^s	For Brakefast 37½ C^s
Supper 37½ Ct^s	Lodging 12½ C^s
Corn p^r quart 6¼ C^s	Fodder & brindle 4 C^s

Liquors, rum, & gin for a half pint 18¾ C^s
And so in proportion for a larger or Smaller quantity
for Brandy for a half pint and so in proportion for a
Smaller or larger quantity 25 C^s

it is Ordered, that the Clerk Cause Copies ~~Copies~~ of the Above rates to be put up in two or More public places in the County.

Ordered, that Payton Skipwith, R. McGillis, and William Johnston be Commissioners for the first District of roads, and Woodford Maybrey, Isaac Crews, and John Floyd be Commissioners of the Second district, and John Brown, Moses Harrel, & Ja^s Williams be Commissioners of the third district.

And Thomas McCall, Nathaniel Green, and Charles Floyd be Commissioners of the fourth District.

———

Unanimously resolved, that Thomas McCall, Charles Floyd, and Nathan^l Greene be Authorised by the Authority of this Court to Ascertain the Shortest Ferry Between the Main Land and the Island of Cumberland, in order that a road May be laid of from thence to the Main Public Road, agreeable to an Act pass'd at Louisville on the 10th day of December 1803.

Resolved, that John Boog be recommended to his excellency the Governor as Tax Collector for the County of Camden for the Years Eighteen Hundred three and Eighteen Hundred and four.

Resolved, that Richard Lang be Nominated a Justice of the peace for the Second District and Woodford Mabrey for the third District.

Ordered Unanimously, that the Clerk of this Court be and he is hereby Authorised to Obtain from the Corporation of the City of Savannah, to be paid out of the County Funds, the ~~County~~ Standard of Weights and Measures as past by them, Within Six Months, agreeable to an Act pass'd at Louis Ville on the tenth day of December 1803, and also a Stamp agreeable to the Above recited act.

———

Jury drawn for January Term 1805

    1. Thomas Rudulph
    2. Henry Hart   25. Herron Herron

Inferior Court Minutes Book 2

3. Asa Halon
5. John Thompkins
6. John Bailey
7. John Crowford
8. Mathew Simpson
9. Jacob Mickler
10. West Sheftel
11. Thomas Tucker
12. John May
13. Willm R. Reddock
14. Willm Motes
15. Roger McCurley
16. Ja^s Burnett
17. John Duksa
18. John Campbell
19. Thos Ellis
20. Isaac Lang
21. John Brown
22. Ed^{wd} Hamilton
23. Burwel Atkinson
24. John Gormon

26. Henry Jones
27. John Eaton
28. Willm Smith
29. F. Hopkins
30. Hezekiah Tucker
31. John Howel
32. Ja^s Prevatt
33. Willm McConnel
34. Willm Culclaser
35. John Hull
36. John Barca
37. Richd Stevens
38. Amos Lindsay
39. Ja^s Hudson
40. John Young
41. Ben^j Grubbs
42. Mills Drury

Resolved, that the Sheriff be Authorised hereby to cause to be erected a pillory, pair of Indian Stocks, and Whipping post in front of the goal, to be paid out of the County funds.

The Court then adjourned without day.

Attest.
Isaac Crews, Clk

Ja^s Seagrove, J. I. C.
William Johnston, J. I. C.
John Floyd, J. I. C.
Payton Shipweth, J. I. C.

Monday, January the Seventh 1805

The Court Met and was opened. Present, their Honors Thomas King, William Johnston, & John Floyd, Esquires, Justices of the Said Court.

The Jury Venire was Called and the following persons Appeared, to wit.

1. John Crowford
2. Willm Motes
3. Ja^s Burnett
4. Richard Stephens
5. John Young
6. Ben^j Grubbs
7. Asa Holton

11. John Hull
12. John Thompkins
13. John Brown
14. Isaac Lang
15. John May
16. John Campbell
17. R. McCurley

Inferior Court Minutes Book 2

    8. Jacob Mickler   18. Timothy Hopkins
    9. Willm Culclazer   19. John Eaton
    10. West Sheftell

The following persons ware Summoned to attend as talles men (Viz).

    1. Willm Thompkins   3. Ja^s Williams
    2. Ja^s King   4. John Hardey
                                  5. John Crews

John Ross   }
    vs   } Attachment
Isaac N. Meserve }

Jury N° 1 Panneled & sworn.

    1. Jno Crofford   5. John Young   9. W. Culclazer
    2. Willm Motes   6. Ben^j Grubbs   10. Jno Howel
    3. Ja^s Burnett   7. Asa Holton   11. West Sheffel
    4. Richd Stevens   8. Jacob Mickler   12. Jno Thompkins

We find for the Plaintiff Eighty One Dollars, With Interest from 9th of April 1803. Jany 7th 1805

                                                       John Crowford, foreman

Robert Rudulph }
    vs   } Attachment
Edward C. Terrel }

Jury N° 2 Sworn, Viz.

    1. John Brown   3. John May   5. R. McCurley
    2. Isaac Lang   4. John Campbell   6. T. Hopkins

---

    7. John Eaton   9. Ja^s King   11. John Hardy
    8. Willm Thompkins   10. Ja^s Williams   12. John Crews

We find for the Plaintiff One Hundred and fifty two Dollars and fifty Cents, with Costs of Suit.

                                                       John Crowford, foreman

Inferior Court Minutes Book 2

Means & Means }
    vs   } Debt
David Garvin & }
Samuel Meers   }

Jury N° 1 sworn.

We find the deed Declared on to be the Deed of the Deft^s and assess One Cent damage. Jefferson, 7th Jany 1805

                                                          John Crowford, foreman

Exor of Richard Gascoigne }
    vs   } Case
Ja^s Hudson   }

We find for the Plaintiff One Hundred and Eighteen Dollars and forty Cents, With lawful Interest from the Seventeenth of January 1803 & Costs of Suit.

                                                         John Crews, foreman

Upon the Petition of Isaac Kershaw Courter for Tavern licence.

Ordered, that petitioner have license, On his Complying with the law.

[In the margin, to the left of the above entry, the clerk wrote the following notation.]

Not issued.

———

Upon the Petition of John Conner for Tavern licence.

Ordered, that the Clerk do Issue licence to the Petitioner, on his Complying with the Law in Such Cases.

[In the margin, to the left of the above entry, the clerk wrote the following notation.]

Not issued.

Jury drawn for June Term 1805

        1. William Smith   25. Peter Knight
        2. Ogden Brown   26. Isham Spalding
        3. Garrett Demott   27. Lewis Thomas
        4. John Bailey, Jn^r 28. William Downs
        5. James Prevatt, Senr 29. Samuel Waters

Inferior Court Minutes Book 2

6. Jacob C. Parker
7. Thomas Holloway
8. George Powell
9. Lewis Levy
10. George Woodruff
11. Abraham Bassent
12. Selby Taylor
13. Samuel Lunsford
14. Thomas Hughs
15. Francis Sterling
16. Francis Le Roi
17. Thomas Studstill
18. Francis Newton
19. Philip Goodbread
20. William Culclasure
21. Charles Homer
22. Stephen West Moore
23. Henry Hart
24. Slauter Cowling
30. Asa Lathrop
31. William Scott
32. John Trevant
33. Ezekiel Hull
34. Samuel Griffin
35. Allen Thomas
36. John Hardy
37. John Thompkins
38. Wm Cook
39. John Conner
40. Robert Watson
41. Peter Lane
42. Nathaniel Greene
43. John Boog
44. George Clubb
45. Horatio Low
46. John Waters
47. Donald Thompkins
48. John Hoge

The Court adjourned Untill tomorrow ten O'Clock.

Examined.
Isaac Crews, Clk

John Floyd, J. I.
William Johnston
Thos King

Tuesday, Jany 8th 1804

The Court Met agreeable to adjournment. Present, their Honors Thomas King, Willm Johnston, and John Floyd, Esquires, Justices of Said Court.

Arch^d Clark, Jrd }
    vs   }
Ja^s Burnett   }

Jud^t by Default.

Copp & King   }
    vs   }
Ja^s & Zach McGirtt }

Jud^t by Default.

Willm Gibson }
    vs   }
Jessey Lee   }

Inferior Court Minutes Book 2

Jud^t by Default.

Exor of Richd Gascoigne }
    vs }
Claud Borel }

Jud^t by Default.

John Ross }
    vs }
Jessey Lee }

Judgement by Default.

———

Robt McFarlane }
    vs }
Jesy Lee }

Jud^t by Default.

On Motion of Mr Clark, Att^y for the Administrator, and refering to the Notification that Application in terms of Law Would be Made, to sell the real Estate of the late Jno Patterson after the expiration of Nine Months.

It is Ordered, that the Petition be granted, the Administrator first Giving Sixty days Notice of Said Sale.

On Motion of Mr Clark, Att^y of the Administrator, and refering to the Nalification that Application in terms of Law Would be Made, to sell the real Estate of the late John Alexander after the expiration of Nine Months. It is Ordered, that the Motion be granted, the Administrator first Giving Sixty days Notice of the Sale.

Resolved, That the second district of road shall run as high up the South side of the great Satilla River as the burned Fort, from thence in a direct line to Traders' hill, and all persons liable to do road duty living above said line on the South of the said River shall be henceforth considered and known to be a part of the third district of Road of Camden County.

———

2nd Resolved, That David G. Jones be appointed Receiver of Tax Returns and John Boog Collector of Taxes for the year 1805.

3rd Resolved, That the magistrates of the respective districts proceed to appoint Constables in the manner that the law directs, No candidates having been offered before the Court.

Inferior Court Minutes Book 2

Upon the Petitions of Eve Wright, Timothy Hopkins, John Eaton, and Elizabeth Long for license to Keep a taverns.

It is ordered, that the Clerk of this Court do Issue Licence to the Petitioners on their Comply Ing with the Law in such Cases.

It is ordered, that James Williams be appointed A Justice of the peace in Capt Hardy's district, And Joseph Jackson be appointed a Justice of the Peace for Capt Ashley's district, and that Donald Tompkins & Ray Sand be appointed for Capt Johnston's District. it is also ordered, that the Clerk do immediately transmit an account of the above Nominations to the Executive.

It is Ordered, that a County Tax be Levied Equal to One Sixth of the General Tax for the Year Eighteen hundred and five.

Ordered, that the Clerk do produce his accounts with the County at the Next Meeting of the Court.

And Also that all persons who have any accounts to Settle with the County do produce them at the Said Next Term of the Court.

The Court then adjourned without day.

Examined.
Isaac Crews, Clk

Thos King
William Johnston
John Floyd

Monday, June the 3rd 1805

The Inferior Court was Opened, present their Honors Thomas King, John Floyd, & William Johnston, Esquires, Justices of Said Court.

The Jury Venire was Called and the following persons Appeared, Viz.

	1. Thomas Hughs	2. John Hardy
3. Francis Sterling	4. Francis Leroy	5. Horatio Lowe
6. Philip Goodbread	7. Thomas Studstill	8. John Walters
9. Garret Demot	10. Peter Knight	11. Willm Downs
12. George Woodruff	13. Asa Lathrop	14. Robt Watson
15. John Bogg	16. Donald Thompkins	17. John Hoge
18. Jacob C. Parker	19. Lewis Levy	20. Jno Conner
21. Ezekel Hull	22. Slauter Cowling	

John Mercer & John May ware summoned as tales Men.

Inferior Court Minutes Book 2

William Neely }
    vs   } Case
Edward Nixon & }
Williford & Cook }

Jury N° 1 empaneled and Sworn.

    1. Thomas Hughs   5. Horatio Lowe   9. Garret Demot
    2. John Hardy   6. Philip Goodbread   10. George Woodruff
    3. Francis Sterling   7. Thos Studstill   11. Peter Knight
    4. Francis Leroy   8. John Walters   12. Willm Downs

We find for the Plaintiff Ninety Dollars, With Interest from 19th March 1805.

                George Woodruff, foreman

Daniel Blue }
    vs   } Case
William Jones, Senr }

I confess Judgement for four Hundred and Seventy Nine Dollars, with Interest from the first Septr 1803. Jefferson, 3rd June 1805

                Wm Jones, Senr

Archibald Clark, Indorse }
    vs   } Case
James Burnett }

Jury N° 2 Sworn.

    1. Asa Lathrop   5. John Hoge   9. Ezekel Hull
    2. Robt Watson   6. Jacob C. Parker   10. Slauter Cowling
    3. John Bogge   7. Lewis Levy   11. John Mercer
    4. Donald Tompkins   8. John Conner   12. John May

We find for the plaintiff the Amount of the Note, Seventy four Dollars $^{50}/_{100}$, & Cost of Suit.

                Lewis Levy

Belthaser Shaffer }
    vs   } Case
James Burnett }

Jury N° 1

Inferior Court Minutes Book 2

We find for the Plaintiff twenty Eight Dollars $^{25}/_{100}$, with Costs.

George Woodruff, foreman

Joseph Thomas }
    vs   } Case
James King   }

Jury No 1

We find for the plaintiff Eighty two Dollars Six & a quarter Cents, with Interest from the 10th Feby 1804, with Costs.

George Woodruff, foreman

John Ross   }
    vs   } Case
Darius Woodworth }

Jury No 2

We find for the Defendant.

Lewis Levy, Foreman

William Gibson, Indorsee }
    vs   } Case
Edward Hamilton   }

Jury No 2

We find for the Plaintiff the Sum of forty two Dollars $^{62½}/_{100}$, with Interest from the Eleventh of March 1804.

Lewis Levy, F

Examined.   John Floyd, J. I. C.
Thos King
William Johnston

The Court then adjourned Untill tomorrow Morning Nine O'Clock.

Isaac Crews, Clk

Inferior Court Minutes Book 2

Tuesday, June the 4th 1805

The Court Met agreeable to adjournment. Present, their Honors Thomas King, John Floyd, & William Johnston, Esquires, Justices of Said Court.

Jones & Neely }
    vs   } Case
Harmon Courter }

Jury Nº 1 empaneled & sworn.

1. Asa Lathrop	5. John Hoge	9. Slauter Cowling
2. Robt Watson	6. Jacob C. Parker	10. John Hardy
3. John Bogge	7. Lewis Levy	11. Francis Leroy
4. Donald Tompkins	8. Ezekel Hull	12. Horatio Lowe

Witness Sworn, Joseph Dorr.

We find for the Plaintiff forty Eight Dollars $^{68¾}/_{100}$, and Costs of Suit.

                                            Lewis Levy, foreman

Robert McFarlane }
    vs   } Attachment
Jessey Lee }

Jury Nº 2 empaneled & sworn.

1. Philip Goodbread	5. Peter Knight	9. John May
2. Thomas Studstill	6. William Downs	10. John Mercer
3. John Walters	7. Thomas Hughs	11. Elihu Hebbard
4. George Woodruff	8. Francis Sterling	12. Christopher Grovenstine

We find for the plaintiff forty five Dollars and forty Seven ½ Cents, and Costs.

                                          George Woodruff, foreman

---

Francis Mussault }
    vs   } Case
John Crews }

I confess Judt for fifty Dollars $^{46¼}/_{100}$, with Costs. Jefferson, 3rd ~~June~~ 1805 June

                                                  Jnº Crews

Inferior Court Minutes Book 2

Timothy Hopkins }
    vs   } Case
Moses Harrel   }

Jury N° 1

We find for the Plaintiff the Sum of four Hundred and twenty four Dollars $81^{3/4}/_{100}$, with Interest from the 29th Jany 1804 & Costs of Suit.

                                                    Lewis Levy, F

On Motion, Mr Charles Stahl personally Appeared and [blot] took and Subscribed the following Oath, Viz.

I, Charles Stahl, do Solemnly Swear that I Will well and truly interpret and translate for and in the Superior and Inferior Courts for the County Aforesaid all and every Such Matters which the Said Courts, or any person or persons Shall demand of Me to interpret or translate and to do all and every duty as Interpreter for and to the Said Superior and Inferior Courts as well in or Out of the Said Courts to the best of My Skill and Knowledge. So help Me God.

Sworn to in Open Court }   Charles Stahl
June the 4th 1805   }
Isaac Crews, Clk   }

On Motion of Mr Clark. It is ordered, that the Sheriff pay the Costs for issuing the Suits in the Cause Case of Copp & Jones vs Nathaniel Atkinson, it appearing that Writs ware lodged in his Office in due time for [blot] Service and he having failed to execute the Same.

On Motion, of Mr Atwater, it is Ordered, that the Sheriff pay the Costs that have Accrued in the two following Cases, Viz. Samuel Higingbothom vs Nathan Atkinson, and the Case of Samuel Higingbothom vs John Hardy, the ~~Sheriff~~ Writs Not having been Served by the Sheriff.

Upon the Petition of Isaac Lang for ~~Tavern~~ licence for retailing, it is ordered, that he have licence, in terms of his petition.

Inferior Court June Term 1805

It is Ordered by the Justices of the Said Court, that the Justices of the peace of the respective districts Within the County aforesaid shall, in each and every Instance Where No fit and proper person has offered or been appointed by the Said Court to act as Constables, that the Said Several Justices of the peace Shall proceed to draw them in manner and form as the Law Directs.

Inferior Court Minutes Book 2

The Court Nominates the following persons as Justices of the peace in this County, Viz.

James Williams and John Brown for Capt Brown's District. Joseph Jackson in Capt Ashley's District in Lue of John Hampton, removed out of the State. John Hardy in Capt Hardey's District, in lue of Hugh Brown, Esqr, resigned.

Timothy Hopkins }
    vs   } case
James Prevatt, Senr }

Judgement by Default. June 1805

Ephrim Brown   }
    vs   } Attachment
James Hutchinson }

Judgement by Default.

William Gibson }
    vs   } Attach^t
Edward Hamilton }

Judgement by Default.

Henry Lainhart }
    vs   }
Thomas Rudulf }

Judgement by Default.

Slauter Cowling }
    vs   } Attachment
Phaup, St Clair & }
Puryear   }

Judgement by Default.

The Court Nominated Ray Sands and Donold Tompkins as Justices of the peace for Capt Johnston's District, in lue of Mr Johnston, appointed Justice of the inferior Court, and Phineas Miller, deceased.

Jury Drawn for Next term Jany 1806.

      1. John Mercer   20. Robt McFarlane
      2. John Eaton   21. Robt Burnet
      3. Saml Ridgeway   22. Charleton Mizell, Junr
      4. John Ross   23. Willm Malcome

Inferior Court Minutes Book 2

5. Edward Rogers
6. Moses Harrel
7. Saml Humphris
8. Willm Pitt Sands
9. Woodford Mabry
10. Nat McCulley
11. Ja^s Smith
12. Ray Sands
13. David Williford
14. Francis Settles
15. Willm Holsreter
16. George Sterret
17. Willm Simpson
18. Ma^{tw} Simpson
19. Robt Stafford
24. Willm McConnel
25. John May
26. John C. Nightingale
27. James Moore
28. Joseph Prevatt
29. Iza Pool
30. John Simpson
31. Arther Moore
32. Flavious Waterman
33. Charles Howell
34. James D. Prevatt
35. R. M. D. J. Elliott
36. Petter Prevatt
37. Danl Mather
38. Joseph Thomas

The following persons having been returned by the Sheriff, as having been Legally Summoned to attend this Court as Jurors, and have Made default, to wit, William Scott, Isham Spalding, John Conner, Allen Thomas, George Clubb, Henry Hart, William Smith, Thomas Holleway, William Culclazer, Charles Homer, Lewis Thomas, and Samuel Griffin.

It is Ordered, that they be fined in the Sum of Ten Dollars Each, Unless they do severally file Good and Sufficient excuses in the Clerk's office of this Court within thirty days, the reasonable Ness of the said Excuses to be Determined at the Next term of this Court, and that the Clerk do post up the foregoing Order in three of the Most public places in the County.

It is Ordered, that the Clerk of this Court do furnish Anna Baley with Ten Dollars out of the County funds for her releaf and that it be paid into hands of One of the overseers of the poor.

It is Also ordered, that Matthew Baley's Marriage licence bond be Sued out before the Sup^r Court. The Court then adjourned Untill the third of July at St Mary's at Chambers.

Examined.

Attest.
Isaac Crews, Clk

John Floyd
Thos King
William Johnston

Inferior Court Minutes Book 2

Wednesday, July the 3rd 1805

The Inferior Court was opened agreeable to adjournment on Monday, June 3rd 1805, present their Honors Thomas King, James Seagrove, Payton Skipwith, & William Johnson, Esquires of said Court.

It is ordered, that the Commissioners of the road in the middle district, layin between Crooked River & the great Satilla River, do make the Bridge across the Crooked River and consider it as belonging to this district, and that one of the said Commissioners be served with this order on or before Monday next.

Randolph McGillis, Tax Collector for the year 1800 & 1801, handed in his accts, which were examined & admitted, leaving a balance due the County on the sum collected of One Hundred & Sixteen Dollars $^{73½}/_{100}$.

Whereas, an omission hath taken place, in not entering on the minutes of this Court an order to the Collector of the general tax for the purpose of collecting the county tax for the years Eighteen Hundred & One, Eighteen Hundred & Three, & Eighteen Hundred & Five. It is hereby ordered, that the Collectors do collect a county tax, for the before mentioned years, One Sixth of the general Tax, and that the Clerk of the Court furnish the respective collectors with a copy of this order.

Exor^s Jo^s Judson }
    vs   } fi fa
Edwd Hamilton }

On Motion Mr Atwater and having qualified that he served the Sheriff with notice to shew cause why the above execution was not returned agreeable to the tenor thereof and the Sheriff having failed to appear. It is therefore Ordered by the Court, that an attachment issue against the Sheriff's body and be held without bail or main prize untill the money on the above execution, with costs to be paid.

James M. Lindsay, late Sheriff of the County, handed in his account against the County for repairing goal, advertising a runaway Negroe, &C, amounting to Forty Eight Dollars & Fifty Cents, which [blot] admitted.

The Court then adjourned untill the first day of monday in September next, to St Mary's at Chambers.

Attest.   Peyton Skipwith, J. I. C.
Augt F. Penkie, Pro Tem   Ja^s Seagrove, J. I. C.
                                                        Thos King
                                                        William Johnston

Inferior Court Minutes Book 2

Monday, Jefferson, January the 6th 1805

The Court was Opened, present their Honors Ja^s Seagrove, Thomas King, William Johnston, and Payton Skipwith, Esq^{rs}, Justices of the Said Court.

The Jury Venire was Called and the following persons appeared, to wit.

    1. W. Wm P. Sands
    2. Ja^s Smith
    3. Robt McFarlane
    4. Richd Elliott
    5. John Simpson
    6. Matt Simpson
    7. Charleton Mizell, Junr
    8. Ja^s D. Prevatt
    9. Willm Holswriter
    10. Joseph Prevatt
    11. Peter Prevatt
    12. Robert Burnett
    13. Willm Simpson
    14. John C. Nightingale
    15. Joseph Thomas
    16. Willm Marcum
    17. John Mercer
    18. John Eaton
    19. Ja^s Moore
    20. Danl Mather

There Not being a Sufficient Number of Jurors present, the following persons ware Summoned as Talesmen.

    1. Ephrim Brown
    2. Philip Goodbread
    3. Richard Lang
    4. Joseph Powers

Ja^s McGirtt }
    vs   } Attachment
John Low }

Jury N° 1 empaneled & sworn, viz.

    1. Willm P. Sands
    2. Ja^s Smith
    3. Robt McFarlane
    4. Richd Elliott
    5. John Simpson
    6. Matt^s Simpson
    7. Charleton Mizell, Junr
    8. Ja^s D. Prevatt
    9. Willm Holswriter
    10. Joseph Prevatt
    11. Peter Prevatt
    12. Robert Burnett

We find for the Defendant, with Costs of Suit.

                            R. M. D. J. Elliott, foreman

Timothy Hopkins }
    vs   } Case
James Pevatt, Senr }

Jury N° 2 Sworn, to wit.

Inferior Court Minutes Book 2

1. Willm Simpson
2. John C. Nightingale
3. Joseph Thomas
4. William Marcum
5. John Mercer
6. John Eaton
7. James Moore
8. Danl Mather
9. Ephrim Brown
10. Philip Goodbread
11. Richard Lang
12. Joseph Powers

We find for the plaintiff fifty Dollars, with cost and Interest from the 1st October 1804.

[faint]   John C. Nightingale, Foreman

Winslow Corbet }
    vs   } Case
Solomon Meers & C° }

Judgement Confessed for fifty Seven Dollars, with Interest from first day of January 1804, One Thousand Eight hundred and four, and Costs of Suit. Jefferson, 6th Jany 1806

Henry Lainhart }
    vs   } Case
Thos Rudulph }

Jury N° 2

We find for the plaintiff Seventy Eight Dollars Six Cents, with Costs.

                               John C. Nightingale, foreman

John Floyd, Ja^s Seagrove, Thos King

———

Payton Skipwith, William Johnston

The Court adjourned Untill Tomorrow Morning Nine O'Clock.

Isaac Crews, Clk

Tursday, January the 7th 1806

The Court Met agreeable to adjournment. Present, the Honorable James Seagrove, Thomas King, William Johnston, John Floyd, and Payton Skipwith, Esquires, Justices of Said Court.

Inferior Court Minutes Book 2

Francis Young, Indorse }
    vs   } Case
Justice Holcomb }

Jury N° 1 Sworn, Viz.

    1. William P. Sands   7. Daniel Mather
    2. John Ross   8. John Eaton
    3. James Smith   9. Ja^s D. Prevatt
    4. R. McFarlane   10. Joseph Prevatt
    5. R. M. D. J. Elliott   11. James Moore
    6. John Mercer   12. Joseph Thomas

We find for the Plaintiff Sixty Dollars, with Costs.

                                            R. M. D. J. Elliott, foreman

George Haning }
    vs   } Attachment
Richard Carnes }

Dismissed Jany 1806.

Slauter Cowling }
    vs   } case by Attachment
John Phaup   }
John St Clair & }
Ellis Puryear   }

Jury N° 2 Sworn, to wit.

    1. John Simpson   7. Robert Burnett
    2. Matthew Simpson   8. Willm Simpson
    3. William Marcum   9. John C. Nightingale
    4. William Holswriter   10. Ephrim Brown
    5. Charleton Mizell   11. Joseph Powers
    6. Peter Prevatt   12. Joseph Thomas

Witnesses Sworn, Thomas Hughs, Isaac Lang, John Eaton, Isaac Crews, Timothy Hopkins.

We find for the Plaintiff five hundred and twenty five Dollars, and Costs of Suit.

                                            John C. Nightingale, Foreman

---

Inferior Court Minutes Book 2

Benjamin Buell }
    vs   } Attachment
David Austin   }

Dismissed Jany 1806.

Daniel McNeal }
    vs   } Attachment
Exo^{rs} Peter Aneil }

withdrawn by the party plff.

William Gibson }
    vs   } attachment
Jessey Lee   }

Discontinued by Plff Att^y.

Francis Mussault }
    vs   } Case
Hughs Thompson }

Settled by the parties.

John Ross }
    vs   } Case
Jesse Lee   }

Dismissed January 1806.

Charles McKinna }
    vs   } Case
McDonald & Co }

Discontinued by Consent of parties.

Peter Turner, paye }
    vs   } Case
William Ashley   }

Discontinued by the parties.

Harmon Courter }
    vs   } case
Ja^s Moore &   }
Willm McConnell }

dismissed.

Inferior Court Minutes Book 2

James Burnett }
    vs   } Case
John Ross   }

Discontinued by the parties.

Ja^s Seagrove, Payton Skipwith, John Floyd, William Johnston-

The Court then Adjourned Untill Tomorrow Nine O'Clock.

Isaac Crews, Clk

~~January~~ Wednesday Jany 8th 1806

The Court Met agreeable to adjournment, present the Honorable James Seagrove, John Floyd, and Payton Skipwith, Esquires, Justices of Said Court. Also, William Johnston, Esqr

The following persons ware drawn as Jurors for the June term 1806, Viz.

1. John D. Young
2. Ja^s Williams
3. Joseph Rane
4. Walter Drummond
5. Smith Cannon
6. Willm Hines
7. Nathan Norton
8. Willm Gillit
9. John Prevatt
10. Jorden Mabrey
11. Robt Brown
12. Ezekel Parish
13. Willm Cone
14. Asa Holton
15. David Mizell
16. Henry Sadler
17. Isaac Lang
18. Stephen Gray
19. John Kade
20. ~~Nathan Atkinson~~
20. Willm Andrews
21. John Howell

---

22. James King
23. Isham Frohock
24. John Hull
25. Josiah Winans
26. Burwell Atkinson
27. David Lewis
28. John Demott
29. Thomas Worth
30. Owen Griffin
31. Timothy Hopkins
32. Joseph Dorr
33. Jacob Clark
34. Jacob Mickler
35. Ephrim Brown
36. Ben^j Grubbs
37. James Ellis
38. Benjamin Turner
39. Willm Neely
40. R. M. Gillis
41. Thomas Bond
42. John Sleigh
43. George B. Damron
44. Joseph Bell

Inferior Court Minutes Book 2

Ordered, that the Justices of the peace in the respective Company Districts in this County do proceed to draw, according to Law, Constables for each district, as No fit and proper persons have Applied for Such Appointments, that the Said Justices do Make a return of the Names of the Several persons so drawn to the Sheriff of this County, Also that the Clerk of this Court Make this order public by advertisement in the respective Company districts in this County.

Ordered, that a County Tax be levied and Collected Equal to One Sixth of the General Tax for the year One thousand Eight hundred and Six, and that the Clerk of this Court furnish the Collector of Taxes for Said year with this order, which Shall be Sufficient

---

Authority for the Collector to enforce the payment of Said Taxes, agreeable to an act for that purpose Made and provided. And also that the Said Collector do give bond and Security to the Court for his faithful performance.

1st The Court proceeded and Nominated John Boog Tax Collector for the County of Camden for the year One thousand Eight hundred and Six.

2nd And David G. Jones, Receiver of Returns of Taxable property for Said year.

3rd William Cone and John Brown, Justices of the peace for Capt Brown's Company district N° 34. And Abraham Bessent, Esqr, for Capt Floyd's Company district N° 31, in lue of John Eaton, Esqr, resigned.

David G. Jones presented his account gainst the County, Amounting to Eight Dollars and Eighty five Cents. Ordered, that the Clerk pay said amount out of the County funds.

Isaac Crews   }
    Vs   } Case
William Gormon }

Judgement by Default.

Daniel Blue   }
    Vs   } Case
Burrows Higingbothom }

Judgement by Default.

Slauter Cowling }
    Vs   } Case
John May   }

Judgement by Default.

Inferior Court Minutes Book 2

Asa Lathrop }
    vs   } Case
Peter Randal }

Judgement by Default.

Ordered, that the Sheriff do pay Over to the Clerk of this Court all Money by him Collected for Road fines in the three districts of road in this County.

Is is further Ordered, that all Moneys Collected for Road fines in the County be paid into the hands of the Clerk of this Court.

Ordered, that the Tavern rates Established June term 1804 be renued for the present year.

Upon a hearing of two Charges exhibited Against James Williams, a resident of Camden County, before this Court on this third day of January Term 1806, they are of Opinion that the Conduct of the Said Williams, Although No evidence has been exhibited Sufficient to ~~Excomunicate~~ Cremate him, is Nevertheless highly reprehensible and, if countenanced by the ~~Authority~~ Existing Authorities of the County, whose duty it is to watch Over the general Interests of their fellow Citizens, would be productive of Great evil to the Community at Large, and are therefore of Oppinion that the Said Williams is an Improper Charecter to

---

To hold any office of honor, profit, or trust within the gift of his fellow Citizens.

It is Ordered, that the Clerk of the Court be allowed for his extra services, agreeable to an act of the General Assembly dated Twenty seventh day of November 1804, the following Sums, to wit: for 1803 twenty dollars, 1804 Forty Dollars, and for 1805 Forty Dollars.

The Clerk produced his Account against the County, Amounting to two hundred and twenty three Dollars Eighty Six Cents, exclusive of the allowance for Extary Services. Ordered to be paid out of the County funds.

Thomas Bond, Constable, produced his account, Amounting to ten Dollars. Ordered, to be paid Out of the County funds.

Examined.   William Johnston, John Floyd,
                                                                    Ja^s Seagrove, Peyton Skipwith

Court then adjourned Without day.

Isaac Crews, Clk

Inferior Court Minutes Book 2

Jefferson, Monday, June 2nd 1806

The Inferior Court was opened, present their Honorors James Seagrove, Thomas King, and John Floyd, Esquires, Justices of Said Court.

The Jury Venire was Called and the following persons appeared and answers their Names.

1. Ephrim Brown	2. Isaac Lang
3. Nathan Norton	4. Joseph Bell
5. John Kade	6. Ja^s Williams
7. William Cone	8. Robert Brown
9. Ezekel Parish	10. Josiah Winans
11. Asa Holton	12. David Lewis
13. Smith Cannon	14. John Sleigh
15. William Neely	16. Burwell Atkinson
17. Joseph Dorr	18. John Demott
19. William Hines	20. William Andrews
21. Ja^s Ellis	22. Thomas Bond
23. Timothy Hopkins	

William Duncan, Indorse }
    vs   } Case
John Ross   }

Jury N° 1 Sworn.

Witnesses Sworn, Robert Ross.

Jurors

1. Ephrim Brown	5. Robt Brown	9. Smith Cannon
2. Isaac Lang	6. Josiah Winans	10. William Neely
3. John Cade	7. Asa Holton	11. Burwell Atkinson
4. William Cone	8. David Lewis	12. Joseph Dorr

Verdict. We find for the Defendant, Costs of Suit.

                                           Ephrim Brown, foreman

---

Samuel Higingbothom }
    vs   } Case
George Ker   }

Jury N° 2 Sworn, viz.

Inferior Court Minutes Book 2

1. John Demott
2. William Andrews
3. Ja^s Ellis
4. Thomas Bond
5. Timothy Hopkins
6. Nathan Norton
7. James Williams
8. Joseph Bell
9. Ezekel Parrish
10. William Hines
11. Charles Coneway
12. Ja^s Smith

Verdict. We find for the plaintiff three Hundred and Sixty Seven Dollars and Seventy five Cents, with Interest from the first day of January Eighteen Hundred and four, and Cost of Suit. June 2nd 1806

Timothy Hopkins, foreman

Daniel Blue }
    vs   } case
Burrewes Higingbothom }

Jury N° 2

We find for the plaintiff Ninety Dollars, with Cost of Suit. Jefferson, 2 June 1806

Timothy Hopkins, foreman

Asa Lathrop }
    vs   } case
Peter Randal }

Jury N° 2

Verdict, we find for the plaintiff One Hundred and Nineteen Dollars, and Cost of Suit. June 2nd 1806

Timothy Hopkins, foreman

Philip Goodbread }
    vs   } Case
Silas Richmond }

Settled by the parties.

Thos King, John Floyd, Ja^s Seagrove

The Court then adjourned Untill tomorrow Morning Eight O'Clock.

Isaac Crews, Clk

Inferior Court Minutes Book 2

Tuesday, June 3rd 1806

The Court Met agreeable to Adjournment, present James Seagrove, John Floyd, and Thomas King, Esquires, Justices of Said Court.

Ephrim Brown }
    vs   } Attachment
James Hutchinson }

Jury N° 1 Sworn, Viz.

1. Isaac Lang	5. Ja^s Williams	9. Josiah Winans
2. Nathan Norton	6. Willm Cone	10. Asa Holton
3. Joseph Bell	7. Robert Brazell	11. David Lewis
4. John Kade	8. Ezekel Parish	12. Smith Cannon

We find for the plaintif One ~~One~~ hundred and Ninety five Dollars and Seventy five Cents, with Cost of Suit.

                                            D. Lewis, foreman

---

On the Petition of Thomas R. Rigby, praying to become a Citizen of the United States, and the same being Certified by a number of respectable Citizens to the Satisfaction of the Court, the following Oath was administered to him by the Court, and he admitted accordingly.

I, Thomas R. Rigby, Do solemnly swear in the presence of almighty God that I have resided within the United States since the month of January 1803, and within the State of Georgia during that period. That I will support the Constitution of the United States. And that I do absolutely renounce and abjure all allegiance and fidelity to any foreign prince, potentate, or sovereignty whatever, and particularly the King of Great Britain, whose Subject I formerly was. And that I will support the Constitution of the State of Georgia.

Sworn to before }   Thos R. Rigby
me in Open Court}
Isaac Crews, Clk }

Alexander Young}
    Vs   } attachment
John Parris   }

I confess Judgement for One hundred and Sixty two Dollars, with Interest from 1st August 1805, and Costs. Jefferson, 2 June 1806

Witness, Arch^d Clarke   John X Parris, his mark

Inferior Court Minutes Book 2

Daniel McNiel }
  vs } case
John Ross }

writ Amended and a term given.

Williford & Cook }
  vs } Debt
Rachel Elliott }

Judgement by Default.

George Enoe }
  vs } case
Francis Young }

Judgement by Default.

Slauter Cowling }
  vs } case
Nathan Upton & }
Lemuel Monson }

Judgement by Default.

Williford & Cook }
  vs }
John Hoge }

Judgement by Default.

Admors Peter Madden }
  vs } Attachment
John F. Pelot }

On Motion of Mr Clark, and Stateing to the Court, that four Bales of Cotton, the property of the Defendant, has been Attached by the Sheriff, and represent the Cotton to be of a perishable Nature.

It is Ordered by the Court, that the Sheriff do immediately proceed to Sell the aforesaid four Bales of Cotton, first giving Legal Notice of the time and place of such Sale, and that he pay the proceeds thereof into the Hands of the plaintiffs, their first giving bond to become responsable for

the Same, in Case they fail to prosecute their action.

Inferior Court Minutes Book 2

On the petition of Isaac Lang, Timothy Hopkins, and Ezekel Hudnal, for Licence to Retail Spiritual Liquors.

It is Ordered, that they have licence, by giving bond and Security, to Keep Orderly guest Houses, and that the Clerk do take Security and issue the licence.

Isaac Lang produced his account for Jail fees for George Knowl, who has Sworn that he was unable to pay his fees, Amounting to Six Dollars Sixty two and a half Cents.

Ordered, to be paid as soon as the funds of the County will permitt.

Ephrim Brown } Inferior Court June Term 1805
   vs   } Case in Attachment
James Hutchinson }

In this Case, it having Appeared to the Court by the Oath of the Plff's Att^y and the records of the Court, that the Original Petition Process bond and affidavit are Either Lost or Miss laid.

It is Ordered, that the present Ones be Considered and Established as Originals, and that the Clerk do sign the process accordingly. June 3rd 1806

                            Thos King, Ja^s Seagrove, John Floyd

---

The Court then adjourned Untill Court in Course.

Isaac Crews, Clk

Jurors Drawn to Serve at the Next term of the Inferior Court, say Jany Term 1807, present James Seagrove and ~~William~~ Thomas King, Esquires, Justices of S^d Court.

Silas Lasley	William King
Harmon Courter	Joseph Mills
John Paris	William Niblack
Frelhrick Slade	Harper Garner
James Bryant	Charles Floyd
George Fleetwood	John Crews
Richard Lang	Francis Mussault
Abner Harrel	John Baley, Senr
Ja^s Campbell	James Jordan
William Mickler	John Brown
Thomas Garner	William Gibson
Langley Bryant	John Mizell
Claborn Wright	John Barco
Mills Drury	William Clark
John Silbert	Ch^s Grovenstine
Adam Cooper	John Gormon

Inferior Court Minutes Book 2

Hugh Brown
Lucius Hitchcock
Hamilton Jones
James Lloyd

Robert Muter
James M. Lindsay
Denis Lowe
James Hudson

Isaac Crews, Clk

Thos King, J. I. C.
Ja^s Seagrove, J. I. C.

Monday, January the fifth 1807

The Court was opened, present their Honors James Seagrove, William Johnston, and John Floyd, Esquires, Justices of Said Court.

To the Honble, the Justices of the Inferior Court for the County of Camden

The petition of James Hannay, of the Town of Saint Mary's

Humbly Sheweth

That Your petitioner was born on the twenty Sixth day of May one thousand seven hundred and Seventy eight, in the Shire of Galloway, in the Kingdom of Great Brittain, of which he was a Subject, and that he landed in the City of Philadelphia in the United States of America on the twenty eighth day of April one thousand eight hundred and one, and that he hath resided for upwards of three Years in the County of Camden.

Your petitioner being desirous to become a Citizen of the United

States, prays that he may be received and admitted a Citizen, according to the Constitution and laws ~~thereof~~ of the United States, and Your petitioner as in duty bound will ever pray &C.

James Hannay

Georgia }
Camden County } ss

James Hannay, being duly sworn, deposeth and saith, that the facts stated in the annexed petition are just and true.

Sworn to before me }
this 5th day of January 1807 }
Isaac Crews, C. I. C. C. C. }

James Hannay

Inferior Court Minutes Book 2

Georgia }
Camden County } ss
Town of Saint Mary's }

Before me, Jn° Ross, Indentant of the town aforesaid, Personally appeared James Burnet, who being duly sworn, doth depose and say that James Hannay, resident of the town aforesaid hath been a resident of the ~~Town aforesaid~~ Same more than one Year and that he hath resided within the United States more than five Years, that he has behaved as a Man of good Moral Character, attached to the principles of the Constitution of the United States and

---

well disposed to the good order and happiness of the same, to the best of his Knowledge.

Sworn to before me }
St Mary's 3 January 1807 }   Ja^s Burnet
Jn° Ross, Intend^t }

We, the subscribers, do certify that we have Known the petitioner, James Hannay, to be a resident for upwards of three Years in the County of Camden, and that we always have Known him to be a man of moral Character and attached to the Constitution of the United States.

Jefferson, 5th January 1807

Hamilton Jones, D. G. Jones, R. M. D. J. Elliott, Arch^d Clark, Jn° Boog, Charles Stahl

The foregoing petition and Certificate, being to the Satisfaction of the Court, the following Oath was administered to him by the Court and be admitted accordingly.

I, James Hannay, do solemnly Swear in the presence of Almighty God that I have resided within the United States since the Month of April one thousand eight hundred and one, and within the State of Georgia upwards

---

of three years. That I will support the Constitution of the United States, and I absolutely renounce and abjure all allegiance and fidelity to any foreign prince, potentate, or Sovereignty whatever, and particularly the King of Great Britain, whose Subject I formerly was. And that I will support the Constitution of the State of Georgia.

Sworn to before me }   James Hannay
in Open Court }
Jany 5 1807 }
Isaac Crews, Clk }

The Jury Venire was Called and the following persons appeared and answered to their Names, viz.

Inferior Court Minutes Book 2

Harper Garner
Denis Lowe
John Brown
Mills Drury
John Silbert
Hamilton Jones
Ja^s M. Lindsay
Silas Lasley

Ja^s Hudson
William Clark
Hugh Brown
William Niblack
Thomas Garner
William Gibson
Philip Goodbread

George Anderson }
   vs   } Case
Richard Pearis   }

I Confess Judgement for One Hundred and fifteen pounds and Eleven Shillings Beheamey Curency (eight Shillings to the Dollar) being two Hundred and Eighty Eight Dollars Eighty Seven and a half Cents, with Interest from the first of January 1802, with Costs of Suit. Jany 5 1807

                                            Clark, Deft's Att^y

Nathaniel Pendleton }
   vs   } Case
George Ker   }

Jury N° 1 Sworn.

    1. Harper Garner   7. Mills Drury
    2. Ja^s Hudson   8. Willm Niblack
    3. Denis Lowe   9. John Silbert
    4. Willm Clark   10. Thomas Garner
    5. John Brown   11. Hamilton Jones
    6. Hugh Brown   12. James M. Lindsay

Verdict. We, the Jury, find in favor of the plaintiff One thousand One Hundred & forty three Dollars forty two Cents, with Interest from 14th December 1804.

                                            Wm Niblack, foreman

---

Williford & Cook}
   vs   } debt
Rachel Elliott   }

Jury N° 1

Silas Lasley Sworn in Lue of Thomas Garner.

Inferior Court Minutes Book 2

Verdict, we find the deed declared on to be the Deed of the Defendant & Assess One Cent Damage, with Costs of Suit. Jefferson, 5th Jany 1807

            Wm Niblack, foreman

Francis Sayre, assignee }
  vs   } Case
William Ashley   }

Jury N° 1

Verdict. We, the Jury, find for the plaintiff three Hundred and forty five Dollars 11¾ Cents, with Interest and Costs. Jany 5, 1807

            Wm Niblack, foreman

Francis Sayre, Indorsee }
  vs   } Case
William Ashley   }

Jury N° 1

Verdict. We, the Jury, find for the plaintiff the Sum of five Hundred and Sixty eight Dollars and Sixteen Cents, being the Amount of principal & Interest of the Notes Declared on up to this Day, with Costs of Suit. Jefferson, 5th Jany 1807

            Willm Niblack, foreman

George Eno }
  vs   } Case
Francis Young }

I Confess Judgement for fifty Six Dollars and Seventy five Cents, with Interest and Costs. Jefferson, 5th Jany 1807

            E. Atwater, Deft's Att^y

Slauter Cowling }
  vs   } Case
Nathan Upton & }
Lemuel Munson }

Jury N° 1

Inferior Court Minutes Book 2

Verdict. We find for the plaintiff the Sum of fifty Dollars, with Interest from the Seventh of March 1806.

$\hspace{6cm}$ Wm Niblack, foreman

Williford & Cook }
$\hspace{1cm}$ vs $\hspace{2cm}$ } Case
John Hoge $\hspace{1.5cm}$ }

Jury N° 1

Verdict, we find for the plaintiff two Hundred & fifty One Dollars and Seventy four Cents, with Interest & Costs. Jefferson, 5th Jany 1807

$\hspace{6cm}$ Wm Niblack, foreman

The Court then adjourned Untill tomorrow ten o'Clock.

Isaac Crews, Clk $\hspace{4cm}$ John Floyd, J. I. C.
$\hspace{7cm}$ William Johnston
$\hspace{7cm}$ Ja^s Seagrove, J. I. C.

———

Tuesday, January 6th 1807

The Court Met agreeable to adjornment, present their Honors James Seagrove, William Johnston, & John Floyd, Esquires, Justices of Said Court.

Catharine McFarlane }
$\hspace{1cm}$ vs $\hspace{2cm}$ } Attachment
Samuel Gold $\hspace{1.3cm}$ }

Jury N° 1 Sworn, to wit.

1. Harper Garner	7. John Paris
2. James Hudson	8. Hugh Brown
3. Denis Lowe	9. Mills Drury
4. William Clark	10. William Niblack
5. James Bryant	11. John Silbert
6. John Brown	12. John Mizell

Verdict. We find for the Plaintiff Six Hundred and four Dollars and thirty three Cents, with Interest at five percent from the twentieth of February 1804, And Damages at fifteen percent, amounting to Ninety Dollars and Sixty four Cents, & Charges of Protest being three Dollars and thirty three Cents, with Costs of Suit.

$\hspace{6cm}$ Wm Niblack, foreman

Inferior Court Minutes Book 2

Ordered, that David G. Joneses Account against the County of thirty One Dollars and twenty five Cents be admitted and paid out of the County funds, it being for Keeping Hair and Mase & Coalt, who was Not able to pay fees.

Solomon Meers }
    vs } Case
Susannah Wright }
Admix of Habakkuh Wright }

Verdict. We find for the plaintiff forty Dollars Seventy Eight Cents ¾, with Costs of Suit. Jany 6, 1807

                                                Wm Niblack, foreman

Philip Goodbread, Clamant }
    vs } fifa replevin
Leven Gunby, plffs in execution }

Jury N° 1

Verdict. We find the property ~~to be~~ Subject to the execution, with Costs of Suit.

Jany 6th 1807   Willm Niblack, foreman

Asa Lathrop, paye }
    vs } Attachment
Josiah Baker }

Judgement by Default.

Jones & Ashley }
    vs } Case
John Howell }

Judgement by Default.

Samuel Boyd and }
Susannah Boyd }
Admors of Danl McGirtt }
    vs } Attachment
James McGirtt }

Judgement by Default.

Inferior Court Minutes Book 2

Copp & King }
    vs } Case
Silas Richmond }

Judgement by Default.

Peter Lane, Indorse }
    vs } Attachment
Josiah Baker }

Judgement by Default.

Peter Lane }
    vs } Attachment
Josiah Baker }

Judgement by Default.

D. G. Jones, Adm^r }
Willm Jones }
    vs } Case
Nathan Atkinson }

Dismissed.

William & Silvester Robinson }
    vs } Attachment
Saml Gold }

Messrs Ogier & Co }
    vs } Attachment
Josiah Baker }

Judgement by Default.

Isaac K. Courter }
    vs } Attachment
Pierre Ordronaux }

Death of Francis Mussault garnishe Suggested.

Judgement by Default.

Inferior Court Minutes Book 2

Jury Drawn for June term.

1. Peter Lane
2. Willm Scott
3. Asa Lathrop
4. John Hardee
5. Saml Griffin
6. John Conner
7. Lewis Thomas
8. Joshua Mizell
9. Thos King
10. Willm Culclazer
11. Nathl Greene
12. Slauter Cowling
13. Samuel Walters
14. John Baley, Senr
15. Ja^s Campbell
16. William Downes
17. Abraham Bessent
18. John Baley, Junr
19. Horatio Lowe
20. Francis Sterling
21. Francis Leroy
22. Henry Hart
23. Stephen W. Moore
24. Thomas Tucker
25. John Tompkins
26. Stephen Loftin
27. Philip Goodbread
28. Allen Thomas
29. Charles Homer
30. Jacob C. Parker
31. Lewis Levy
32. Ogden Brown
33. James Prevatt, Senr
34. Isham Spalding
35. Garret Demott
36. Peter Mickler
37. ~~Willia~~ John Hoge
38. Henry Jones
39.
40.

James M. Lindsay }
    vs   } Submission & award
John Gormon   }

On Motion of Mr Clark and refering to the award returned in the above case. It is Ordered by the Court, That the award of the arbitrators be received

---

The amount being One hundred and six Dollars and seventy Eight Cents, and paying one half of the Lawful fees arising on said Suit to the Said James Lindsay. And, It is further Ordered, that the afore Said award be made a rule of this Court, in Terms of the Judiciary Law and Submission of the Parties.

John McClellan }
    vs   } Submission & award
George Campbell }

On Motion of Mr Atwater and producing to the Court the Submission of the parties on which the award was founded. It is Ordered by the Court, That the award be received and that the said Defendant pay to the plaintiff the sum of Two thousand two hundred & Sixty three Dollars and twelve and one half Cents, as expressed by the award. And that the Same be made a rule of this Court, in Termxs of the Judiciary Law.

Ordered, That David G. Jones be and he is hereby nominated to receive the Returns for the years 1805,

Inferior Court Minutes Book 2

1806, and 1807. And that William Niblack be appointed a Justice of the peace in the 31st District Company of Militia Commanded by Captain Crews, in the room of Isaac Lange, resigned.

Ordered, That the overseers of the Poor of this County be notified to appear at the next Inferior Court, Prepared to report to the Court the number and Condition of the poor under their Care and what amount of funds they are possessed of for their support.

And, That Thomas H. Wilson be appointed Overseer of the poor in the thirtieth district Company of Militia Commanded by Capt W. Johnston, in the room of William Delony, deceased.

Also, That Abraham Bessent be appointed Overseer of the Poor in the thirty first District of Militia Commanded by Capt Crews, in room of Woodford Mabry, deceased.

Also, That a County Tax be levied for the years 1805, 1806, & 1807 equal to One Sixth of the general Tax, and that the Collector of the general Tax for Said Years do collect the Same.

The Court then adjourned Untill tomorrow Ten O'Clock.

Isaac Crews, Clk   John Floyd
                                               Ja^s Seagrove
                                               William Johnston

Wednesday, January 7th 1807

The Court opened agreeably to adjournment. Present, their Honors James Seagrove, John Floyd, and William Johnston, Esq^{rs}, Justices of said Court.

Accounts were produced by Isaac Lang, Goaler, against Joseph Frank and Michael Banbury, Amounting to One hundred and thirty one Dollars & $87½/100$ for Goal Fees, which were ordered to be paid to said Lang out of the County funds.

The State	}
vs	} Breaking Goal & escaping
George Campbell &	}
Roger McCurley	}

It being represented by the Sheriff of the County, that the Prisoners abovenamed had been lawfully confined in Goal and that, from the assistance rendered them by a certain person or persons unknown, they were enabled to effect an escape. And, it appearing that the Prisoners had left considerable property behind.

Inferior Court Minutes Book 2

It is therefore Ordered by the Court, that the Sheriff forthwith take possession of the Goods & Chattels of the aforesaid prisoners wheresoever the Same be found, and after giving ten Days Notice Expose to Sale

---

such property, Applying the Amount thereof in the first place to the payment of the Goal fees and Secondly to the payment of Such repair as may have been Necessary to place the goal in the like good Order.

Returning the Surplus, if Any, in the hands of the Clerk of this Court, to be paid Over to the parties or their Legal representatives.

Ordered, that the Clerk of the Court do employ a proper person to have the Windows of the Court House Securly hung with Strong Iron Hinges, with proper Inside fastenings, and and to sash and glaze the four Windows in the Court room, that the doors to be secured, One With a Strong Stock Jack and the Other with a Bar on the inside, that it Shall be the duty of the Goaler to Keep the Said Court House Shut and locked up when unocupied on public Business, and that the reasonable expence incured by the Above Mentioned repairs Shall be paid out of the County funds.

And, it is further Ordered, that the Clerk doth have the Necessary repairs on the Goal Compleated as soon as possible.

Ordered, that the Justices of the peace in the respective Company Districts in this County do draw according to Law Constables for each District.

The following persons have been returned by the Sheriff as having been duly Summoned to Attend at this term as Jurors and have Made Default, Viz. Charles Floyd, Langley Bryant, James Jordan, Christopher Grovenstine, John Gormon, John Barker, Abner Harrel, John Crews, Harmon Courter, Lucius Hitchcock, Adam Cooper, James Lloyd, William King. It is Ordered, that they be fined in the Sum of Twenty Dollars Each, Unless they do Sevearlly file their excuses on Oath with the Clerk within thirty Days, in terms of the Law.

Ja[s] Seagrove
William Johnston
John Floyd

The Court then Adjourned Untill Court in Course.

Isaac Crews, Clk

Inferior Court Minutes Book 2

Jefferson, June 1st 1807

The Inferior Court was opened, there being Only One of the Justices of Said Court present, to wit, John Floyd, Esqr, the Court was adjourned Untill Court in Course.

Isaac Crews, Clk

Chambers, 27th June 1807, St Mary's

Present, their Honors James Seagrove and Thomas King, Justices of the Inferior Court.

The State   }
    vs   } Charged with Cattle Stealing
David Davis }

The prisoner having been brought up by Writ of Habeus Corpus.

The papers pertaining to the offence being examined, the Court ware of the Opinion that the Charge was not Sufficiently Substantiated to warrant an order of the Court, that the prisoner be bound in a recognizance to appear at the Next Superior Court to answer the Charge.

It is therefore Ordered, that the Prisoner be Discharged on payment of Fees.

Signed.   Thos King, Ja^s Seagrove

The Above is a true Copy of the original proceedings, Recorded June 29th 1807.

Isaac Crews, C. I. C. C. C.

Monday, January the forth 1808

The Court was opened, present Their Honors Thomas King, John Floyd, Peyton Skipwith, Esquires, Justices of Said Court.

The Jury Venire Was Called, there Not being a Sufficient Number of Jurors Attending to proceed to trials, & The Jurors present ware discharged untill Tomorrow Morning Nine O'Clock.

The Court then Adjourned Untill Tomorrow Nine O'Clock.

Isaac Crews, Clk   John Floyd, Thos King, Peyton Skipwith

Inferior Court Minutes Book 2

Tuesday, January the fifth 1808

The Court Met agreeable to adjournment, present Their Honors Thomas King, John Floyd, and Peyton Skipwith, Esquires.

In Consequence of the failure of the Court at the Term of June last, No Jury had been drawn for the present Court, ~~and of~~ and on an investigation the present Court, an Opinion of that

---

The former Jury Cannot ~~be~~ Legally Serve at the present Term, , Therefore the Jurors Attending ware discharged Accordingly.

Harper Garner }
    vs   } case
Robert Burnet }

Judgement by Default.

White Roceter   }
    vs   } case
John Henry Gerbel }

Judgement by Default.

It is ordered, that in conformity to an act of the Legislature passed on the third of December 1806, the Clerk of the Court do charge in the Bill of Costs, on all Suits brought in the Superior & Inferior Courts of this County, Such Sums of Money as are therein imposed, and that the Sheriff collect Such Sums of money so imposed and pay them over to the Clerk, by him to be accounted for to the Justices of the Court, and that he open an account for the purpose accordingly.

Ordered, that the Clerk advertise in four or more public places in the County, that all persons wishing to Keep Taverns, or Sell Spirituous Liquors by retail, in Said County, to Come before

---

before this Court at their Next term and Obtain a licence for so doing, agreeable to an act of the Legislature passed in December 1791, or the Law will be inforced indescremenately against [blot] all delinquents.

Jury Drawn for June Term 1808

1. Nathl Greene	20. John Cade
2. George Gates	21. Randolph McGillis
3. Benjamin Grubbs	22. William Watson
4. Abner Harrall	23. Walter Drummond

Inferior Court Minutes Book 2

5. William Downs
6. Elihu Hubbard
7. Burwell Atkinson
8. William Hines
9. Smith Cannon
10. Isham Spalding
11. Henry Jones
12. Lewis Levy
13. Peter Thompson
14. James Hudson
15. Peter Hagan
16. Isaac K. Courter
17. Nicholas S. Bayard
18. Peter Prevatt
19. Isaac Poole

24. Francis Young
25. Saml Griffin
26. Robt McFarlane
27. Abraham Bessent
28. Robt Brown
29. Thos Hughes
30. James M. Lindsay
31. John Gilbert
32. Henry McIntosh
33. John Prevatt
34. Joseph Bell
35. Nathan Norton
36. Thos Rudulph

James Douglass }
Adm^r of John Douglass }
    vs } case
Randolph McGillis }

Judgement by default.

Elizabeth Gordon, Admi^x }
    vs }
James Seagrove }

Judgement by Default.

James Willy, Indorse }
    vs }
King & Jones }

Judgement by Default.

Scott & Co }
    vs } Case
Joseph Dorr, Admo^r }
of Joseph Judson }

Judgement by Default.

William Mein & }
Robert Mackay, Survivor }
    vs } case
Joseph Dorr, admo^r of }
Joseph Judson }

Inferior Court Minutes Book 2

Judgement by Default.

Thomas Ogier }
    vs   } Case
Josiah Baker }

Judgement by Default.

Elias Baker }
    vs   } Attach[t]
Sylvanus Crowel & }
Mathias Crowel }

Judgement by Default.

Slauter Cowling }
    vs   } Case
Exors William Gormon }

Judgement by Default

———

Slauter Cowling }
    vs   } Attach[t]
Josiah Baker }

Judgement by Default

Robert Burnet, Exor }
William Gormon }
    vs   } attach[t]
John Gormon & }
Willoughby Hoge }

Judgement by Default.

Robert L. Burnet, Exor }
William Gormon }
    vs   } attach[t]
Willoughby Hodge & }
William Marcum }

Judgement by default.

Thomas Garner }
    vs   } Case
Lonstreet & Griffin }

Inferior Court Minutes Book 2

Judgement by Default.

Edward Barnwell }
    vs   } Attach^t
John C. Houston }

Judgement by Default.

Daniel Copp, Indorse }
    vs   } Attach^t
Thomas Doyle   }

Judgement by Default.

John Holzendorf }
    vs   } Attach^t
Jehu Underwood }

Judgement by Default.

---

on the petition of Isaac Lang, Timothy Hopkins, and Elizabeth Baley for Tavern Licence. It is ordered, that the Clerk do issue the Licence, on their Complying with the Law, in such cases.

On Motion of Mr Clark and Setting forth to the Court that a certain negroe slave Dick had been levied on as the property of James McGirth, at the suit of the admor & Admix of Daniel McGirth, and that one Zachariah McGirth has enterposed his claim to the said negroe, and that he had in all things complyed with the provisions of the Law, as to the requisites necessary to be observed in the establishment of the said Zachariah McGirth's Claim.

And, it further Appearing to the Court that, notwithstanding the afore Said security having been given by the Claimant Such Sheriff still hold not only the Bonds, but Also the Negroe belonging to the Claimant.

It is therefore ordered by the Court, that the said Sheriff Do forthwith deliver to the party claimant, or his leagal Representative, the aforesaid negroe Dick within

---

Ten Days from the date hereof or, that in default thereof, an Attachment as for Contempt of this Court Do issue against him.

Ordered, that the Justices of the peace in the respective Company Districts do draw according to Law Constables for Each District, and make return of the Names of the persons so drawn to the Sheriff of this County without Delay.

Inferior Court Minutes Book 2

Ordered, that Isaac Lang's Account against the County be admitted and paid, Amounting to Seventeen Dollars thirty seven and a half Cents.

Ordered, that Samuel Kean be and he is hereby Nominated as Tax Collector for the Year One thousand Eight Hundred and Eight, and that Joseph Crews be and he is hereby Nominated receiver of Returns of Taxable property for said Year.

The Court then adjourned untill tomorrow Nine O'Clock.

Isaac Crews, Clk   Peyton Skipwith, Thos King, John Floyd

Wednesday, January 6th 1808

The Court Met agreeable to adjournment. Present, their Honors Thomas King, John Floyd, and Peyton Skipwith, Esquires, Justices of Said Court.

On the petition of John Köth, praying to become a Citizen of the United States, and the same being certified by a Number of respectable Citizens, to the Satisfaction of the Court, the following oath was administered to him by the Court and be admitted accordingly.

I, John Köth, do Solemnly swear, in the presence of Almighty God, that I have resided in the United States since the Month of January 1794, and ~~the whole time~~ within the State of Georgia during that period. That I will Support the Constitution of the United States, and that I absolutely renounce and abjure all allegiance and fidelity to any foreign power, potentate, prince, or Sovereignty, and particularly the Emperor of Germany, whose Subject I formerly was. And, that I will support the Constitution of the State of Georgia.

Sworn to before me }   Jon Köth
in open Court   }
Isaac Crews, Clk   }

It is Ordered, that Daniel Miller be recommended and is hereby recommended as a Justice of the peace for the thirty first Company District of Militia Commanded by Capt Crews, in Lue of Abra^m Bessent, Esqr, Removed out of the District.

It is Ordered, that John Tompkins be and he is hereby recommended as Justice of the peace for the thirty second district of Militia in Said County Commanded by John Tompkins, in Lue of Donald Tompkins, resigned.

It is Ordered, that John Crews and William Cone, Junr be and they are hereby recommended as Justices of the peace for the thirty forth District of Militia Commanded by Willm Cone, Junr, in Lue of William Cone, Senr, Resigned, and John Brown, Esqr, resigned.

Inferior Court Minutes Book 2

It is Ordered, that Jessey H. Harison be and he is hereby recommended as a Justice of the peace for Thirty ~~Second~~ Third District of Militia in Said County Commanded by John Hardy, in Lue of Thos R. Rigby, removed.

It is Ordered, that a County Tax be levied and Collected for the year 1808 Equal to One Sixth of the general Tax, and that the Tax Collector for year do Collect the Same.

Ordered, that David G. Jones' account against the County be admitted and paid, amounting to forty four Dollars Eighty Seven and a half Cents.

William & S. Robinson }
    vs   } Attachment
Samuel Gould   }

On motion of Mr Clark, Stating that attachment had issued in the above, and that Daniel Copp, Garnishee, had been Served with notice, and he Did at the last Term Render in on oath, agreeably to Law, a Schedule of Bonds, Notes, &c being in his hands the Property of the Said Samuel Gould.

It is therefore Ordered by the Court, that the said notes, accounts, bonds, &c so rendered by the Garnishee be filed in the Clerk's Office Within thirty Days from the Adjournment of this Court, and that Suits be instituted thereon, and it is further Ordered, that the Plf's Att^y in the above case have the Direction of the said Actions to Judgment, and the Moneies so recovered thereonshall be paid in the Clerk's Offices, subject to the further Order of this Court. And, it is further Ordered, that the Garnishee be Served with a Copy of this Order.

Ogier & Compay }
    vs   } Attach^t
Josiah Baker   }

On motion of Mr Clark, Stating that Attachment had issued in the Above case, And that John Ross, a Garnishee had been

---

Served with notice, and that he did at the last Term render in on Oath, agreeable to Law, a schedule of Notes, Accounts, &c being in his hands, and which had been deposited by the said Josiah Baker.

It is therefore Ordered by the Court, that the said Notes, Accounts, &c, so Rendered by the said Garnishee, be filed in the Clerk's Office within thirty Days from the Adjournment of this Court, and that suits be instituted thereon, and the Monies so recovered thereon shall be Deposited in the Clerk's Office, subject to the further Order of this Court. And, it is further Ordered, that a Copy of this Order be Served on the said Garnishee.

Inferior Court Minutes Book 2

John Holzendorf }
    vs   } Attach^t
Jehu Underwood }

On Motion of Mr Clark, Stating that Attachment had issued in the Above Case, and that Archabald Bain, a Garnishee, had been served with Notice, and that he did at this Term render in on Oath, Agreeable to Law, a Schedule of Notes ~~Accounts &c~~ being in his hands, and which had been Deposited by the said Jehu

Underwood. It is therefore Ordered by the ~~said~~ Court, that the Note so rendered by the said Garnishee, now filed in the Clerk;'s Office, that suit be instituted by the Plf's Attorney thereon, and the Monies ~~& there~~ thereon recovered shall be deposited in the Clerk's Office, subject to the further Order of this Court.

The Court then adjourned Without day.

Isaac Crews, Clk Thos King, John Floyd, Peyton Skipwith

Georgia   }
Camden County } Inferior Court at Chambers, in the Town of St Mary's, 20th February 1808.

Present, their Honors James Seagrove, Peyton Skipwith, Thomas King, & William Johnston, Esq^{rs}.

On former order of Court, the Defendant in Execution, Charles Homer, an Insolvent Debtor, was brought up by Writ of Habeous Corpus, and No Creditor Shewing Cause Why he Should Not be discharged, the Court after Administering to him the following Oath prescribed by Law.

I, Charles Homer, do Solemnly Swear in the presence of Almighty God that I am

I am Not possessed of Any real or personal Estate, debts, or Effests, Securities, or Contracts Whatsoever, any wearing apparel, bedding for My Self and family and the Working tools or implements of My trade or Calling, to gether with the Necessary equipments for a Militia Soldier excepted, other than are Contained in the Schedule Now Delivered, and that I have Not, directly or indirectly, Since My imprisonment or before, Sold, leased, assigned, or Other wise disposed of, or Made over in trust for My Self, or otherwise, any part of My Lands, estate, goods, Stock, Money, debts, Securities, or Contracts, Whereby Any Money may hereafter become payable, or any real or personal estate, whereby to have or expect any benefit or profit to My Self, My Wfe, or My Heir.So help me God.

Sworn to in Open Court   }   ~~Peyton Skipwith~~
this 20th day of February 1808 }

———

the prisoner having delivered up all his property and taken the foregoing Oath.

Ordered, that he be deliberated from his imprisonment and Seta at Large, According to the Act of the General Assembly in that Case Made and provided.

William Johnston
Peyton Skipwith
Ja^s Seagrove

St Mary's Chamber, 29th Feby 1808, Inferior Court

State   }
 vs   } Attachment for Not Obeying the Order of the Court
D. G. Jones }

The prisoner being brought ~~before~~ up by virtue of a Habeas Corpus, proceeded to investigate the Causes of his Confinement.

On examination, the Circumstances leading to his Confinement, they appeared as follows, that Jospeh Crews, Deputy Sheriff, had levied an Attachment against One James McGirt at the suit of the Admor & Admix of Daniel McGirt on a Certain Negro Named Dick, took him into possession, and Shortly after placed him in the Hands of Saml Boyd, the Admor on the Said Estate, that One

———

One Zachariah McGirt interposed a Claim to the Said Negro and gave Security agreeably to Law, to establish his Claim thereto, oor pay all Costs and damages, which Might arise, that Not Withstanding this, the Deputy Sheriff Suffered the aforesaid Negro Dick to remain in possession of the Said Boyd. That at the last term of the Infr Court, the attorney for the Clamant prayed the Court to order a Delivery of the Said Negro Dick to the Clamant or his legal representative, or that in default an Attachment do issue against the Sheriff. As for a Contempt of the Court that such Order had been regularly Served, and that the Same was Not Complied with on the part of the Sheriff or his deputy.

It further appearing that the process and Other papers had been placed in the Hands of Joseph Crews, Deputy Sheriff, who alone had Conducted the Case thro Every Stage and that he alone Ought to be punished for his mal-feasance in office.

Inferior Court Minutes Book 2

The Court therefore Order, that David G. Jones, Sheriff as aforesaid, be released and discharged from from imprisonment, and that an Attachment as

---

for a Contempt of this Court do forth with issue ag^t Joseph Crews, Deputy Sheriff.

It is Ordered by the Court, that the Sheriff of the County proceed immidiately to put such repairs on the public jail in the Town of Jefferson as will Make it Secure for the safe Keeping of prisoners and that the jail in the Town of St Mary's be a place of Confinement untill those repairs Shall be made on the jail in the Town of Jefferson aforesaid.

William Johnston
Peyton Skipwith
Ja^s Seagrove

Inferior Court Camden County, Chambers 10th March 1808

Joseph Crews, late Deputy Sheriff of this County, against whom an Attachment for a Contempt had issued, being Now brought up and having upon Oath in the presence of the Court purged him Self of the Contempt with Which he Stands charged.

On Motion of Counsel for the prisoner. It is Ordered, that he be released & discharged.

Ja^s Seagrove, Peyton Skipwith

Monday, June the 6th 1808

The Court was opened. Present, William Johnston, John Floyd, & Peyton Skipwith, Esquires, Justices of Said Court.

The Jury Venire facias was Called and the following persons Appeared and [blot] answered to their Names, Viz.

    1. John Prevatt   2. Thomas Hughs

---

3. Samuel Griffin	10. Robert Brown
4. John Cade	11. Robt McFarlane
5. Ja^s Hudson	12. I. K. Courter
6. Smith Cannon	13. Willm Hines
7. George Gates	14. Willm Downs
8. Nathan Norton	15. Benjamin Grubbs
9. James Lindsay	16. Willm Watson

Inferior Court Minutes Book 2

There being No Cases on the doquet that can be tried under the present Acts of the Legislature passed at Milledge Ville on the [blank] 1808.

Therefore the Jurors ware dismissed.

The Court then adjourned Untill Court in Course.

Isaac Crews, Clk   Peyton Skipwith
                                    John Floyd
                                    William Johnston

At Chambers, June the Seventh 1808. Present, their Honors James Seagrove, Peyton Skipwith, and William Johnston, Esquires, Justices of Said Court.

On the petition

———

On the petition of Alexander Deblieux, praying to be admitted Citizen of the United States, and the same being certified by a Number of respectable Citizens to the Satisfaction of the Court, the following oath was Administered to him accordingly.

I, Alexander Deblieux, do Solemnly Swear in the presence of Almighty God, that I have resided with the United States and in Louisiana since the Month of August 1802, and within the State of Georgia kore than two years. That I will support the Constitution of the United States and that I absolutely renounce and abjure all allegiance and fidelity to any foreign power, potentate, prince, or sovereignty, and particularly the Emperor of France, whose Subject I formerly was. And, that I will support the Constitution of the State of Georgia.

                                    Deblieux

Isaac Crews, Clk   Ja^s Seagrove
                                    William Johnston
                                    Peyton Skipwith

———

Monday, January the Second 1809

The Court was Opened, Present Their Honors James Seagrove, Thomas King, John Floyd, & William Johnston, Esquires, Justices of Said Court.

There being No Jury, the Court proceeded to Call the appearance doquit.

Inferior Court Minutes Book 2

Timothy Hall }
   vs   } Case
James Smith }

Judgement by Default. Jany Term 1809.

James Seagrove }
   vs   } Trover
Samuel Boyd }

Judgement by Default. January Term 1809.

John Holzendorf }
   vs   } Case
Samuel Griffin }

Judgement by Default.

Alex^r Leckie, Indorse }
   vs   } Case
Ray Sands }

Judgement by Default.

Alex^r Leckie, Indorse }
   vs   } Case
Ray Sands }

Judgement by Default.

Alex^r Leckie, Indorse }
   vs   } Case
Charlotte P. Mabry, }
Administratrix of }
Woodford Mabry }

Judgement by Default.

___

Alexander Ogden }
   vs   } Case
Lewis Levy }

Judgement by Default. January Term 1809

Inferior Court Minutes Book 2

Samuel Dewherst, }
Admor of John White }
    vs   } Case
Harmon Courter }

Judgement by Default.

Sarah Howley }
    vs   } Attachment
James Hutchinson & }
Moses Harrel }

Death of James Hutchinson, ~~Suggested~~ One of the Defendants, Suggested and Judgement by Default against Moses Haral.

J. Head }
    vs   } Trespass Esarmes &C
A. Lathrop & }
G. Roberts }

Death of A. Lathrop Suggested & Judgement against George Roberts by Default.

Hudnall, Paxton, & Weyman }
    vs   } Case
Slauter Cowling }

Writ amended & term given.

Timothy Hopkins }
    vs   } Case
Arthur Moore }

Judgement by Default.

Admor Joseph Mitchell }
    vs   } Case
James Baird }

Judgement by Default.

———

Ezekiel Hudnall }
    vs   } Slander
Jarey Ives }

Bail Discharged & plea filed.

Inferior Court Minutes Book 2

Jury drawn for June Term.

1. Ogden Brown
2. William Ashley
3. William Neely
4. Thos H. Miller
5. David Lewis
6. Thomas Clark, Junr
7. Charles Floyd
8. John Boog
9. Ja^s D. Prevatt
10. Hugh Brown
11. William Culclazier
12. Joseph Rain
13. William Clark
14. William Cone, Junr
15. Arthur Moore
16. Henry Garvey
17. Ezekiel Hudnall
18. William Gibson
19. Thomas Bond
20. Francis Sterling
21. William Smith
22. James Hanney
23. Charles Howell
24. Charles Homer
25. Ezekiel Parish
26. Francis Settle
27. Joseph Thomas
28. Thomas King, Merch^t
29. Henry Hart
30. William Gillet
31. Daniel Copp
32. Donold Tompkins
33. Ja^s Elliott
34. Philip Goodbread
35. R. M. D. J. Elliott
36. Ja^s Bryant
37. Timothy Hopkins

The Court then adjourned Untill Tomorrow Nine O'Clock.

Isaac Crews, Clk

Ja^s Seagrove
Thos King
William Johnston
John Floyd

Tuesday, January the third 1809

The Court Met agreeable to adjournment. Present, their Honors James Seagrove, Thomas King, John Floyd, & William Johnston, Esq^{rs}, Justices of Said Court.

Ordered, that the Justices of the peace in the different Company districts do draw Constables for their respective districts, as the Law directs, No persons having offered their Services in That Capacity to this Court.

Ordered, that a County Tax be levied & Collected for the Year 1809 Equal to One Sixth of the general Tax, & that the Collector of the general Tax do Collect & pay Over the Same to this Court.

The Sheriff of the County, by his Memorial to the Court, represented the ruinous & insecure State of the Court House and and Goal, and the responsibility that he labored Under, when in the Execution of his duty, in Consequence thereof and having prayed that Some Appropriation be made to enable him to remedy the evil.

Inferior Court Minutes Book 2

It is therefore Ordered by the Court, that the County funds that Now are, or that May hereafter be Collected, be Appropriated for that purpose. And, it

---

is further Ordered, that the Clerk of the Inferior Court of this County Do pay to the Order of the Said Sheriff all Moneys that May Come in his hands or possession Either from fines or other assessments, provided that the Said Amount do Not exceed the Sum of two Hundred Dollars.

Ordered, that a Tax for the relief of the poor be levied & Collected Equal to One fourteenth of the general Tax for the year One Thousand Eight Hundred & Nine. And, that the Collector of Taxes for said year do Collect and pay Over the Said Tax to the Overseers of the poor for the Town of St Mary's, in lue of Robert McFarlane, Esqr, deceased.

Ordered, that Daniel Miller & Timothy Hopkins, Esq^{rs} be & they are hereby Appointed Overseers of the poor for the 31st district.

~~Ordered~~ The Petition of James Nobles, praying the benefit of the insolvent act.

Ordered, that the Creditors of the said Nobles be notified to appear at St Mary's in Camden County on the twentieth day of January next, to shew cause, if any they have, why

---

the said Nobles be not discharged Agreeable to terms of the act.

Ordered, that the Clerk of this Court do report immediately to the Court the reasons why he has not delivered to this Court a list of persons liable to serve as Jurors, in Order that the said list might be corrected & Jurors drawn in terms of the Law, in consequence of Such neglect or omission, the said Court were prevented at the preceeding and present Term of Court from drawing said Jurors, as pointed out and directed by Law. In consequence of which Order, the said Clerk presented the following report, to Wit.

The list has not been furnished by the receiver of Tax returns for said County, nor from the Collector of Taxes. Therefore, he, the said Clerk, was unable to render the list to the Court for Correction, in terms of the Law, made & provided in such cases.

Wherefore, it is resolved, as the opinion of this Court, that the Receiver of Taxes, whose duty it was

---

to render to the said Clerk a Digest, as specified in the fourth Section of Tax Law, have by such neglect incured the fines & penaltys inflicted by the said section. And, it is further Ordered, that these proceedings be made of record, & that the Clerk of the said Court do fourthwith transmit to the Att^y Genl a Copy thereof, in Order that such

Inferior Court Minutes Book 2

measures may be pursued & adopted as are best calculated to punish or prevent such neglect or omissions in future.

The Court then adjourned to Meet agt Chambers in the Town of St Mary's on the twentieth of January Ins^t.

Isaac Crews, Clk   Ja^s Seagrove
                                    Thos King
                                    John Floyd
                                    William Johnston

St Mary's, at Chambers, Friday, January the 20th 1809

The Court Met agreeable to adjournment. Present, their Honors James Seagrove, Thos King, John Floyd, & William Johnston, Esq^{rs}, Justices of Said Court.

James Nobles, a Debtor, having being brought up, rendered to the Court a Schedule of his Effects, of which the following is a Copy, and are in the words following, to wit.

Camden County

Schedules of the Estate & Effects of James Nobles, an insolvent Debtor, rendered to the Inferior Court for the Benefit of his Creditors, previous to his discharge.

One Canoe, 22 feet long, 3½ feet Wide

One thousand W. O. Staves, 16 Oars 15 feet Long

Open Account against J. P. Randall $7-0

Four Cows & Calves, Four thousand Shingles Mor & less

A tract of Land, Said to be ~~left~~ Devised by Hannah Nobles, his Grandmother, of Effingham County, Situated in Bulloch County, Georgia

I, James Nobles, do Solemnly Swear in the presence of Almighty God, that I am Not possessed of any Reil or personal Estate, debts, Credits, or Effects, Securities, or Contracts Whatsoever (My wearing apparel, bedding for My Self & family, & the Working Tools or Implements of My Trade or Calling, together With the Necessary Equipments of a Militia Soldier Excepted) Other than are Contained in the Schedule Now delivered, and that I have Not, directly or indirectly, Since my imprisonment or before

---

Sold, Leased, assigned, or other wise disposed of, or Made Over in Trust for My Self, or Other wise, any part of Lands, Estates, goods, Stock, Money, debts, Securities, or

Inferior Court Minutes Book 2

Contracts, whereby any Money may hereafter become payable, or any real or personal Estate, whereby to have or Expect any benefit or profit, to My self, My wife, or my Heir. So help me God.

Sworn in Open Court }	James X Nobles, his mark
this 20th Jany 1809 }	[His mark consists of a large circle,
Isaac Crews, Clk }	with a capital X in it]

And, it further appeared that the Creditors of the said James Nobles had been regularly Served with the notice to appear at this Day to shew cause, if they any they had, why the prayer of the said Debtor should not be granted, and they having been severally Called made default. It is therefore Ordered by the Court, That the Prisoner be forthwith released and discharged from his Imprisonment, on his Paying fees, And if unable to do so, that the same be paid out of the sales arising from his Effects.

Ordered, that Charles Magill be and he is hereby Appointed Rdeceiver of the returns of Taxable property for the County of Camden for the year One thousand Eight Hundred & Nine.

And, that Randolph McGillis, Esqr be & he is hereby Appointed Collector of Taxes for the years 1808 & 1809, for the year Eighteen hundred and Eight, in lue of Samuel Kean, Died.

The Court then adjourned Untill Court in Course.

Isaac Crews, Clk	Thos King
	Ja^s Seagrove
	John Floyd
	William Johnston

Georgia }	
Camden County }	Court at Chambers in the Town of St Mary's, 16th of March 1809

The Prisoners, James Brown, Adam Hays, William Winslow, & John Right, Seamen, having been brought up & also the Opposite party, & a full investigation being had.

It is Ordered, that the four Prisoners be discharged from Confinement, on their paying all costs arrising on their imprisonment & being brought up.

Ja^s Seagrove
Thos King
William Johnston

Inferior Court Minutes Book 2

Georgia }
Camden County } Inferior Court at Chambers, May 23rd 1809

Present, their Honors James Seagrove & William Johnston, Esq[rs]

On the Petition of Thomas Bond, an Insolvent Debtor, to receive the benefit of the act in that case Made & provided & being brought up, under writ of Habeas Corpus.

Ordered, that the Creditors of the Said Thomas Bond be Notified to appear at the Next Inferior Court, to be held at Jefferson, in and for the County Aforesaid, On the Sixth day of June Next, to shew Cause why the prayers of the petitioner Should Not be Granted.

S[t] Mary's, May 23rd

             Ja[s] Seagrove, William Johnston

At Chambers, S[t] Mary's, May 3rd 1809

Present, their Honors James Seagrove, Thomas King, & William Johnston, Justices of the Inferior Court.

State }
 vs   } warrant Charge the prisoner with useing threats
Zachariah McGirt } ag[s] the life of Samuel Boyd

The Prisoner, having Prayed the Benefit of the writ of Habeas Corpus, was in Consequence brought up. On Motion of the prisoner's Counsel, And it Appearing that the Affidavit on which the Warrant had issued is both Vague and Uncertain & Not Sufficient to Justify the detention of the person of the prisoner.

It is therefore Ordered by the Court, that the Prisoner be forth with discharged from his Confinement & that the prosecuter pay Costs.

             Ja[s] Seagrove
             Tho[s] King
             William Johnston

Georgia, Camden County Inferior Court, Town of S[t] Mary's, At Chambers, May 26th 1809

Present, Their Honors James Seagrove & Thomas King, Esquires

Inferior Court Minutes Book 2

John Street }
    vs   } Trespass
Daniel Daney }
Jacob Lewis & }
John Philips }

The Prisoners having been Brought up by Writ of Habeas Corpus.

On Motion of the Plaintiff's Attorney, Ordered, that the defendants be brought to Morrow at 10 O'clock to have their Hearing.

                                          Ja^s Seagrove, Thos King

May 27th 1809

The Court Met according to adjournment. Present, their Honors James Seagrove, Thomas King, & William Johnston, Esquires.

The Prisoners, Daniel Dane, Jacob Lewis, and John Phillips, ware brought up, & after hearing the parties, Plaintiff & Defendants, the Court Ordered that the prisoners be discharged on paying their Own Costs.

                                            Ja^s Seagrove
                                            Thos. King
                                            William Johnston

Georgia, Camden County, Inferior Court at Chambers, May 30th 1809

Present, their Honors James Seagrove & William Johnston, Esquires.

George Webber }
    vs   } Case
Nathaniel Verry } Bail

The Prisoner, having been Brought before the Court under writ of Habeas Corpus, & the Case being investigated & boath parties heard.

Ordered, That it Appearing that the Cause of Action having Originated in the Spanish Dominions & both parties, Plaintiff and Defendant being foreigners, the prisoner be discharged & Each party pay their own Costs. The Court Considering the parties Not to come Under the Jurisdiction of this State.

                                            J. Seagrove, William Johnston

Inferior Court Minutes Book 2

Jefferson, Monday, June 5th 1809

Court was Opened. Present, James Seagrove, Thomas King, John Floyd, & William Johnston, Esquires, Justices of Said Court.

The Jury Venire was Called and discharged Untill tomorrow Nine O'Clock.

The Court proceeded to the selection of Grand Jurors agreeable to An Act of the Legislature of 1805.

The Commission of John Ross [faint], Justice of the Inferior Court, was read and Ordered to be recorded as follows, to wit.

Georgia. By his Excellency, Jared Irwin, Governor and Commander in Chief of the Army & Navy of this State & the Militia thereof.

To John Ross, Esquire, Greeting.

By Virtue of the power & the Authority in me Vested by the Constitution of the State aforesaid and in pursuance of Your Appointment by the General Assembly On the 19th day of November Eighteen Hundred & Eight.

I do hereby Commission you, the Said John Ross, One of the Justices of the Inferior Court, of the County of Camden, in

---

in the said State. You are therefore hereby hereby Authorised and required to do and perform all and Singular the duties incumbent on You, as a Justice of the Said Court, According to Law & the trust reposed in you, this Commission to Continue in force during good behavior, or so long as you Shall reside in the County for which are Appointed, Unless removed by sentence on impeachment, or by the Governor, On the address of two thirds of Each Branch of the General Assembly. Given Under My Hand & Seal this Fifth day of December in the Year of our Lord Eighteen Hundred and Eight and in the thirty third year of American Independence.

                                                            by the Governor
Jared Irwin   Hor. Marbury, Secy

The Court then adjourned Untill Tomorrow Morning Nine O'Clock.

Isaac Crews, Clk   Thos King
                                                        John Floyd
                                                        J. Seagrove
                                                        William Johnston

Inferior Court Minutes Book 2

Tuesday, June 6th 1809

The Court Met according to adjournment. Present, their Honors James Seagrove, Thomas King, John Floyd, & William Johnston, Esquires, Justices of Said Court.

The Jury Venirey was Called & the following Jurors appeared, Viz.

1. William Ashley	13. Francis Settle, Ex^d
2. Charles Howell	14. William Clark
3. William Gibson	15. Ez. Hudnall
4. Thos H. Miller	16. Donald Tompkins
5. David Lewis	17. Ja^s Bryant
6. John Boog	18. Hugh Brown
7. ~~Ezekiel Ha~~ Ezekiel Parris	19. Philip Goodbread
8. Thomas King	Arthur Moor
9. William Cone, Junr	Francis Sterling
10. Richd Elliott	[faint]
11. Willm Culclazier	
12. William Gillis	

The following persons ware Summoned as Talles men, viz.

John Conner	Thomas Goodbread
Ja^s Helvingston	Samuel Boyd
William Hines	

Francis Settle, appeared And Made Oath that he is upwards of Sixty Years of Age.

Ordered, that he be excused and that his Name be taken from the Jury List.

On the Petition of James C. W. Stuart, praying to be admitted a Citizen of the United States, and the Same being certified by a number of respectable Citizens to the Satisfaction of the Court, the following oath was administered to him accordingly.

I, James Charles William Stuart, do Solomnly Swear in the presence of Almighty God, that I have resided in the United States for ~~Several~~ Seven years past, and within the state of Georgia more than three years. That I will support the Constitution of the United States and that I absolutely renounce and abjure all allegiance and fidelity to any foreign power, potentate, prince, or Sovereignty and particularly the King of England, whose Subject I formerly was. And, that I will Support the Constitution of the State of Georgia.

Sworn in   }
Open Court   }   James C. W. Stuart
Isaac Crews, Clk }

Inferior Court Minutes Book 2

Copp & King }
    vs   } Case
Silas Richmond }

Jury N° 2 Sworn generally.

William Clark	Francis Sterling
Ezekiel Hudnall	John Conner
Donald Tompkins	James Helvingston
Hugh Brown	William Hines
Philip Goodbread	Thomas Goodbread
Arthur Moore	Samuel Boyd

Verdict, we find for the plaintiff One hundred and fifteen Dollars and forty One Cents, with Interest from the thirteenth of June 1805 & Costs of Suit. June 5th 1809

                                              Ezekiel Hudnall, foreman

Peter Lane }
    vs   } Attachment
Josiah Baker }

Jury N° 1 Sworn, to wit.

William Ashley	Charles Howell
William Gibson	Thos H. Miller
David Lewis	John Boog
Ezekiel Pearis	Thomas King
Willm Cone, Junr	R. M. D. J. Elliott
William Culclazur	William Gillet

Verdict, we find for the plaintiff One hundred and thirty Dollars and Seventy two Cents, with Interest from the 19th June 1806 and Costs of Suit. June 6th 1809

                                              Willm Gibson, foreman

Samuel Humphreys }
    vs   } Case
Longstreet & Griffin }

Jury N° 2

Verdict, we find for the plff five hundred & Seventy Dollars, with Interest from the Sixteenth of June 1806 & Costs of Suit. June 6th 1809

                                              Ezekiel Hudnall, foreman

Inferior Court Minutes Book 2

Isaac Cook }
    vs } Case
John Demott & }
Thomas King, Esqr }

I Confess Judgement for One Hundred Dollars, with Interest from the 8th March 1806 and Costs of Suit. June 6th 1809

                                                  Clark, deft's Att^y

---

Jones & Ashley }
    vs } Case
John Howell }

Jury N° 2

Verdict. We find for the Plaintiff forty Nine Dollars ~~fifty~~ forty four and three quarter Cents, with Interest from the 8th Novr 1806 and Costs of Suit.

Jefferson, 6th June 1809   Ezek^l Hudnall, foreman

Admors Peter Madden }
    vs } Attachment
John F. Pelott }

Jury N° 2

Verdict, we find for the Plaintiff five Hundred Dollars, with Interest & Costs of Suit. Jefferson, 6th June 1809

                                                  Ezek^l Hudnall, foreman

Joseph Dorr }
Admor of Jo^s Judson }
    vs } Case
Nathan Atkinson }

Jury N° 1, Philip Goodbread in place of R. M. D. J. Elliott.

Verdict. We find for the plaintiff

Six Hundred & Eighty four Dollars Eighty Six & an half Cents, with Interest from 8th Jany 1805, & Costs of Suit.

June 6th 1809   Willm Gibson, foreman

Inferior Court Minutes Book 2

Isaac Crews }
    vs   } Slander
John Messer }

Jury N° 2

Verdict. We, the Jury, find for the Plaintiff two Hundred & fifty Dollars, With Costs of Suit.

6th June 1809   Ezek^l Hudnall, foreman

Sadler & Sands }
    vs   } Case
Joseph Dorr }

I Confess Judgement for Seventy Dollars, with Interest from twenty Nine of June 1803, & Costs of Suit.

June 6th 18709   Joseph Dorr

~~Hudnall~~
Hudson Ragland }
    vs   } Case
James Seagrove }

I Confess Jug^t for One hundred & five Dollars & fifty Cents & Interest on the Same, & on two Hundred thirty Eight Dollars, from the first of January 1805 to 13th Jan 1806, & Costs of Suit. June 6th 1809

                                                                                   Clark, Plff's Att^y

Timothy Hall }
    vs   } Case
James Smith }

I confess Jug^t for three Hundred & Eighteen Dollars & forty Eight & One half Cents, with Interest from the tenth of January Eighteen Hundred & Eight & Costs of Suit.

June 6th 1809   Stahl, Deft^s Att^y

Minis & Hunter }
    vs   } Case
James Seagrove }

I confess Judgement for three Hundred & twenty One Dollars & Eleven Cents, with Interest from the 29th Decr 1809 & Costs. 6th June 1809

Inferior Court Minutes Book 2

Clark, Deft's Atty

William B. Smith }
    vs   } Case
James Seagrove, Esqr }

I confess Judgement for two hundred & six dollars, with Interest from the thirteenth of April 1804 & Costs.

6th June 1809   Clark, Deft's Atty

Messrs Ogier & Co }
    vs   } attachment
Josiah Baker   }

Jury No 1 One

Verdict. We find for the plaintiff Seven hundred & Sixty Dollars, with Interest from 31st Jany 1806, & Costs of Suit.

June 6th 1809   William Gibson, foreman

White Rosseter }
    vs   } Case
John Henry Gerbel }

Jury No 1

Verdict. We find for the plaintiff two Hundred Dolls and Sixteen Cents. wth Interest from 30th July 1806 & Costs of Suit.

June 6th 1809   Willm Gibson, foreman

William B. Smith   }
    vs   } Case
Randolph McGillis, Esqr }

I confess Judgement for One hundred and Sixty five Dollars, with Interest from the first of November 1804, & Costs. 6th June 1809

R. McGillis

Hunter & Minis }
    vs   } Case
James Seagrove }

Inferior Court Minutes Book 2

I confess Judgement for three hundred & One Dollars and fifty five Cents, with Interest from the 6th March 1805, & Costs of Suit. June 6th 1809

                 Clark, ~~Plff's~~ Deft's Atty

Wiliam & Silvester Robinson }
  vs   } Attachment
Samuel Gould   }

Jury No 1

Verdict, we find for the plaintiffs two Thousand two Hundred and Eighty One Dollars $^{40}/_{100}$, with Costs of Suit.

June 6th 1809   Willm Gibson, foreman

James Douglass, Admor }
John Douglass   }
  vs   } Case
Randolph McGillis   }

I confess Judgement for two Hundred Dollars, with Interest from the first of January 1806 & Costs of Suit.

June 6th 1809   R. McGillis

James Douglass, Admor }
John Douglass   }
  vs   } Case
Thomas King, Esqr   }

I confess Judgement for fifty Dollars, with Interest from the first of Jany 1806 & Costs.
June 6th 1809

                 Clark, Deft's Atty

Executor of Richd Gascoigne }
  vs   } Case
Francis Settle   }

Jury No 2

Verdict. we, the Jury, find for the plaintiff thirty Dollars Nine & three fourths Cents, with Costs of Suit.

June 6th 1809   Ezekl Hudnall, foreman

Inferior Court Minutes Book 2

James Willy, Indorse }
    vs   } Case
King & Jones }

I confess Judgement for fifty four Dollars and twenty five Cents, with Interest from the 19th of January 1804 & Costs.

June 6th 1809   Thos King, Junr

Timothy Hopkins }
    vs   } Case
Abram Pratt }

Jury No 1

Verdict. We find for the plaintiff One Hundred and twenty Dollars & fifty Eight Cents, with Interest from 15th July 1809 & Costs of Suit.

June 6th ~~1809~~ 1807   Willm Gibson, foreman

Peter Lane }
    vs   } Attachment
Josiah Baker }

Jury No 1

Verdict. We find for the plaintiff One Hundred & Eighty Six Dollars and eighty One & ¼ Cents, with Costs of Suit.

June 6th 1809   Willm Gibson, foreman

Leven Gunby }
    vs   } Debt
William Neely }

Jury No 2

Verdict. We find the deed declared on to be the deed of the Defendant & assess One Cent damages & Costs of Suit.

June 6th 1809   Ezekl Hudnall, Foreman

David G. Jones }
    vs   } Case
Charles Stahl }

Inferior Court Minutes Book 2

I confess Judgt for Eighty two Dollars $^{50}/_{100}$, with Interest from first March 1806 & Costs.

June 6th 1809   Charles Stahl

Hamilton Jones }
    vs   } Case
Charles Stahl   }

I confess Judgement for Seventy four Dollars $^{94}/_{100}$, with Interest from 13th March 1806 & Costs.

June 6th 1809   Charles Stahl

On Motion of Mr Stahl, Ordered that Thomas Bond, an Insolvent debtor, Now in the Common Joal, be brought up in pursuance of Notice, On a former Order of this Court at Chambers in St Mary's.

The Prisoner, Thomas Bond, was brought into Court & produced the following Schedule & took the following Oath, Viz.

Schedule of the property of Thomas Bond, an Insolvent Debtor, that prays the Benefit of the Act in that Case Made & provided, Viz.

A Crop of Corn Now in the Ground of a bout four acres.

I, Thomas Bond, do Solemnly Swear, in the presence of Almighty God, that I am Not possessed of any real or personal Estate, debts, Credits, or Effects, Securities, or Contracts Whatsoever. My wearing Apparel, bedding for My Self & family, & Working Tools or implements of My trade or calling, together with the Necessary Equipments of a Militia Soldier, Excepted; Other than are Contained in the Schedue Now Delivered and that I have Not, Directly or indirectly, Since my imprisonment

---

Imprisonment or before, Sold, leased, Assigned, or Other wise disposed of, or made Over in Trust for My Self or Otherwise, Any part of My Lands, Estates, Goods, Stock, Money, debts, Securities, or any real or personal Estate, whereby any Money hereafter May become payable, or any real or personal Estate, whereby to have or expect any Benefit or profit, to My Self, My wife, or My heirs. So help me God.

Sworn to in Open Court   Thos Bond
June 6th 1809
Isaac Crews, Clk

Thomas Bond having taken taken the Oath prescribed by Law, It is Ordered that he be discharged according.

Inferior Court Minutes Book 2

Court then adjourned Untill Tomorrow Morning Nine O'Clock.

Isaac Crews, Clk

John Floyd
Thos King
Ja^s Seagrove
William Johnston

Wednesday, June 7th 1809

The Court met agreeable to adjournment. Present, their Honors James Seagrove, Thomas King, John Floyd, & William Johnston, Esquires, Justices of Said Court.

Hunter & Minis }
    vs   } Case
James Smith   }

I confess Judgement for One Hundred & fifty Eight Dollars and Eleven Cents, with Interest from the first day of January Eighteen Hundred and four & Costs of Suit.

June 7th 1809   Stahl, Deft^s Atty

Mintwin & Bown   }
    vs   } Case
Randolph McGillis }

I confess Judgement for three Hundred & twenty two Dollars thirty seven and a half Cents, with Interest from the tenth of Jany 1806 & Costs of Suit. June 7th 1809

                                                    R. McGillis

Mintwin & Bown, Indorsee }
    vs   } Case
Randolph McGillis   }

I confess Judgement for One hundred & forty Dollars & thirty Cents, with Interest from the fifth of January 1806 & Costs.

June 7th 1809   R. McGillis

Williford & Cook   }
    vs   } Case
John Ross, Admor of }
Peter Knight   }

Jury N° 1

Inferior Court Minutes Book 2

Verdict. We find for the Plaintiffs Three Hundred and thirteen Dollars and thirty Eight Cents, with Interest from the date the Notes become due, & Costs of Suit.

June 7th 1809   Will[m] Gibson, foreman

Scott & Company }
    vs   } Case
Joseph Dorr, Admor }
Joseph Judson   }

Jury N° 1

Verdict. We find for the plaintiffs two Thousand three hundred & thirty Dollars & Ninety One Cents, with Costs of Suit.

June 7, 1809   Will[m] Gibson, foreman

William Mein &   }
Robert Makay, Survr[s] }
    vs   } Case
Joseph Dorr, Admor }
Joseph Judson   }

Jury N° 1

Verdict. We find for the plaintiffs five Hundred & fifteen Dollars & thirty five Cents, with Costs of Suit. June 7th 1809

                                                              Will[m] Gibson, foreman

Robert & John Bolton }
    vs   } Debt
Joseph R. McCay   }

Jury N° 1

Verdict. We find the deed Declared on be the deed of the Defendant & assess One Cent Damages, with Costs of Suit.

June 7th 1809   Will[m] Gibson, foreman

William Culclazier }
    vs   } Case
John Howell   }

Jury N° 1

Inferior Court Minutes Book 2

Timothy Hopkins Sworn on the Jury in Lue of William Culclazier.

Verdict, we find for the Plaintiff Ninety Dollars, with Interest from the first day of January 1807 & Costs of Suit.

June 7th 1809   Willm Gibson, foreman

William Culclazier }
      vs   } Case
Elizabeth Gordon }

Jury N° 1

Verdict for the plaintiff Two hundred and thirty Seven Dollars & forty three Cents, with Interest on 425.$^{20}/_{100}$, from 1st Jany 1807 to 8 dec^r 1807 and Interest of two hundred & thirty seven Dollars $^{43}/_{100}$ from the 8th Decr 1807, & Costs of Suit.

~~Jun 7~~ June 7, 1809   Willm Gibson, foreman

Isaac K. Courter }
      vs   } Attachment
Pierre Ordonaux }

Jury N° 1

William Culclazier on the Jury in Lue of William Gibson.

Verdict, we find for the Plaintiff One hundred & Eighty Eight Dollars and Costs of Suit.

$188 7th June 1809   Thos H. Miller, foreman

Harper Garner }
      vs   } Special Action on the Case
Robert Burnet }

Jury N° 2

Witness Sworn William Cone, Junr & Wm Marcum.

Verdict. We, the Jury, find for the Plaintiff One hundred Dollars, with Costs of Suit. June 7th 1809

                                                           Ezekiel Hudnall, foreman

Inferior Court Minutes Book 2

William B. Smith }
    vs   } Case
Abram Pratt   }

Jury N° 1

William Gibson on the Jury in lue of Timothy Hopkins.

Verdict, we find for the plaintiff Seven hundred and Seventy three dollars and fifteen Cents, with Costs of Suit with ~~Costs~~ Interest.

___

Interest on One ~~One~~ Hundred & forty Seven Dollars of this Sum from the 26th May 1804. And on the defendant's delivering to the Plaintiff's Attorney the Notes or Judgements against R. McGillis, James Seagrove, Copp & King, William Naylor, and and H. Jones, acco^t, Francis Mursault, rec^t, for four Watches, & H. Jones, rec^t, for One Watch (the Other having been recd by S^d Pratt) as per defendant's Rect of 26th May 1804, Within ten days from this date, they are to be Considered as part payment of this Judgement.

June 7th 1809   Willm Gibson, foreman

Roberson & Long }
    vs   } case
Thomas Hughs   }

I confess Judgement for three Hundred & Ninety One Dollars & Eighty One Cents, & Interest from first of January 1804 & Costs of Suit. June 7th 1809

                                                                                  Th^o Hughs

Cunningham & Oneale }
    vs   } Case
Hughs & Crews   }

We Confess Judgement for Six Hundred & forty One Dollars and Nine Cents, with Interest from the twenty Eighth of June 1804 & Costs of Suit.

June 7th 1809   Th^o Hughs, Isaac Crews

___

John Jord^n Kern }
    vs   } Case
Thomas Hughs   }

Inferior Court Minutes Book 2

I confess Judgement for Six hundred & fifteen Dollars & forty Seven Cents, with Interest from the twenty fourth of April 1804 & Costs of Suit.

June 7th 1809   Thos Hughs

Timothy Hopkins }
    vs   } Case
Thomas Hughs }

I confess Judgement for the Sum of forty Eight Dollars & twenty five Cents, With Interest & Cost.

Jefferson, 7th June 1809   Tho Hughs

Samuel Boyd &   }
Susannah Boyd,   }
Danl McGertt, admors }
    vs   } Attachment
James McGirtt   }

Jury No 2

Timothy Hopkins & William Marcum On the Jury in lue of Samuel Boyd & Arthur Moore.

Witnesses Sworn, William Ashley, Thos King, R. M. D. J. Elliott

Verdict, we the Jury find

———

for Plaintiff One Hundred & thrity three Dollars & Eighty Seven & One half Cents, with Costs of Suit.

June 7, 1809   Ezekl Hudnall, foreman

                                                                   John Floyd
                                                                   Thos King
                                                                   Jas Seagrove
                                                                   William Johnston

The Court then adjourned Untill Tomorrow Morning Nine O'Clock.

Isaac Crews, Clk

Inferior Court Minutes Book 2

Thursday, June the Eighth 1809

The Court Met agreeable to adjournment. Present, James Seagrove, Thomas King, John Floyd, & Willm Johnston, Esquires, Justices of Said Court.

Slauter Cowling }
    vs   } Attachment
Josiah Baker   }

Jury N° 1, as yesterday.

Verdict, we find for the Plaintiff three hundred and thirty five Dollars Sixty three Cents, with Interest from 30th July 1807 & Costs.

June 8th 1809   Willm Gibson, foreman

Thomas Ogier }
    vs   } Case
Josiah Baker }

Jury N° 2

Verdict, we find for the Plaintiff five Hundred Dollars, with Interest from 31st January 1806 & Costs of Suit.

8th June 1809   Ezek^l Hudnall, Foreman

Thomas Garner   }
    vs   } Case
Longstreet & Griffin }

Jury N° 2

Verdict. We find for the Plaintiff Eighty Seven Dollars fifty Seven & a quarter Cents, with Interest from the 21st September 1806 & Costs.

8th June 1809   Ezek^l Hudnall, Foreman

Robert Burnett   }
Exor Willm Gormon}
    vs   } Attachment
John Gormon &   }
Willoughby Hodge }

Jury N° 1

Inferior Court Minutes Book 2

Verdict. We find for the Plaintiff two hundred & seventy Nine Dollars & thirty Seven & ½ Cents, with Interest from 1st May 1807 & Costs.

June 8th 1809   Willm Gibson, foreman

John Holzendorf }
    vs   } Attachment
Jehu Underwood }

Jury N° 2

Verdict. We find for the Plaintiff three Hundred & Nine Dollars & fifty four Cents, with Interest from 15th July 1806 & Costs of Suit. 8th June 1809

                                     Ezek^l Hudnall, Foreman

Robert L. Burnett   }
Exor William Gormon }
    vs   } Attachment
Willoughby Hodge & }
William Marcum   }

Jury N° 1

Verdict. We find for the Plaintiff Seventy four Dollars and twenty five Cents, with Interest from the 9th Feby 1807 (Seven) & Costs. June 8th 1809

                                       Willm Gibson, foreman

Daniel Copp, Indorse }
    vs   } Attachment
Thomas Doyle   }

Jury N° 2

Verdict. we, the Jury find for the plaintiff three Hundred Dollars, with Interest from the twenty fifth of June 1806, With Cost of Suit. June 8th 1809

                                     Ezek^l Hudnall, Foreman

John Holzendorf }
    vs   } Case
Samuel Griffin }

Jury N° 2

Inferior Court Minutes Book 2

Verdict. We find for the Plaintiff the Sum of two hundred & three Dollars twelve & a half Cents (and for forty One dollars One and three quarter Cents Interest to this day) & Costs of Suit.

8th June 1809   Ezek^l Hudnall, foreman

Edward Barnwell }
    vs   } Attachment
John C. Houston }

Jury N° 1

Verdict. We find this to be the Deed of the defendant & Assess One Cent damages, with Costs of Suit, and that Execution issue against James Seagrove, Garnishe, for twenty Six Dollars & fifty cents.

June 8th 1809   Willm Gibson, foreman

Philip Goodbread }
    vs   } Slander
Claborn Wright }

Witnesses Sworn, Thomas Goodbread, Arthur Moor, Robert Stafford, John Beesley, Amos Latham.

Jury N° 1

Verdict. We find for the Plaintiff One Dollar damages, with Costs of Suit.

June 8th 1809   Willm Gibson, foreman

The Jury list, as served on the fifth Ins^t, the Names of the Jurors was placed in the Jury Box in Appartment N° 1.

The following persons ware drawn for January Term 1810. 1810 Viz.

1. John Bailey, Junr	16. John Oaks
2. John Prevall	17. John Barco
3. John Frank	18. John Pratt
4. Richard Pellum	19. Chris^t Grovenstine
5. Ogden Brown	20. Ned Williams
6. Samuel Griffin	21. James King
7. Joseph Crews	22. Willm F. Kelley
8. Edwd W. Weyman	23. John Hardee
9. Willm Mickler	24. David Mizell
10. ~~Thomas Bond~~	25. John Crews
11. Ja^s Erskins	26. John Brown

Inferior Court Minutes Book 2

12. Charlton Mizell
13. N. R. Green
14. Sol Ostean
15. Thomas Garner

27. Alex^r Elliott
28. John Johnston
29. Shared Sheffield
30. Isham Frohock

---

31. Benjamin Grubbs
32. Berry Elzey
33. Danl Mather
34. Isaac Greene

35. Peter Prevatt
36. Danl Grant
37. Jessey H. Harrison
38. Robt Brown

James Seagrove }
    vs   } Trover
Samuel Boyd }

Jury N° 1

Verdict. We find for the Plaintiff Three Hundred Dollars & Costs of Suit.

June 8th 1809   Willm Gibson, foreman

Daniel Copp }
    vs   } Attachment
Thomas Doyle }

On Motion of Mr Stahl, Plaintiff's Attorney, that David Lewis, Garnishe in the Above Case, had Made return On Oath that he was in possession of Several Specialties, the property of the Defendant.

Ordered, that at least so much thereof as will Satisfy the Judgement Obtained be within ten Days delivered to the plaintiff's Att^y and be Sued.

Alexander Lechie, Indorse }
    vs   } case
Ray Sands }

Jury N° 2

Verdict. We, the Jury, find for the Defendant, With Costs of Suit.

June 8th 1809   Ezek^l Hudnall, foreman

Alexander Lechie, Indorse }
    vs   } Case
Ray Sands }

Inferior Court Minutes Book 2

Jury N° 2

Verdict. We, the Jury, find for the Defendant, with Costs of Suit.

June 8th 1809   Ezek^l Hudnall, Foreman

Alexander Lechie, Indorse }
    vs   } Case
Charlotte P. Mabry, Admix }
Woodford Mabry   }

Jury N° 1

Verdict. We find for the Plaintiff four Hundred Dollars, with Interest from the first day of Jany 1804 & Costs.

June 8th 1809   Willm Gibson, foreman

Alexander Ogden }
    vs   } Case
Lewis Levy   }

Jury N° 1

Verdict. We find for the Plaintiff One hundred and thirty four Dollars & Seventy five Cents, with Interest from the 27th Jany 1807 & Costs of Suit.

June 8th 1809   Willm Gibson, foreman

Samuel Dewhurst   }
Admor John White   }
    vs   } Case
Harmon Courter   }

Jury N° 1

Verdict. We find for the Plaintiff One hundred Dollars, with Interest from 6th June 1807 & Costs of Suit.

June 8th 1809   Willm Gibson, foreman

Timothy Hopkins }
    vs   } Case
Arthur Moore   }

Jury N° 1

Inferior Court Minutes Book 2

Verdict. We find for the Plaintiff thirty Eight Dollars and twenty Six ¼ Cents, with Interest from 6th Feby 1808 & Costs.

June 8th 1809   Willm Gibson, foreman

Alexander Lechie, Indee }
  vs   } Case
David G. Jones, Admor }
William Jones   }

Jury No 1

Verdict. We find for the plaintiff Six Hundred and Sixteen Dollars & forty four Cents, with Interest from 1st Jany 1804 & Costs of Suit.

June 8th 1809   Willm Gibson, foreman

Ezekiel Hudnall }
  vs   } Slander
Jerry Ives   }

Jury No 1

Verdict. we find for the Plaintiff fifty Dollars, with Costs of Suit.

June 8th 1809   Willm Gibson, foreman

Slauter Cowling }
  vs   } Debt
Hudnall & Weyman }

Same }
 vs } debt
Same }

The parties, Plaintif & Defendants, agree to Submit the Matter in dispute in the above actions and all other Matters in dispute to the final End & determination of Elihu Atwater and Archd Clark, Esquires, Indifferently Chosen on the part of the plaintiff & on the part of the defendants, and it is further Ordered, that Either party be permitted to proceed to that refferance on gieving the adverse party five days previous Notice of the time & place of Such Meeting, and it is further Ordered, that the award to be rendered be made a rule of the next Inferior Court.

Ezekl Hudnall   Timothy Hopkins, agent
                  for S. Cowling

Inferior Court Minutes Book 2

Copp & King }
    vs   } Attachment
Wiley Thompson }

On Motion of Mr Clark and Stating to the Court that Attachment had issued and been regularly Served and that the Original papers had been lost or mislaid. It is therefore Ordered by the Court, that a Copy of the original Writ be Substituted, that the same be placed on the Docquet of the present Term, and that the Case progress.

The Court then adjourned Untill Nine O'clock tomorrow Morning.

Isaac Crews, Clk   Thos King
                                                        Ja^s Seagrove
                                                        John Floyd
                                                        William Johnston

---

Friday, June 9th 1809

The Court met agreeable to adjournment. Present, Their Honors James Seagrove, Thomas King, John Floyd, & Willm Johnston, Esquires, Justices of Said Court.

Tunno & Cox   }
    vs   } Case
Admors Woodford Mabry }

Judgement by Default. June 9th 1809

Ezek^l Hudnall & Co }
    vs   } Case
Danl Mather   }

Judgement by Default. June 9th 1809

Hudnall, Paxton, & Weyman }
    vs   } Case
Daniel Mather   }

Judgement by Default. June 9th 1809

                                              Error   { William Johnston
                                                                { Ja^s Seagrove
                                                                { William Johnston

On the petition of Francis Sterling, for the right of Establishing a Ferry from the Town of Jefferson to Cross the river Satilla as far as Brown's Ferry. It is Ordered, that the

Inferior Court Minutes Book 2

petitioner's Prayer be granted and that he have exclusive right to establish the Said Ferry from the Town of Jefferson.

---

and that the following ratats be the Established prices, to wit.

Man & Horse 50 Cents; Single Man 25; a led Horse 25; Horse, Chair, & Man 1.00^{cts}; four wheel Carriage 1 Dollar, with two horses 1.50; Horned Cattle 10^{Cts} each; Sheep, hogs, or goats 4 Cents Each.

Ordered, that Timothy Hopkins, Isaac Lang, & Darius Woodworth Each have licence to retail Spirituous Liquors, On their Complying With the law in that Case.

Order'd, that Isaac Crews' account of Nine Dollars eighty One & ¼ Cents be admitted and paid out of the County funds and also the Sum of two hundred Dollars for his extra Services as Clerk of the Inferior Court, Superior Court, and Court of Ordinary, being fifty Dollars p^r Year for the Years 1806, 1807, 1808, & 1809.

Asa Holton, Sheriff of the County of Camden, having rendered his Account Against the County, and the same Appearing Just and reasonable.

It is Ordered by the Court, that the same be passed and the Clerk

---

of the Inferior Court do pay to the order of the Said Asa Holton, Sheriff, the Sum of One hundred and thirty two Dollars & twelve Cents in full for his Account up to this day.

Charles Stahl, State Interpretor, having rendered his Account Against the County and the same ~~being~~ Appearing Just, it is Ordered by the Court, that the Same be passed and that the Clerk of the Inferior Court do pay to the Order of the Said Charles Stahl forty Dollars, in full for his account up to this day.

Ordered, that the Clerk of the Court do pay unto the ~~said~~ William Johnston, out of any County Monies which he May have in his hands, the sum of thirty Seven dollars and fifteen Cents, being the ballance due him for Building a Court House & Goal in the Town of St Mary's.

John Boog, having presented his Account as deputy Sheriff of the County, for Services performed for the Benefit thereof, and the Same appearing Just & reasonable. It is therefore Ordered, that the same do pass

---

And that he be paid the same Sum of Seventy two Dollars, being the ballance remaining due him Out of the County funds.

Inferior Court Minutes Book 2

Ordered, that William Cone, Junior be & he is hereby Nominated a Justice of the Peace of the 32 district, Capt Thompkins' Comp^y, in room of Richard Lang, Esqr, resigned, and Also that John Hagan be and he is hereby Nominated a Justice of the Peace in [blank] district, lately Commanded by Capt William Cone, Junr, In lue of William Cone, Esqr, removed Out of the District.

Ordered, that the Clerk of this Court doth forthwith proceed immediately Against all persons Indebted to the County, Agreeable to Law in Such Case Made and provided.

The Jail of the County not being in the Necessary State of Safety to receive prisoners and in Great want of repair. It is Ordered, that the Sheriff advertise that Within the Space of One Month from this date proposals will be received by him from any person who may

---

wish to Contract for the repair of the said Jail, and that the preference will be given to the lowest price offered, the Contractor giving bond and Security for the faithfull performance of the Contract.

The Court then adjourned Untill Court in Course.

Isaac Crews, Clk

John Floyd
Thos King
Ja^s Seagrove
William Johnston

At Chambers, Town of St Mary's, Septr 4th 1809

Present, their Honors William Johnston & Thos King, Esq^{rs}, Justices of the Inferior Court.

I, Isaac Kershaw Courter, do Solemnly Swear that I will faithfully execute all Writs, warrants, precepts, and processes directed to me as Deputy Sheriff of the County of Camden, and true returns Make, and in all things well and truly and without Malice or partiality perform the duties of the Office of Deputy Sheriff of Camden County during My Continuance in office as Deputy Sheriff, and take Only My Lawfull fees. So Help Me God.

Isaac K. Courter

Sworn to before us }
this 4th day of Septr 1809 }
Isaac Crews, Clk }

Thos King, J. I. C.
Willm Johnston, J. I. C.

Inferior Court Minutes Book 2

Monday, January 1st 1810

Court was Opened, there being No Justices of the Court present. The Court was adjourned Untill tomorrow Morning Ten O'clock.

Isaac Crews, Clk

Tuesday, January 2nd 1810

The Court was Opened Agreeable to adjournment. Present, James Seagrove, Thomas King, and William Johnston, Esquires, Justices of Said Court.

The Jury Venire was Called and the following persons appeared, to wit.

   James King   Robert Brown
   David Mizell   John Brown
   Sherrard Sheffield   Berry Elzey
   Edwd Williams   John Crews
   Solomon Osteen   Charleton Mizell
   Daniel Mather   John Prevatt

Henry Austin, admor   }
of Davis Austin   }
  vs   } Case
James Helvingston   }
Admor Jacob Helvingston }

Non suit.

Slauter Cowling   }
  vs   } Case
John Gormon &   }
R. L. Burnet, Exors }
of Willm Gormon   }

Jury N° 1 Sworn.

   1. James King   7. Robert Brown
   2. David Mizell   8. John Brown
   3. Sherrard Sheffield   9. Berry Elzey
   4. Edwd Williams   10. John Crews
   5. Solomon Osteen   11. Charlton Mizell
   6. Danl Mather   12. John Prevatt

Witness Sworn, Isaac Crews

Verdict. over

Inferior Court Minutes Book 2

Verdict. We find for the Plaintiff Sixty thee Dollars and Sixty Six Cents, with Costs of Suit.

Jefferson, Jany 2nd 1810   John Crews, foreman

Elias Baker   }
 vs   } Attachment
Mathews Crowell & }
Sylvanus Crowell }

Jury N° 1

Verdict. We find for the Plaintiff One hundred and forty dollars, with Cost of Suit.

Jefferson, 2nd Jany 1810   John Crews, foreman

Sarah Howley   }
 vs   } Attachment
James Hutchinson }
& Moses Harrel }

Jury N° 1

Verdict. We find for the Plaintiff five hundred Dollars, with Interest from Eighth day of January One thousand Eight Hundred and three, With Costs.

Jefferson, 2nd January 1810   John Crews, foreman

Tunno & Cox }
 vs   } Case
The Admix of }
Woodford Mabry }

Verdict. We find for the Plaintiffs Six Hundred and Eighty five Dollars, with Interest from first February 1806 & Costs.

Jefferson, 2nd Jany 1810   John Crews, foreman

George Starrat, Survivor}
 vs   } Case
Francis Settle   }

Inferior Court Minutes Book 2

I confess Judgement for twenty four Dollars and Ninety three Cents, with Interest from 31st December 1806 & Costs.

2nd January 1810   Fr. Settle

William Cook &   }
David Williford, Indorsees }
    vs   } Case
David Lews   }

Jury N° 1

William Niblack on the Jury in Lue of Edward Williams.

Witness Sworn, Arch[d] Clark.

Verdict. Jefferson, January 2nd 1810

We find for the Plaintiff the sum of five hundred and ten Dollars $^{72}/_{100}$, with Interest from the twenty ~~third day~~ fifth May 1802, with Costs of Suit.

                                     John Crews, foreman

On the petition of Robert Ripley, praying to become a Citizen of the United States, & the Same being Certified to the Satisfaction of the Court, the following Oath was administered to him in Open Court, and be Admitted Accordingly.

I, Robert Ripley, do Solemnly Swear in the presence of Almighty God, that I have resided within the Untied States Eight Years last past and within this State Eighteen Months, that I will Support the Constitution of the United States, and that I Absolutely renounce and Abjure all allegiance & fidelity to any foreign power, potentate, prince, or Soverignty, and particularly to the King of Great Britain, whose Subject I formerly was, and that I will Support the Constitution of the State of Georgia. So help me god.

Sworn to in Open Court }   Robert Ripley
Jan[y] 2nd 1810   }
Isaac Crews, Clk   }

Inferior Court Minutes Book 2

The following Communication was handed to the Court, Gen¹ John Floyd. And Ordered to be recorded and filed, Viz.

Camden County, Jany 2nd 1810

Gentlemen,

Having for the last Six Years served with you as one of the Justices of the Inferior Court of this County, which ~~office~~ Office I have been impelled to retain untill the present period, with No other view than a Sence of the duty that I owed to the County to Perform my Tour of public service thereunto required.

With a Consciousness of having, during my Continuance in office, faithfully Executed my best Judgement and Attention in the discharge of its duties.

I flatter My self that it will Not be deemed inexpedient that I should Now relinquish the task, Especially as the public interest cannot sustain any injury thereby, as the Vacancy can be readily and more Judiciously filled. You will therefore receive and Consider this as my resignation and Act Accordingly. That you may Long Continue your public Usefulness & the full enjoyment of Every Blessing is the Ardent wish of

———

of Gentlemen.

Your Ms^t Ob^t Ser^t,

John Floyd

James Seagrove, Thomas King,
& William Johnson, Esquires,
Justices of the Inferior Court

The Court then adjourned Untill Ten O'Clock Tomorrow.

Isaac Crews, Clk   Thos King
                                                   Ja^s Seagrove
                                                   William Johnston

Wednesday, January 3rd 1810

The Court met agreeable to adjournment. Present, James Seagrove, Thos King, & William Johnston, Esquires, Justices of Said Court.

John Sterrat   }
    vs   } case
Samuel Boyd   }

Jury N° 1, as Yesterday.

Inferior Court Minutes Book 2

Verdict. We find for the Plaintiff One hundred and fifty Six Dollars and forty three Cents, with Interest from 11th April 1809 & Costs of Suit.

3rd January 1810   John Crews, foreman

Ezekiel Hudnall & Co }
     vs   } Case
William Niblack   }

Jury No 1

Winesses Sworn, Edwd W. Weyman, Daniel Miller.

Verdict. We find for the Plaintiffs forty Nine Dollars Sixty two and a half Cts, With Costs of Suit.

January 3rd 1810   John Crews, foreman

Ezekiel Hudnall & Co }
     vs   } Case
Daniel Mather   }

I confess Judgement for fifty four Dollars for and the quarter Cents, with Costs of Suit. 3rd Jany 1810

                                                 Daniel Mather

Hudnall, Paxton, }
&Weyman   }
     vs   } Case
Daniel Mather   }

I confess Judgement for Sixty Dollars & fifty four and an half Cents, With Costs of Suit. January 3rd 1810

                                                 Daniel Mather

---

Nimrod Stanhope Miller is hereby Nominated and Appointed to take the Census or Enumerated of All free White persons and people of Colour residing within the County of Camden.

And the following Oath was Administered to him in Open Court (Viz)

Inferior Court Minutes Book 2

I, Nimrod Stanhope Miller, do Solemnly ySwear on the Holy Evangelists of Almighty God, That I will truly and faithfully perform the trust reposed in me in takeing the Census for the County of Camden, as required of me ~~as required~~ by Law. So help me God.

Sworn to in Open Court } N. S. Miller
Jany 3rd 1810 }
Isaac Crews, Clk }

Timothy Hopkins }
    vs } Case
Samuel Boyd }

I confess Judgement for the the Sum of One hundred and Eleven Dollars and fifty five Cents, & Costs.

3rd Jany 1810 Samuel Boyd

Hudnall, Paxton, }
Weyman }
    vs } Case
John Browne }

Jury N° 1

Verdict. we find for the Plaintiffs thirty Nine Dollars and fifty Nine and a quarter Cents, with Costs of Suit.

Jany 3rd 1810 J. Crews, foreman

Hudnall, Paxton, }
Weyman }
    vs } Case
William Niblack }

Jury N° 1

Witnesses Sworn, Charles Floyd, David Miller.

Verdict. We find for the Defendant Sixty four Dollars twenty four Cents, with Costs of Suit. 3rd January 1810

                                         John Crews, foreman

Inferior Court Minutes Book 2

Ezekiel Hudnall & C° }
    vs   } Case
Amos Latham   }

Jury N° 1

Verdict. We find for the Plaintiffs One hundred and Six dollars and twenty two Cents, with Costs of Suit.

                                        John Crews, foreman

———

M. Shearer }
    vs   } Case
Abram Pratt }

Jury N° 1

Verdict. we find for the plaintiff One hundred and Eighty five Dollars fifty Eight Cents, with Interest from the 11th May 1808, with Costs of Suit.

3rd Jany 1810   J. Crews, foreman

Hudnall, Paxton, }
& Weyman   }
    vs   } Case
Berrey Elzey   }

Jury N° 1

William Watson Sworn on the Jury in Lue of Berrey Elzey.

Verdict. We find for the defendant One Dollar forty five Cents, the Costs of Suit. Jefferson, 3rd Jany 1810

                                        John Crews, foreman

Ethan Clark   }
    vs   } Case
George Ker, Senr }

Jury N° 1

Berrey Elzey on the Jury in his place.

Inferior Court Minutes Book 2

Verdict. We find for the plaintiff One Hundred and twenty five Dollars, with Costs of Suit.

Jefferson, Jany 3rd 1810   John Crews, foreman

Hunter & Mims }
    vs   } fi fa
James Smith }

Mims & Hunter }
    vs   } fi fa
Ja^s Seagrove }

Ja^s Wylly }
    vs   } fi fa
King & Jones }

Alexander Leckie }
    vs   } fi fa
Admor of Jones }

Hunter & Mims }
    vs   } fi fa
Ja^s Seagrove }

Hudson Ragland }
    vs   } fi fa
James Seagrove }

Timothy Hall }
    vs   } fi fa
James Smith }

On Motion Mr Atwater, Attorney for the Plaintiffs in the Above cases, it appearing that returns are Not made. It is Ordered, that the Sheriff, Asa Holton, Esqr do make returns thereon, Within Sixty Days from this date, or else Attachment issue against him as for a Contempt of this Court.

William Watson }
    vs   } Case
George Ker }

Jury N° 1

Verdict. We find for the Plaintiff five Hundred and Eighty One Dollars fourteen and a half Cents, with Costs of Suit.

Jefferson, 3rd Jany 1810   John Crews, foreman

Copp & King }
    vs   } Attachment
Wyley Thompson }
~~William Watson~~ }

Jury N° 1

Inferior Court Minutes Book 2

Verdict. We find for the Plaintiffs Two hundred thirty five Dollars and Eighty five and an half Cents, with Costs of Suit, with Interest from 6th September 1804.

Jany 3rd 1810   John Crews, foreman

                                                              Ja^s Seagrove
                                                              William Johnston
                                                              Thos King

The Court then adjourned Untill Tomorrow Morning Nine O'Clock.

Isaac Crews, Clk

Thursday, January 4th 1810, the Court Met agreeable to adjournment. Present, James Seagrove, Thomas King, and William Johnston, Esquires, Justices of Said Court.

It is Ordered, that Ephrim Cook be and he is hereby Nominated as Justice of the Peace for the 33rd District of Camden County, Commanded by Capt John Hardee.

And, that Donold Thompkins, Esqr be and he is hereby Nominated a Justice of the peace in the [blank] district, Commanded by Capt John Thompkins.

No persons having Offered for the appointment of Constables to this Court.

It is Ordered, that the Justices of the Peace in the several Captain's districts within this County, or any One of them in Each District, do Without delay proceed and Draw Constables for the respective Company districts, as the Law directs.

Upon the application of William Club for Tavern Licence.

It is Ordered, that have Licence, on his Complying With the Law in that Case, to Commence on the twenty Sixth day of September last and End on the 26th September next, he having at that time taken the Oath prescribed by Law to be taken by Retailers &c.

The following persons were drawn as Jurors for Junne Term 1810, Viz.

      1. Richard Pelham   20. Zac^k Motes
      2. Andrew Mc[blot]allan   21. Brelain Brinkley
      3. John Boog   22. Stephen Gray
      4. Adam Cooper   23. Thomas Hughs
      5. David G. Jones   24. Garret Demott
      6. Duncan Curry   25. James Williamson
      7. William Neely   26. Nathan Norton
      8. Lewis Levy   27. George Gales

Inferior Court Minutes Book 2

9. Francis Young
10. Peter Mickler
11. Henry Jones
12. Charles Floyd
13. Stephen W. Moore
14. Silas Weeks
15. James Whitten
16. Mills Drury
17. David Hall
18. Jacob Robertson
19. Edward Shearman

28. Hezekiah Ponder
29. Alex^r Kean
30. Hardy Lanier
31. Thos Clark
32. John Oaks
33. John Thompson
34. Jacob Clark
35. Josiah Wilkinson
36. Danl Brockington, J^r
37. Henry Sadler

On Motion of Mr Clark, Att^y for the morgagee, praying for the foreclosure of a Mortgage the Equity of redemption of the Mortgage Executed by Samuel Boyd to Silvanus Church for Securing the payment of a Sum of Money Contained in the Several Notes. It is ordered by the Court, That Execution founded thereon do issue in Terms of the Judiciary Act.

Slauter Cowling }
    vs } debt on replevin Bond
Ezekiel Hudnall }
& D. Tompkins }

refered.

Same }
    vs } Debt on Repleven Bond
E. Hudnall }
& John Tompkins }

Agreeably to the reference Made at the last term of the Inferior Court. We, the Undersigned arbitrators named by the said Court, Proceeded in the investigation of all matters of Difference in the aforesaid actions, as Well as all other matters of whatsoever denomination that exist between the said parties, And having deliberately and maturely Considered the same, Have awarded and do hereby award, That the said Ezekiel Hudnal do Transfer, assign, and Set over unto the Said Cowling, or his Attorney, a Judgment

---

obtained at this present Term of the Inferior Court by Ezekiel Hudnall and Company against Amos Latham for the Sum of One hundred & Six Dollars & twenty two Cents, it appearing to the Undersigned, that Ezekiel Hudnal hath the Control of the said Judgment and that it originated in consequence of Suppoed Rent being due to the said Latham. And that the said Slauter Cowling do pay to the said Ezekiel Hudnal, on account of Ezekiel Hudnal and Company, One hundred and Seventeen Dollars and Ninety Cents.

Inferior Court Minutes Book 2

And we do further award that all actions, Suits, quarrels, and controversies whatsoever had moved, arisen, and depending for any Matter, Cause, or thing, Either in Law or Equity, Shall Cease, and determined, and that Each party Shall pay their own Costs & charges in any Ways relating to Controversies to or Concerning the premises. And lastly, we do award that general releases be executed in due form after the performance of the parties to these Presents.

$Arch^d$ Clark, Elihu Atwater

On motion, it is Ordered, that

———

the foregoing award be received and that the same be Entered up as the Judgment of this Court.

The Court then adjourned Untill Court in Course.

Isaac Crews, Clk Ja^s Seagrove
                                    William Johnston
                                    Thos King

Camden County, 4th January 1810

Gentlemen,

It is Not without a Suitable degree of regret, that I feel myself impelled to withdraw from all kind of Public appointments under the State of Georgia; the Honor I have enjoyed of Serving as a Magistrate for upwards of Twenty Years and a Justice of the Inferior Court of Camden ever since its first formation. I now resign to the source from whence derived, and this I do under a full conviction that I have Conscientiously fulfilled the Oath I took to administer Equal justice to all without favour or affect to any, as far as my Understanding enabled me to do. I had it in Contemplation to have resigned my seat on Your Honorable Bench

———

Some time past; but finding an Attempt Made on My Public Character by a low, groveling, vitious faction in this County delayed My intention untill a public investigation Should be had. This having taken place and the leaders of the faction having failed in their plans against me, I am Now left at liberty to do What to me seems fit I should. It is With exceeding regret that I take leave of You, My much respected friends, And long associated Brothers of the bench of Camden, but I have Not ceased for a Moment (since the event took place) to feel the Indignity & insult offered, that heretofore Much respected bench, by the Appointment of a Certain John Ross in the room of Our Worthy brother Judge Peyton Skipwith, deceased. It is My sincere wish that you May get an honest, respectable Gentleman to fill My seat Now Vacated. But, as Appointments go Nowadays, It is a Matter scarcely to be Expected. I am Much of Opinion that, at present, "the Post of Honor is a private Station."

Inferior Court Minutes Book 2

Along with My Commission, I do decline for Evermore serving as a Grand Juror, as I cannot Think of hearing My self and brother Jurors insulted

---

and Abused in Open Court by One of the bar in presence of his Honor the Judge, With Out the least Check for Such, for such Outrageous treatment of as respectable and honest a Grand Jury as Ever sat in Georgia.

I Now bid a dieu to Publick life after afaithful service in America as a Soldier, & Citizen, in Most Stations for forty Eight years, Out of Sixty two, the last twenty five in Georgia.

Wishing You, My ~~Much~~ Worthy & Much Esteemed friends, together With the rest of the Honest, Virtuous, and Well disposed Citizens of Camden, Every possible happiness, I remain Yours and their

Devoted, faithful friend & Humble Servt

Ja^s Seagrove

The Honorable Thomas King, William Johnston, & }
John Floyd, Esq^{rs}, Justices of the Inferior Court }
Camden County }

P. S. It is My request that this My Resignation and Observations thereon be made of record in your Honb^{le} Court.

               Ja^s Seagrove

Entered by Order of Court }
4th Jany 1810 }

Isaac Crews, Clk

Jefferson, June 4th 1810, Monday

The Court was Opened. Present, their Honors John Ross, William Scott, Stephen W. Moore, Justices of Said Court.

The Court then adjourned until tomorrow 9 O'Clock.

Tuesday, June 5th

The Court met pursuant to adjournment. Presnt, their Honors John Ross, William Scott, and Stephen W. Moore, Justices of Said Court.

Inferior Court Minutes Book 2

The Dedimus Potestatum directed to the Court to qualify William Mickler Sheriff Elect of the County being produced, the same was taken up and the Said Sheriff having Produced Satisfactory Security, for the faithful discharge of his duties, the following oath was duly administered and Subscribed by him, to Wit.

I, William Mickler, do Solemnly Swear that I will faithfully Execute all Writs, Warrants, Precepts, and Processes directed to Me as Sheriff of the

County of Camden, and true returns Make, and in all things Will and truly, and Without Malice pr Partiality, perform the duties of the Office of Sheriff of Camden County, during My Continuance in office, and take Only My Lawful fees. So Help Me God.

Sworn in Open Court }   Willm Mickler
5th June 1810   }

before us   Jn° Ross, J. I. C.
               Wm Scott, J. I. C.
               Step W. Moore, J. I. C.

On the Petition of Adam Walsby, praying to be admitted a Citizen of the United States, and the same being Certified to the Satisfaction of the Court, the following Oath was administered to him Accordingly.

I, Adam Walsby, do Solemnly Swear in the Presence of Almighty God, that I have resided Within the United States since the Eighth day of March Eighteen Hundred and One, and Within the State of Georgia More than five Years Last Past, that I Will Support the Constitution of the United States, and that I Absolutely renounce and Abjure All Allegiance & fidelity to any foreign power, potentate, prince, or Soverignty and Particularly the King of England

England, Whose Subject I formerly was, and that I will Support the Constitution of the State of Georgia. So Help Me God.

Sworn to in Open Court }
June 5th 1810   }   Adam Walsby
Jn° Ross, J. I. C.   }
Wm Scott, J. I. C.   }
Step W. Moore, J. I. C. }

Daniel Blue   }
      vs   } Attachment
Robert L. Burnett & }
Willoughby Hodge   }

Inferior Court Minutes Book 2

Mr Atwater, Appearing for the defendants, and Bonds being given. On Motion of Said Atwater to dismiss said Suit, On the ground that the defendants, or One of them, Ware Within the County when the Writ of Attachment Was issued. It is Ordered, that the fact be tried by a Jury at the Next Term, There Not being a Sufficient Number of Jurors Present at this Term.

Nathl Pidge }
    vs   } Attachment
Thomas Doyle }

Judgement by default, June 5th 1810.

Jacob Miller }
    vs   } Case
George Roberts }

Judgement by default, June 5th 1810.

David Lewis, Adm^or }
of Peter Madden   }
    vs   } Attachment
Thomas Doyle   }

Judgement by default, June 5th 1810.

Wood & Stodert }
    vs   } Case
George Roberts }

Judgement by default, June Term 1810.

Elijah Stoddard }
    vs   }
George Roberts }

Judgement by Default, June Term 1810.

John Smith }
    vs   }
Calvin Ballard }

Judgement by Default, June 5th 1810.

John Baldwin }
    vs   }
Calvin Ballard }

Inferior Court Minutes Book 2

Judgement by Default, June Term 5th 1810.

T. Hall & A. Hitchcock }
Adm[rs] Hitchcock   }
    vs   }
W[m] McClure   }

Term given & writ to be amended, June Term 1810.

Jury Drawn for January Term 1811

1. Nathaniel Sephens
2. Thomas H. Miller
3. William Simpson
4. Ja[s] Moore
5. Benj. Honeker
6. Ingle Hart Cruse
7. Nathn[l] Beal
8. Silvanus Church
9. John Beesley
10. David Davis
11. Thomas Little
12. James Smith
13. David Mizele
14. John Sparkman
15. Lewis Thomas
16. Henry McIntosh
17. Joseph Rain
18. Ja[s] Brooks
19. John Mizele
20. Tho[s] Rogers
21. Jacob Miclker
22. William Marcun
23. John Filchett
24. Isaac Lang
25. Joseph Thomas
26. Levy Johns
27. John Tompkins
28. James Elliott
29. Joseph McCullough
30. John Motes
31. Dan[l] Brockington, Sen[r]
32. James Stuart
33. David Lang
34. Ransom Cason
35. Isham Spalding
36. Ezekiel Smith
37. Will[m] Niblack
38. Will[m] Andrews
39. Denis Lowe
40. Hezekiah Ponder
41. Duncan Currey
42. John Boog
43. Adam Cooper
44. Charles Floyd
45. Sherrard Sheffield
46. Andrew McClellan
47. Ja[s] Helvingston
48. John Brown
49. Alex[r] Kean
50. Alex[r] Elliott

Whereas, no appointments for a Receiver of Tax returns has been Made for the years Eighteen Hundred and Nine and Ten, and No Collector for the years eighteen Hundred and Eight, Nine, and Ten.

It is Ordered, that William Scott, Jun[r] be appointed Collector of Taxes for the Years 1808, 1809, & 1810.

Inferior Court Minutes Book 2

And that Isaac Crews be appointed receiver of Returns of Taxable Property for the years 1809 & 1810.

The Court then adjourned Untill Court in Course.

Isaac Crews, Clk   Jn° Ross, J. I. C.
                                    Wm Scott, J. I. C.
                                    Step W. Moore, J. I. C.

———

Monday, January the 7th 1811

The Court was Opened. Present, their Honors John Ross, William Scott, & Stephen W. Moore, Esquires, Justices of Said Court.

The Court adjourned Untill Tomorrow Morning ten O'Clock.

Isaac Crews, Clk   Wm Scott, J. I. C.
                                    Step W. Moore, J. I. C.
                                    Jn° Ross, J. I. C.

Tuesday, January the 8th 1811

The Court Met agreeable to adjournment. Present, their Honors John Ross, William Scott, & Stephen W. Moore, Esquires, Justices of Said Court.

The Jury Venire was Called and the following persons Answered, to wit.

1. John Brown	William Andrews
2. David Mizele	William Simpson
3. David Lang	James Helvingston
4. Denis Lowe	Silvanus Church
5. John Filchet	William Niblack
6. Isaac Lang	John Mizele
7. Joseph Rain	Ja^s Moore
	Andrew McClellen

———

John Miller   }
    vs   } Case
Moses Harrel   }

Jury N° 1 Sworn, Viz.

| John Brown | Isaac Lang | Ja^s Helvingston |
| David Mizele | Joseph Rain | William Niblack |

Inferior Court Minutes Book 2

    David Lang   William Andrews   John Mizele
    John Filchet   William Simpson   Ja^s Moore

Witnesses Sworn, Isaac Crews.

Verdict. We find for the Plaintiff One Hundred and fourteen Dollars Sixty One Cents, with Interest from first January 1804, and Costs of Suit. 8th Jany 1811

                                             Willm Niblack, foreman

George Ker, Senr }
     vs   } Case
William Watson }

Non suit.

Lodewick Ashley }
     vs   } Attachment
James Williamson }

Jury N° 1

Verdict. We find for the Plaintiff the Sum of Six hundred and fifty Six Dollars and thirty Nine Cents, with Costs of Suit.

Jefferson, 8th Jany 1811   Wm Niblack, foreman

———

Timothy Hall }
     vs   } Case
William Neely }

Jury N° 1

Verdict. We find for the plaintiff fifty Eight Dollars, with Interest from the twelfth Day of June Eighteen Hundred and Nine.

Jany 8th 1811   Wm Niblack, foreman

Jacob Miller }
     vs   } Case
George Roberts }

Jury N° 1

Inferior Court Minutes Book 2

Verdict. We find for the Plaintiff One Hundred and Ninety two Dollars $^{25}/_{100}$, with Interest from Second May 1810 & Costs.

8th January 1811   Wm Niblack, foreman

Samuel Evans }
   vs   } Case
William Marcum }

Jury N° 1

Verdict. We find for the plaintiff forty Seven Dollars and fifty Cents, With Interest from first December 1808.

8th Jany 1811   Wm Niblack, foreman

David Lewis }
Adm^{or} of P. Madden }
   vs   } Attachment
Thomas Doyle }

Jury N° 1

Verdict. We find for the Plaintiff three Hundred and thirty Seven Dollars Sixty two and a half Cents, With Costs.

Jany 8th 1811   Willm Niblack, foreman

Wood & Stoddard }
   vs   } Case
George Roberts }

Jury N° 1

Verdict. We find for the plaintiffs two Hundred and twelve Dollars, with Interest from 1st Decr 1809 & Costs of Suit.

January 8th 1811   Wm Niblack, foreman

Elijah Stoddard }
   vs   } Case
George Roberts }

Jury N° 1

Inferior Court Minutes Book 2

Verdict. We find for the plaintiff One Hundred and four Dollars, With Interest from 11th May 1810.

January 8th 1811   Wm Niblack, foreman

John Smith }
    vs   } Case
Calvin Ballard }

Jury N° 1

Verdict. We find for the plaintiff One hundred and forty four Dollars Sixty four [blot] Cents, with Costs of Suit.

January 8th 1811   Wm Niblack, foreman

John Baldwin }
    vs   }
Calvin Ballard }

Jury N° 1

Verdict. We find for the plaintiff Ninety [blot]ollars, with costs of Suit.

8th Jany 1811   Wm Niblack, foreman

Elizabeth Gordon, Exix }
    vs   } Case
James Seagrove   }

Jury N° 1

Verdict. We find for the plaintiff One hundred and Seventy One Dollars and fifty Cents, With Interest from first January 1807 and Costs. 8th January 1811

                                         Wm Niblack, foreman

Ezekiel Hudnall & C° }
    vs   } Case
Mills Drury   }

Judgement by Default. Jany 8th 1811

Inferior Court Minutes Book 2

Walter Simpson }
    vs   } Attachment
Levin Gunby }

Judgement by Default. Jany 8th 1811

Lilley & Sibley }
    vs   } Attachment
Thomas Doyle }

Judgement by Default. January 8th 1811

Francis G. Delesslen   }
    vs   } Attachment
George Sterrat, Survivor }

Judgement by Default. Jany 8th 1811

Ordered, that the Justices of the peace in the Several districts in this County do draw Constables for to fill Such Vacancies as May be, in the Mode pointed Out by Law, as No proper persons have applied to this Court for such Appointments.

Isaac Crews, Clk   Wm Scott, J. I. C.
                                                          Step W. Moore, J. I. C.
                                                          Jno Ross, J. I. C.

Ordered, that a County tax be levied & Collected for the year 1811 Equal to One Sixth of the General Tax, and that a poor Tax be levied & Collected for said Year Equal to One Sixteenth fourteenth of the General Tax.

At Chambers in St Mary's, Friday, March 1811

Present, their Honors John Ross, Abraham Bessent, and Stephen West Moore, Esquires, Justices of Said Court.

Jurors Drawn for June Term 1811, to wit.

1. Stephen Sparksman
2. Eli Cason
3. Stephen Gray
4. Danl Brockington, Junr
5. Thomas Garner
6. Ezekiel Smith
7. John Cade
8. Richard Pellum
9. James Vincent
10. Thomas Tucker
21. Ransom Cason
22. Philip Goodbread
23. I. K. Courter
24. Solomon Ostean
25. Henry Jones
26. William Cone, Junr
27. Simon L. Mott
28. Berry Walker
29. Charles Howell
30. John Bailey, Junr

Inferior Court Minutes Book 2

11. William F. Kelly
12. John Browne
13. Isaac Johns
14. Moses Harrison
15. Joseph McCullough
16. David Hall
17. Francis Young
18. Ja^s Nobles
19. Nathaniel Stephens
20. William Gillet

31. Levi Sparksman
32. Josiah Winans
33. John Oaks
34. Adam Cooper
35. James Brooks
36. Charlton Mizele, Junr
37. Duncan Currey
38. Ephrem Taylor
39. Thomas King
40. Daniel Greene

Jefferson, Monday, June 3rd 1811

The Court was Opened, present, their Honors John Ross, William Scott, & Abraham Bessent, Esquires, Justices of Said Court.

The Court adjourned Untill to morrow Morning half after ~~Nine~~ Eight O'Clock.

Isaac Crews, Clk

Jno Ross, J. I. C.
William Scott, J. I. C.
Abra^m Bessent, J. I. C.

Tuesday, June 4th 1811

The Court Met Agreeable to adjournment. Present, their Honors John Ross, William Scott, & Abraham Bessent, Esquires, Justices of Said Court.

The Jury Venire was Called & the following Jurors Attended, to wit.

1. William Kelly
2. Charlton Mizele, Junr
3. Philip Goodbread
4. William Gillet
5. Ephrem Taylor
6. Thomas Tucker

7. David Hall
8. John Brown
9. Stephen Sparksman
10. Littleberry Walker

Joseph Reid }
   vs   } Trespass on the Case
Isaac K. Courter } Malicious Prosecution

Jury N° 1 Sworn.

Inferior Court Minutes Book 2

1. William F. Kelly
2. Charlton Mizele, Jun[r]
3. Philip Goodbread
4. William Gillet
5. Ephrem Taylor
6. Thomas Tucker
7. David Hall
8. John Brown
9. Stephen Sparksman
10. Littleberry Walker
11. Nathan Norton
12. Denis Lowe

Witness Sworn, Charles Stahl.

Exemplification from the Indendants' Court of S[t] Mary's red in Evidence.

Verdict. We find for the plaintiff, Joseph Reid, fifty Dollars, with Costs of Suit.

4th June 1811   David Hall, foreman

Adam Walsby }
   vs   } Case
Michael Lynch }

Jury N° 1

Verdict. we find for Adam Walsby, Plaintiff, One hundred and twelve Dollars, With Costs of Suit.

4th June 1811   David Hall, foreman

John Head   }
   vs   } Trespass Vi et Armis &c
Asa Lathrop & George Roberts}

We find for the Defendant, with Costs of suit.

4th March 1811

We consent that this Action be placed on the appeal, Without bond or Costs.

                                           Clark, deft's att[y]
                                           Atwater, by request of
                                           Ge° Ker, Esq[r]

Ezekiel Hudnall & C° }
   vs   } Case
Tho[s] Bond   }

I confess Judgt for Fifty three Dollars twenty and three quarter Cents, & Costs.

4th June 1811   Stahl, Deft's atty

Inferior Court Minutes Book 2

Nathaniel R. Pidge }
    vs   } Attachment
Thomas Doyle   }

Jury Nº 2 Sworn.

    1. John Hardee   5. George Woodworth   9. Samuel Boyd
    2. Isaac Lang   6. Mills Drury   10. John Conner
    3. John May   7. Francis Sterling   11. John Bailey
    4. Allen Thomas   8. William Andrews   12. John Browne

Verdict. We, the Jury, find for the Plaintiff Nine hundred and twenty three Dollars and two & a half Cents, With Costs of Suit.

4th June 1811   John Hardee, foreman

Daniel Blue   }
    vs   } Attachment
Robert L. Burnett & }
Willoughby Hodge   }

Jury Nº 1

Verdict, we find favor of the Plaintiff, Daniel Blue, the Sum of two hundred and Ten Dollars, With Interest from 9th February 1806 and Costs of Suit.

June the 4th 1811 David Hall, foreman

William Aitcheson }
    vs   } Attachment
Henry W. Paxton   }

Jury Nº 1

Verdict. we find for the Plaintiff Twelve hundred & Eighty three Dollars and Nineteen Cents, With Interest from 24th October 1807 & Costs.

4th June 1811   David Hall, foreman

Walter Simpson }
    vs   } Attachment
Levin Gunby   }

Jury Nº 2

Inferior Court Minutes Book 2

Verdict. we find for the Defendant, With Costs of Suit.

4th June 1811   John Hardee, foreman

I consent this action be placed on the appeal Doquet, without payment of Costs.

                                                            Atwater, for Deft

---

Lilley & Sibley }
    vs   } Attachment
Thomas Doyle   }

Jury N° 1

Verdict. We find for the Plaintiff fifty Eight Dollars, with Interest from twenty first June 1807 & Costs.

4th June 1811   David Hall, foreman

Lilley & Sibley, Indorsees }
    vs   } Attachment
Thomas Doyle   }

Jury N° 2

Verdict. We find for the Plaintiff One Hundred and Sixty Dollars, with Interest from 11th August 1807 and Costs of Suit. 4th June 1811

                                                            John Hardee, foreman

Stephen Waterman, Indorse }
    vs   } Case
Wade Hampton   }

Jefferson, 4th June 1811

I confess Judgement for the sum of two hundred and four Dollars, with Interest from the first day of February 1810 & Costs.

                                                            John Atkinson, Atty for Deft

I consent to Stay Execution for Seven Months from this Date. june 4th 1811

                                                            Clark, Plff's Atty

---

179

Inferior Court Minutes Book 2

Francis G. Celusline }
    vs   } Attachment
George Sterrat, Surv^r }

Jury N° 1

Verdict. We find for the Plaintiff One Thousand Dollars, with Interest from the fourth day of March Eighteen Hundred and Six, With Costs of Suit. June 4th 1811

                                          David Hale, foreman

Copp & King 2nd }
    vs   } Case
Woodland & King 3rd }

Jury N° 2

Verdict. We find for the Plaintiffs against Thomas King 3rd One hundred and twenty two Dollars Eight and three fourths Cents, With Interest from Thirty first of December Eighteen Hundred and four & Costs of Suit.

June 4th 1811   John Hardee, foreman

John Carnehan }
    vs   } Case
John G. Fitzgerald & }
Catharine Fitzgerald }

I confess Judgement for the sum of One Hundred and five Dollars and 57/100, with Interest from first January One thousand Eight Hundred and Nine & Costs.

4th June 1811   Stahl, Deft's Atty

I consent to a Stay of Levy for Six Months from from this date. 4th June 1811

                                          Clark, Plff's Atty

I. K. Courter }
    vs   } Scirefacias
Exor Francis Mussault }

Jury N° 1

Inferior Court Minutes Book 2

Verdict. We find for the Plaintiff One hundred and Eighty Eight Dollars, With Interest from Seventeenth June 1809 & Costs.

4th June 1811   David Hale, foreman

Francis Mussault }
    vs   } Attachment
Josiah Baker   }

No parties. June 1811

G. Tufts & Co }
    vs   } Case
Asa Lathrop   }

Continued by Consent of Parties. June 1811

Isaac K. Courter }
    vs   } Slander
Joseph Reid   }

Discontinued by Consent of Plff's Atty.

John Howell   }
    vs   } Debt
Hayns Lernard }

Settled, as suggested by Defendant's Counsel. June 1811

[illegible] }
    vs   } Attachment
[illegible] }

Continued, for want of a quorum, a Member of this Court being interested for the Estate of the plaintiff. June 1811

Ezekiel Hudnall & Co }
    vs   } Case
Mills Drury   }

Continued by Consent of Parties. June 1811

E. Hudnall & Co }
    vs   } Case
Denis Lowe   }

Continued by Consent of Parties. June 4th 1811

Inferior Court Minutes Book 2

Hudnall, Paxton & C° }
    vs   } Case
Denis Lowe   }

Continued by Consent of Parties. June 1811

Elihu Hebbard   }
    vs   } Attachment
Jahu Underwood }

Judgement by Default. June 1811

George Roberts, Indorsee }
for the use of   }
Elihu Hebbard   }
    vs   } Attachment
Jahu Underwood   }

Judgement by Default. June 1811

Executors F. Mussault}
    vs   } Attachment
James Cashen   }

Judgement by Default. June 1811

George Gates }
    vs   } Case
James Gilman }

Judgement by Default. June 1811

William Hobkirk }
    vs   } Trover
Silvanus Church }

Plea filed.

Edward Shearman }
    vs   } Case
James Gilman   }

Plea filed. June 1811

Thomas Wilder}
    vs   } Case
David G. Jones }

182

Inferior Court Minutes Book 2

Plea filed. June 1811

Asa Holton }
   vs } Case
Eleazer Waterman }

Settled.

Lilley & Sibley }
   vs } Case
Langley Bryrant }

Judgement by default. June 1811

On the Petition of Isaac Lang, Timothy Hopkins, Darius Woodworth & Sons, & Allen Thomas for Francis [blot].

It is Ordered, that the Clerk of this Court do issue license to the aforesaid Applicants, on them Complying with the requisites of the Law in that Case Made and provided.

Ordered, that the Defaulting Jurors be fined in the sum of ten Dollars Each, Unless they Severally file a Sufficient Excuse with the Clerk of this Court within thirty days from the adjournment of this Court.

The Court then adjourned Untill Court in Course.

Isaac Crews, Clk

William Scott, J. I. C.
Jn° Ross, J. I. C.
Abra^m Bessent, J. I. C.

Jury drawn for January Term 1812

1. Zachariah Moles
2. William Watson
3. Alex^r Elliott
4. John Beesly
5. Nathan^l Beal
6. John Sleigh
7. James Erskin
8. Levy Johns
9. Isaac Tucker
10. Charles Magill
11. James D. Prevatt
12. Hardy Laneer
13. David Mizell
14. Isham Spalding
15. Daniel McMillin
21. John Thompson
22. Isaac Green
23. William Andrews
24. John Prevatt
25. Lewis Thomas
26. Christopher Grovenstine
27. Thomas Clark
28. John Barco
29. John Demott
30. James Williamson
31. Britain Brinkley
32. William Drummond
33. William Hines
34. Arthur Moore
35. John Ashley

Inferior Court Minutes Book 2

16. James Elliott
17. Jacob Clark
18. Berry Elzey
19. Jacob Rolinson
20. John Campbell

36. Nathan Norton
37. Jehu Sparksman
38. James Helvingston
39. Amos Lindsay
40. Mills Drury
41. David Crum

Jefferson, Monday, January 6th 1812

The Court was Opened. Present, their Honors John Ross, William Scott, and Abraham Bessent, Esquires, Justices of Said Court.

The Jury Venire was Called and the following Jurors Attended, to wit.

Mills Drury
William Hines
William Andrews
John Prevatt
Daniel McMillin
Berry Elzey

Nathaniel Beal
Zachariah Motes
John Campbell
Isaac Green
Nathan Norton
Ephrem Taylor

Elihu Hebbard, paye }
    vs   } Attachment
Jehu Underwood }

Jury N° 1 Sworn

1. Mills Drury
2. William Hines
3. William Andrews
4. John Prevatt
5. Danl McMillin
6. Berry Elzey

7. Nathaniel Beal
8. Zachariah Motes
9. John Campbell
10. Isaac Green
11. Nathan Norton
12. Ephrem Taylor

Verdict. We find for the Plaintiff Sixty One Dollars and ~~forty~~ four cents, with Interest from 14th June 1806 & costs.

Jefferson, 6th Jany 1812   John Campbell, foreman

Thomas Wilder }
    vs   } case
David G. Jones }

I confess Judgement for the Sum of Two hundred & Thirteen Dollars and Seventy five Cents, with Interest from the first day of January 1810, with Costs of Suit.

Inferior Court Minutes Book 2

Jefferson, 6th Jany 1812   D. G. Jones

Gardner, Tufts & C°   }
    vs   } Case
Asa Lathrop   }

On Motion of Mr Atwater, and it Appearing that the defendant, Asa Lathrop, is dead and that Asa ~~Lathrop~~ Holton, the Executor on his Estate, has been duly Summoned in by Scire Facias. It is Ordered, that Asa Holton be Made defendant and the Case to progress to Trial.

Gardner, Tufts & C°   }
    vs   } Case
Asa Holton, Exor of   }
Asa ~~Holton~~ Lathrop   }

Jury N° 1

Verdict. We find for the plaintiff against Asa Holton, Executor, One hundred & forty Dollars, with Interest from the first of December 1803 & Costs.

January 6th 1812   John Campbell, foreman

———

Thomas Vincent   }
    vs   } Case
Daniel Copp   }

Jury N° 1

Verdict. We find for the Plaintiff Three hundred and Eighty Dollars, with Interest from the twenty Seventh of May Eighteen Hundred and Six & Costs of Suit. January 6th 1812

                                                         John Campbell, foreman

Nathaniel Pendleton   }
Plaintiff in Execution   }
    vs   } fi fa
George Ker, Junr &   }
Isabell Fotheringham   }
Claimants   }

Jury N° 1 Sworn.

John Thompson sworn in Lue of Isaac Greene.

Inferior Court Minutes Book 2

Verdict. We find the property Served on subject to this Execution and Assess One cent Damages & Costs. 6th January 1812

                                        John Campbell, foreman

I consent that an Appeal be Entered without Payment of Costs or further form.

                                        Clark, Plff's Atty

                                        Abra^m Bessent, J. I. C.
                                        John Ross, J. I. C.
                                        Wm Scott, J. I. C.

The Court then adjourned Untill Tomorrow Morning half after Nine O'Clock.

Tuesday, January the 7th 1812

The Court Met agreeable to adjournment. Present, their Honors Abraham Bessent, William Scott, John Ross, & Stephen W. Moore, Esquires, Justices of Said Court.

Ezekiel Hudnall & Co }
       vs   } Case
Mills Drury   }

I confess Judgement for twenty six Dollars sixty three ~~cents~~ and three quarter cents, with costs of suit.

Jefferson, 7th Jany 1812   Mills Drury

Alexander Lechie, Ind   }
plaintiff in Execution   }
       vs   } fi fa
William Jones, Junr }
as guardian of   }
William Goodgame Jones }
Claimant   }

Jury N° 1 Sworn, Viz.

        1. John Thompson   5. William Andrews   9. Berry Elzey
        2. Lewis Thomas   6. John Prevatt   10. Nathan^l Beal
        3. Mills Drury   7. Nathan Norton   11. Zach Motes
        4. William Hines   8. Danl McMillin   12. John Campbell

Witnesses Sworn, William Ashley, Jo^s Dorr, John Bailey.

Verdict over

Inferior Court Minutes Book 2

Verdict. We find the property Subject to this Execution, with cost and sute.

John Campbell, foreman

On the Petition of John Bashlot, praying to be a citizen of the united States, the following Oath was administered to him and he was admitted accordingly, to wit.

John Bashlott do solemnly Swear in the presence of Almighty God, that I have resided in the State of Georgia three years last past, that I will support the Constitution of the United States, and that I absolutely renounce and Abjure all Allegiance and fidelity to any foreign Power, Potentate, Prince, or Sovereignty, and particularly the Sovereign Authority of France, whose subject I formerly was, and that I will Support the Constitution of the State of Georgia.

Sworn to in Open Court }
January 7th 1812 } Jan Bachelott

~~Sworn to~~ }
Step W. Moore, J. I. C. }

On the Petition of Samuel McClellan, praying to be admitted a Citizen of the United States, the following Oath was administered to him and he accordingly admitted.

I, Samuel McClellan, Do solemnly swear in th epresence of almighty God, That I have resided in the United States since the year one thousand Seven hundred & seventy Nine and in the State of Georgia upwards of Seven years, And that I do absolutely renounce and abjure all faith, allegiance, and fidelity to any foreign Prince, Power, Potentate, or Sovereignty whatsoever, and particularly to the King of Great Britain, whose subject I formerly was, And that I will support the Constitution of the State of Georgia.

Sworn in Open }
Court this 7 Jany 1812 } Samuel McClellan

Abra^m Bessent, J. I. C.
John Ross, J. I. C.
Step W. Moore, J. I. C.

Samuel Boyd, Admor }
Susannah Boyd, Admix }
of Daniel McGirt }
plaintiffs in Execution }
    vs } fi fa
Francis Young, Claimant }

Inferior Court Minutes Book 2

Jury N° 1 Sworn.

~~Verdict~~.

Witnesses Sworn, William Ashley, Lodewick Ashley, William Niblack, James Seagrove.

Verdict. We find the property Served on Subject to the Execution, with costs of Suit.

John Campbell, foreman

Hudnall, Paxton, & }
Weyman }
    vs } case
Denis Lowe }

I confess Judgement for One hundred and forty dollars and Eleven Cents, with costs of Suit.

7th Jany 1812   Denis X Lowe, his mark

Witness, A. Clark.

E. Hudnall & C° }
    vs } Case
Denis Lowe }

I confess Judgement for Sixteen Dollars and forty Cents, Without Costs. 7th Jany 1812

Witness, A. Clark.

Denis X Lowe, his mark

Williford & Cook }
    vs } fi fa
Admor of Peter Knight }
John Ross, Claimant }

On Motion of Mr Clark, it is ordered by the Court that the Above Action be placed on the Sheriff's claim docket of this Court.

Benjamin Honeker }
    vs } Attachment
Charles Seton }

On Motion of Mr Atwater, the Attorney for the Plf. It appearing that Benjamin Honeker is dead and Abraham Bessent is the administrator on his Estate and that the defendant

Inferior Court Minutes Book 2

is Now residing Out of the State, so that Sci fac cannot be served on him, it is Ordered, that on ~~Motion~~ Notice being Published in One of the Public Gazettes for three Months, that the case progress in the name of Ab^m Bessent, administrator of Benjamin Honeker.

William Hobkirk }
    vs   } Trover
Silvanus Church }

Settled. 6th Jany 1812

Lilley & Sibley }
    vs   } case
Langley Bryant }

death of the defendant Suggested 6th January 1812.

Asa Holton, Exor of }
Asa Lathrop   }
    vs   } Case
Luther P. Rockwood }

Judgement by default. January 7th 1812

                                      Abra^m Bessent, J. I. C.
                                      John Ross, J. I. C.
                                      Step W. Moore, J. I. C.
                                      Wm Scott, J. I. C.

The Court then adjourned Untill Tomorrow Morning Eight O'Clock.

                                      Isaac Crews, Clk

Wednesday, January the 8th 1812

The Court Met agreeable to adjournment. Present, their Honors John Ross, Abraham Bessent, Stephen W. Moore, Esquires, Justices of Said Court.

Hunter & Mims }   Mims & Hunter }
    vs   } fi fa   vs   } fi fa
James Seagrove }   James Seagrove }

Hudson Raglen }
    vs   } fi fa
James Seagrove }

It being Stated to the Court that Asa Holton, late Sheriff of said County, hath by his deputy, M. Stephens,

Inferior Court Minutes Book 2

returned the Above Executions, Satisfied as to One third part their Amount, together with One third the Interest & Costs, and that he has Not Paid Over the Amount so satisfied to the Plaintiffs or their Att^y, but that the same Still remains due, which the said Asa refuses to pay over.

It is Ordered, that the bond of the Said Asa and his Securities be Sued for the Plaintiffs in the Above Executions.

Inferior Court

Copp & King }
    vs   } Ca sa
Thomas King }

On Motion of Mr Atwater, Plaintiffs' Attorney, and it Appearing that a ca sa has been delivered to William Mickler, Esquire, Sheriff, and that the Same is Not returned this Term.

It is Ordered, that the said Sheriff do Make return of said ca sa, within thirty days from this date, Or that Attachment issue against him as for contempt of this Court.

Ordered, that the Magistrate or Magistrates in Each District do immediately draw Constables, Whose duty it shall be to attend the Inferior and Superior Courts, when duly required, two of Whom Shall be Summoned by the Sheriff to attend the Inferior Courts of the County.

Ordered, that the Sheriff be fined in the Sum of Ten Dollars for Neglecting to summon twenty One Jurors drawn to Serve this Term.

Ordered, that the defaulting Jurors be fined in the Sum of Twenty Dollars, Unless Sufficient Excuse for their Non Attendance be filed in the Clerk's office Within thirty Days.

John Sleigh. John Sleigh excused by the Court on a/c of infirmity.

Ordered, that George Dilworth be and he is hereby Appointed a Justice of the Peace in the district Commanded by Capt Hardee.

                                              John Ross, J. I. C.
                                              Abra^m Bessent
                                              Step W. Moore

Inferior Court Minutes Book 2

Jurors drawn for June Term 1812, present Abra^m Bessent, John Ross, & Stephen West Moore, Esquires, Justices of Said Inferior Court.

1. David Davis
2. William Clark
3. Silas Johns
4. Edward Williams
5. John Filchett
6. David Lang
7. John Moles
8. Inglehart Cruse
9. Benjamin Grubbs
10. John Clarke
11. Henry Hart
12. Garret Demott
13. John Ellis
14. Danl Brockington, Senr
15. John Conner
16. C. N. Drury
17. John Johnston
18. James Moore
19. James Whitten
20. Josiah Wilkinson
21. James Roberts
22. William Simpson
23. Allen Thomas
24. John D. Young
25. Silas Weeks
26. Dennis Lowe
27. Francis Sterling
28. William Marcum
29. Samuel Boyd
30. John Holzendorf
31. James Stewart
32. William Watson
33. John Beesley
34. James Erskin
35. Isaac Tucker
36. Levi Johns
37. Charles Magill
38. James D. Prevatt
39. Hardy Laneer
40. Jacob Clark

Jefferson, Monday, 1st June 1812

Court was Opened. Present, John Ross, Abraham Bessent, & William Scott, Esquires, Justices of Said Court.

The Jury Venire was Called and the following Jurors Attended, to wit.

1. James Moore
2. Samuel Boyd
3. John Filchett
4. Denis Lowe
5. William Simpson
6. John Motes
7. Silas Weeks
8. Daniel Brockington
9. James Stewart
10. Isaac Tucker
11. N. S. Drury
12. P. Goodbread

Executor of Mussault }
    vs   } Attachment
James Cashin   }

Jury N° 1 Sworn as above.

Inferior Court Minutes Book 2

Verdict. We find for the plaintiff One hundred thirty Dollars Eighty and One quarter Cents, with Costs of Suit. 1st June 1812

Samuel Boyd, foreman

James Baird, Indorsee }
    vs   } Case
Matthew Carter   }

Jury Nº 1

Verdict. We find for the plaintiff One hundred and fifty Dollars, with Interest from the first day of December Eighteen hundred and Ten & Costs of Suit. June 1st 1812

Samuel Boyd, foreman

Robert Rudulph }
    vs   }
Paul Chase   }

Jury Nº 1

Witness Sworn, William King.

Verdict. We, the Jury, find for the Plaintiff three hundred and Seventy five Dollars, with Costs of Suit. June 1st 1812

Samuel Boyd, foreman

I agree to credit Fifty Six Dollars 53¼ Cents.

Clark, Plff's Atty

The Court then adjourned Untill Tomorrow Nine O'Clock.

Abra^m Bessent
Wm Scott
John Ross

Tuesday, June 2nd 1812

The Court Met agreeable to adjournment. present, Their Honors John Ross, William Scott, & Abraham Bessent, Esquires, Justices of Said Court.

Inferior Court Minutes Book 2

Jury N° 1 Sworn, to wit.

1. John Filchett	7. Benjamin Grubbs
2. John Motes	8. William Simpson
3. John Conner	9. Dan¹ Brockington
4. Isaac Tucker	10. J. D. Young
5. Denis Lowe	11. James Moore
6. Silas Weeks	12. Philip Goodbread

Chancy B. Shepard }
    vs   } Attachment
William Cone, Junr }

Jury N° 1, as above.

Verdict. We find for the plaintiff One hundred Dollars, with Interest from the twenty second of August Eighteen hundred and ten & Costs of Suit. June 2nd 1812

                                          John Conner, foreman

James Baird }
    vs   } Case
John Crews }

I confess Judgement for One hundred and four Dollars and Eighty two and an half Cents, with Interest from the Third day of March Eighteen hundred and ten & Costs of Suit.

June 2nd 1812   John Conner, foreman

John Floyd   }
    vs   } case
Alexander Niger }

Jury N° 1

Witnesses Sworn, John Filchett, Dan¹ Grant, Charles Floyd, Archibald Clark, John Bashlot.

Verdict. We find for the Plaintiff One hundred and fifty Dollars, with Costs of Suit.

2nd June 1812   John Conner, foreman

On Application of Gen¹ John Floyd, Mr Charles Floyd, Daniel Grant, & William McNish.

Inferior Court Minutes Book 2

It is Ordered, that the Petitioners do Employ their Own hands liable to Perform Road duty

for the present year in repairing the road duty leading from the house ~~of~~ [smudge] Landing to the main Post Road leading through Camden County, provided they employ the said Hands twelve ~~Hands~~ Days in the said Year in so repairing said Road (and provided the Hands be first employed on Wakers Swamp and there Continued Untill it be Completed) and that the persons that may be in the employ of the said petitioners as owners, as well as the Hands above alluded to Shall be Exempt from performing duty on the Main Post Road aforesaid for the present year.

General John Floyd, William McNish, & Daniel Grant to Superintend the same & report to the Commissioners of Post Road their Actings and Doings.

Jefferson, 2nd June 1812

Copp & King }
  vs   } Sci fa
Wyley Thompson & }
L. Ashley   }

It appearing in this case that No return of the Writ in the Above Case has been Made. It is therefore Ordered, that the Sheriff of this County do forthwith Make return, say Within ten days of the aforesaid Writ, or that in default an Attachment as for Contempt do forth with issue against him.

William Price }
  vs   }
Samuel Tayson }

On Motion of Mr Atwater, plaintiff's Attorney, and it Appearing that Bail had been legally

Ordered in this case and that the Deputy Sheriff, William Mickler, had made Service and Neglected to take Bail, to Which said Atwater Makes Exceptions.

John Everingham }
  vs   } Attachment
Asa Hosmer   }

On Motion of Mr ~~Atwater~~ Clark, Attorney ~~Attorney~~ for the plaintiff, Stating to this Court, that by the return of the Writ in the Above case, a Certain Negro Named Philip has been Attached as the property of the Defendant, and it appearing that the said property is of a Perishable Nature, It is therefore Ordered by the Court, that the Sheriff do proceed to a Sale of the Aforesaid Negro According to Law, and the Moneys Arising

Inferior Court Minutes Book 2

from such Sale be deposited in the Clerk's office by the Sheriff or Other Officer to Abide the further Order of this Court.

John Ross
Wm Scott, J. I. C.
Abra^m Bessent

omitted.

Ordered, that Isaac Lang, Timothy Hopkins, Darius Woodworth and Son, Allen Thomas, and Charles Dishon have license to retail Spirituous Liquors, on their Giving Bond and Security as the Law directs.

The Court then Adjourned Untill Court in Course.

———

At Chambers in St Mary's, Monday, July the 4th 1812. Present, John Ross, Stephen W. Moore, Abraham Bessent, Esquires, Justices of S^d Court.

Upon the petition of John Pottle to be [smudge] to be admitted as a Citizen of the United States and he having been recommended as a Man of Good Morel character and Attacht to the Constitution of the United States, the following oath was administered to him, & he was admitted accordingly.

I, John Pottle, On the Holy Evangelists of Almighty God, do declare that I will Support the Constitution of the United States, That I do absolutely and Entirely renounce and Abjure all Allegiance and Fidelity to Every Foreign Prince, Potentate, State, or Sovereignty Whatever, and particularly the King or Regent of Great Britain, That more than Five Years have Elapsed since My Residence in the United States first Commenced, and that my Residence Within Camden County has been More than One Year, That I will Bear true and faithful Allegiance to the United States and the Constitued authorities thereof, According to the best of my skill and Judgement. So Help Me God.

Sworn in Open Court }
6th July 1812 }   John Pottle

John Ross, Abra^m Bessent

———

At Chambers, St Mary's, 9th September 1812

Present, John Ross, Abraham Bessent, & Stephen W. Moore, Esquires, Justices of S^d Court.

Inferior Court Minutes Book 2

The following persons were drawn as Jurors for January Term 1813, to wit.

1. William Drummond	25. John Motes
2. Christopher Grovenstine	26. William Clark
3. David Crum	27. John Ennis
4. James Helvingston	28. Allen Thomas
5. John Sparksman	29. John D. Young
6. Britain Brinkley	30. Dan[l] Brockington, Sen[r]
7. John Barco	31. James Whitten
8. Jacob Rollinson	32. Jacob Clark
9. James Williamson	33. James Moore
10. Duncan Curry	34. John Conner
11. Alexander Elliott	35. David Davies
12. Thomas Settles	36. James Roberts
13. Mills Drury	37. John Filchett
14. Thomas Godbread	38. Josiah Wilkinson
15. Isham Spalding, Jun[r]	39. Silas Weeks
16. John Prevatt	40. John Holzendorf
17. Levi Johns	41. Henry Hart
18. Isaac Tucker	42. John Johnston
19. Edward Williams	43. James Stewart
20. John Busby	44. Silas Johns
21. Samuel Boyd	45. James Erskins
22. Francis Sterling	46. William Watson
23. William Marcum	47. James D. Prevatt
24. Dennis Lowe	48. Charles Magill

Monday, January 4th 1813

The Inferior Court Was Opened. Present, their Honors John Ross, Abraham Bessent, and William Scott, Esquires, Justices of said Court.

The Court adjourned Untill Tomorrow Morning Nine O'Clock.

Isaac Crews, Clk

Tuesday, January the 5th 1813

The Court Met agreeable to adjournment. Present, Their Honors William Scott, John Ross, & William Ashley, Esquires, Justices of said Court.

The Jury Venire was Called & the following Jurors Attended, to wit.

1. Allen Thomas	8. James Stewart
2. John Filchett	9. James Moore
3. John Motes	10. John Busby
4. John Ennis	11. Jacob Clark

Inferior Court Minutes Book 2

    5. Isham Spalding, Junr   12. James Halvingston
    6. Mills Drury
    7. Duncan Curry

Ordered, that James Halvingston & James Stewart be excused.

Archibald Clark for   }
Patrick McOwen   }
13. vs   } Case
Edward W. Weyman }

Jury N° 1 Sworn.

    1. Allen Thomas   7. Duncan Curry
    2. John Filchett   8. James Moore
    3. John Motes   9. John Busby
    4. John Ennis   10. Jacob Clark
    5. Mills Drury   11. John May
    6. Isham Spalding   12. Nathan Norton

Verdict. We find for the plaintiff Nine Hundred and twenty five Dollars and thirty One Cents, with Interest from twenty sixth August 1811 and Costs of Suit.

Jefferson, 5th January 1813   John May, foreman

Archibald Clark for   }
Patrick McOwen   }
14. vs   } Case
Edward W. Weyman }

Jury N° 1

Verdict. We find for the plaintiff Nine Hundred & twenty five Dollars and thirty One Cents, With Interest from 26th August 1811 & Costs of Suit.

Jefferson, 5th Jany 1813   John May, foreman

William McLuer, Indorse }
    vs   } case
Donald Tompkins   }

Jury N° 1

Verdict. We find for the plaintiff One hundred and twenty Seven Dollars and twenty Cents, with Interest from 28 February 1811 and Costs of Suit.

5th Jany 1813   John May, foreman

Inferior Court Minutes Book 2

William McLure }
    vs   } Case
John Tompkins }

Jury N° 1

Verdict. We find for the Plaintiff Three Hundred and forty Eight Dollars & fifty five Cents, With Interest from 28th Feby 1811 & Costs.

5th Jany 1813   John May, foreman

George Stewart }
    vs   } Case
Stover & Reynolds }

Jury N° 1

Verdict. We find for the Plaintiff One Hundred and ten Dollars and Seventy Eight Cents, With Interest from 28th Jany 1811 & Costs.

5th Jany 1813   John May, foreman

William Downs }
    vs   } case
Daniel Copp }

Jury N° 1

Verdict. we find for the plaintiff two Hundred and Seventy five Dollars, with Interest from the Eleventh day of January last & Costs of Suit. January 5th 1813

                                     John May, foreman

Levin Gunby }
    vs   } Case
George Roberts }

Jury N° 1

Verdict. We find for the Plaintiff One hundred Dollars, with Interest from the Eleventh of April 1807 & Costs of Suit.

Jany 5th 1813   John May, foreman

Inferior Court Minutes Book 2

Jury N° 1

C. B. Shepard }
   vs } Case
James Williamson }

Jury N° 1

Verdict. We find for the Plaintiff One Hundred and Sixty Six Dollars & Sixty Cents, With Interest from the Third of June Eighteen Hundred & Ten & Costs of Suit.

January 5th 1813   John May, foreman

Asa Holton, Exor of }
Asa Lathrop }
   vs } Case
Luther P. Lockwood }

Jury N° 1

Verdict. We find for the Plaintiff Ninety Dollars and forty three and three quarter Cents, With Interest from 26th Ap^l 1811 & Costs.

5th January 1813   John May, foreman

Abraham Bessent, Exor of }
John Eaton }
   vs } Case
William Cone, Junr & }
Fredrick Slade }

Verdict. We find for the plaintiff Eighty Seven Dollars thirty Seven & One half Cents, with Interest from the twenty Sixth of October Eighteen hundred And Seven & Costs of Suit.

January 5th 1813   John May, foreman

George Stewart }
   vs } Attach^t
Strover & Reynolds }

On Motion of Archibald Clark, Att^y for the plaintiff in the above case.

It is Ordered by the Court, that Judgement be entered against Edward W. Weyman as Garnishe

Inferior Court Minutes Book 2

Guarnishe for Sixty four dollars & seventy five Cents and Costs, it being the Amount Acknowledged by him as being in his Hands.

Abraham Bessent }
Exor of Benjamin Honeker }
    vs   } Attachment
Charles Seton }

Jury N° 1

Witnesses Sworn, Duncan Curry, Jacob Clark, and John Ross.

Verdict. We find for the plaintiff One Hundred and Sixty Dollars, with Costs of Suit.

5th January 1813   John May, foreman

Nathan Bixby }
    vs   } Case
Samuel S. Wagner }

It is agreed between the parties, plaintiff & defendant in this case, that the Examin of John Randolph be taken before the Court, and that the same be admitted at the of the Trial of the said Case, & that the said Case be Continued.

Thomas Whelwell }
7   vs   } Case
Charles Deshon }

Jury N° 1

John Conner & Isaac Lang Sworn on the Jury in lue of Jacob Clark & Allen Thomas.

Verdict. We find for the Plaintiff Sixty Three Dollars, With Interest from 29th March 1812 and Costs of Suit.

5th January 1813   John May, foreman

———

Micajah Bond }
    vs   } Case
James Stafford }

Jury N° 1

Verdict. We find for the Plff five Hundred and fifty five Dollars, With Interest from the first day of January Eighteen hundred & Eleven & Costs of Suit.

January 5th 1813   John May, foreman

Inferior Court Minutes Book 2

The Governor of Georgia }
Nº 1   vs   } Debt
Asa Holton, Et al   }

Jury Nº 1

Verdict. We find the deed declared on to be the Deed of the defendants & Assess One Cent Damages. Jany 5th 1813

                                                    John May, foreman

Littleton Myrick   }
    vs   } Case
Hugh Brown, Indorse }

Jury Nº 1

Witness, David Brown.

Verdict. We find for the plaintiff fifty Dollars, With Interest & Costs of Suit.

January 5, 1813   John May, foreman

Isaac Crews, Clerk of the   }
Court of Ordinary, for   }
the use of Elihu Atwater   }
admix Francis Waterman   }
    vs   } Debt
James Hannay, David Lewis }
& James Smith   }

Continued.

John Holzendorf, Plff in Execution }
    vs   } Claim
Israel Barber, Claimant   }

Jury Nº 1 Sworn as the law directs.

Witness, Wade Hampton.

Verdict. We find the property Levied on Not Subject to this Execution. 5th January 1813

                                                    John May, foreman

Inferior Court Minutes Book 2

Williford & Cook }
Plffs in Execution }
    vs   } Claim
John Ross, Admor of }
Patrick Hacket }

We, the Undersigned Referees, by Archibald Clark, Esqr, Agent for Messrs Williford and Cook, and John Ross, Esqr, Claimant in the Above case, Do award, After giving due Notice of the time of Meeting Agreeable to Sheriff's Return, that the Right of property is in John Ross aforesaid, Vizt. The House &c as expressed or particularlized in the Conveyance of Asa Holton, Sheriff of Said County, Bearing date the 24th december 1807.

Given Under Our Hands & Seals this }   Abra^m Bessent
2nd of January 1813   }   Hen^y Sadler

Examined 6 January 1813   John Ross
     Abra^m Bessent
     Wm Ashley

The Court then adjourned Untill Tomorrow Nine O'Clock A. M.

Isaac Crews, Clk

Wednesday, January 6th 1813

The Court Met agreeable to adjournment. Present, John Ross, Abraham Bessent, & and William Ashley, Esquires, Justices of Said Court.

Nathan Bixby }
    vs   } Attachment
Daniel Edes }

Judgement by default.

Timothy Hopkins }
    vs   } Attachment
Jacob Campbell }

Judgement by default.

Elihu Atwater }
    vs   } Attachment
William Price }

Judgement by default.

Inferior Court Minutes Book 2

F. M. Arodundo & Son }
    vs   } Case
Lodewick Ashley }

plea filed.

Eleazer Waterman }
    vs   } Case
Josiah Smith }

plea filed.

Vincent Pendergrass }
    vs   } Case
Seymour Picket }

~~plea filed~~. Not served.

William Cone, Sen[r] }
    vs   } Case
McKeen Greene }

Settled.

John Cheely }
    vs   } case
Thomas Farless }

Not served.

Joseph Reid }
    vs   } case
Gabriel Priest }

Not served.

Robert Rudulph }
    vs   } Attachment
Zapheniah Kingsley }

Judgement by default.

Horatio Lowe }
    vs   } Attachment
Robert Kershaw }

Judgement by default.

Inferior Court Minutes Book 2

Joseph Reid }
    vs   } Trover
Elizabeth Arons & }
William Carney }

Joseph Rain }
    vs   } Attachment
Charles Jones }

Judgement by default.

Sadler & Sands }
    vs   } Case
Robert Walker }

Judgement by default.

Williford & Cook } Refered
Plff in Execution }
    vs   } Claim
John Ross, Claimant }

The Award of the Referees was Rendered, Ordered to be Recorded. Jany 5th 1813

Thomas Vincent }
    vs   } Ca sa
Daniel Copp }

On Motion of Mr Atwater, Attorney for the plaintiff, & it Appearing that the Sheriff, Hugh Brown, Esquire, had possession of said Process in time to have made due return On the same, but has Neglected to do so. It is Ordered, that said Sheriff do pay over the Amount thereof to the plff's Att^y Within Thirty Days, or that Attachment issue.

Joseph Reid }
    vs   } Trover
Elizabeth Arons & }
William Carney }

On Motion of Mr Atwater and it Appearing that the Sheriff has Neither taken Bail of the defendant, Elizabeth Arons, or made return of Service on her.

It is therefore Ordered, that the Sheriff be considered & held as Bail for the said Elizabeth or her Appearance to Answer said Suit, Unless he Make due returns Within ten days from this date.

Ordered, that the Names of Defaulting Jurors be published at Jefferson, also at St Mary's, And that they Each be fined in the sum of Twenty Dollars, Unless Good &

Inferior Court Minutes Book 2

Sufficient Excuse be filed On Oath in the Clerk's Office Within Thirty [blot] days from the date of said publication.

Ordered, that a County Tax be levied and Collected by the Tax Collector Equal to One third of the General Tax for the year 1812 & 1813.

And a poor Tax Equal to One fourteenth for said Years.

John Ross
Abra^m Bessent
Wm Ashley

At Chambers, St Mary's, January 11th 1813

Present, John Ross, Abraham Bessent, & the following persons were drawn as Jurors for June Term 1813.

1. William F. Kelly
2. Garret Demott
3. Inglehart Cruse
4. William Andrews
5. John Oaks
6. Stephen Sparksman
7. Philip Goodbread
8. Charles Howell
9. Danl McMillen
10. Isaac K. Courter
11. Richard Pellum
12. Amos Lindsay
13. John Cade
14. Hardee Laneer
15. John Campbell
16. Benjamin Grubbs
17. John Demott
18. Ransom Cason
19. Henry Jones
20. Arthur Moore
21. David Lang
22. Charlton Mizele, Junr
23. James Brooks
24. David Mizele
25. Francis Young
26. Isaac Johns
27. Thomas Garner
28. John Clark
29. Daniel Greene
30. Nathan^l Beal
31. David Hale
32. Eli Cason
33. Nathan Norton
34. Nathl Stephens
35. Joseph McCullough
36. Charles N. Drury
37. James Vincent
38. Stephen Gray
39. Levi Sparksman
40. Adam Cooper
41. James Nobles
42. Danl Brockington, Junr
43. Ezekiel Smith
44. Berry Elzey
45. Lewis Thomas
46. John Baley, Junr
47. Josiah Winans
48. Isaac Greene

It is Ordered, that William Mickler, Esquire, late Sheriff and at present deputy Sheriff, do pay over all fines by him Collected, or required so to do by the Order or Sentance of

Inferior Court Minutes Book 2

the Superior Court, Within Thirty days from this date, or in default thereof an Attachment do issue as for a Contempt, And that he be immediately served with a Copy hereof.

John Ross
Abra^m Bessent
Step W. Moore

Monday, June the 7th 1813

The Court was Opened, Present, their Honors John Ross, Abraham Bessent, & William Scott, Justices of Said Court.

The Jury Venire Was Called and the following Jurors appeared, to wit.

John Bailey, Junr	David Mizele
David Lang	Levi Sparksman
Daniel McMillin	Stephen Sparksman
Isaac Greene	William Andrews
Nathan Norton	John Oaks
Daniel Greene	Nathaniel Beal
Arthur Moore	Charlton Mizele, Junr
Stephen Gray	
Benjamin Grubbs	
Philip Goodbread	

———

Ordered, that John Oaks & Nathaniel Beal be Excused, on Account of the Indisposition of their families.

Nathan Bixby   }
    vs   } case
Samuel S. Wagner }

Jury N° 1 Sworn.

1. John Bailey	2. David Lang
3. Daniel McMillin	4. Isaac Greene
5. Nathan Norton	6. Arthur Moore
7. Stephen Gray	8. Benjamin Grubbs
9. Philip Goodbread	10. David Mizele
11. Levy Sparksman	12. Stephen Sparksman

Witnesses Sworn, to wit, James Bixby & David Tucker.

The Examination of Randolph also red.

Inferior Court Minutes Book 2

Verdict. We find for the Plaintiff twenty five Cents Damages, With Costs of Suit. June 7th 1813

David Mizele, foreman

Edward Richardson }
  vs   } Attachment
Benjamin F. Hard }

Jury N° 1

Verdict. We find for the plaintiff Fifty Eight Dollars & Costs of Suit.

7th June 1813   David Mizele, foreman

Timothy Hopkins }
  vs   } Attachment
Jacob Campbell }

Jury N° 1.

Verdict. We find for the Plaintiff Eighty Dollars, With Interest from 1st Jany 1812 & Costs of Suit. 7th June 1813

David Mizele, foreman

Sadler & Sands }
  vs   } Case
Robert Walker }

Jury N° 1

Verdict. We find for the Plaintiff Eighty Dollars and forty Eight and Three fourth Cents, With Interest from Thirty first of December 1806 & Costs of Suit. June 7th 1813

David Mizele, foreman

George Roberts, for }
Use of Elihu Hebbard }
  vs   } Attachment
Jehu Underwood }

Continued. June 1813

George Gates }
  vs   } Case
James Gilman }

Inferior Court Minutes Book 2

Continued. June Term 1813

Isaac K. Courter }
    vs   }
Don Justo Lopez }

Continued. June Term 1813

Micah Stone }
    vs   } Case
Nathan Bixby }

Continued. June Term 1813

Josiah Smith }
    vs   } Trover
John Best }

Continued. June Term 1813

James A. Brush }
    vs   } Case
Stephen Waterman }

discontinued June Term 1813

William Price }
    vs   } Trespass
Samuel Tayson }

Continued. June Term 1813

Nathan Bixby }
    vs   } Attachment
Daniel Edes }

Continued. June Term 1813

Elihu Atwater }
    vs   } Attachment
William Price }

Continued. June Term 1813

F. M. Aredondo & Son }
    vs   } Attachment
Lodewick Ashley }

Inferior Court Minutes Book 2

Continued by Consent. June Term 1813

John Ross
William Scott, J. I. C.
Abra^m Bessent

The Court then adjourned Until Eight O'Clock Tomorrow Morning.

Tuesday, June the 8th 1813

The Court was Opened agreeable to Adjournment. Present, Their Honors John Ross, William Scott, Abraham Bessent, William Ashley, Esquires, Justices of Said Court.

Ordered, that the Several Justices of the Peace in Camden County, do forth with proceed to draw Constables in Each District to Supply all existing Vacancies.

Daniel Beasley }
    vs   } Trover
James Moore }

Daniel Beasley }
    vs   } Trover
Philip Goodbread }

The Parties in the Above Cases ~~agreeable~~ by their Attornies agree that the Same be Continued Untill the Next term, that all of formality in the Taking ~~of~~ the Examinations of Certain Witnesses, Under Commission from this Court and Now Opened be waved, And that the parties be at Liberty to improve upon the Trial Such Parts thereof as are legal, and according to the Rule of Evidence.

Clark, Deft's Atty
Atwater, Plff's Atty

Eleazer Waterman }
    vs   } Case
Josiah Smith }

Jury No 1, as Yesterday.

Verdict. We find for the defendant Costs of Suit.

June 8th 1813   David Mizele, foreman

Joseph Rain }
    vs   } Attachment
Charles Jones }

Inferior Court Minutes Book 2

Jury N° 1, as Yesterday.

Verdict. We find for the Plaintiff One hundred and Seventy five Dollars & Costs. One hundred and Three Dollars Eighty One and a quarter Cents of Which Amount, we find against James Lloyd, a guarnishee in the Above case.

8th June 1813   David Mizele, foreman

Robert Rudulph   }
    vs   } Attachment
Zapheniah Kingsley }

Jury N° 1

Verdict. We find for the Plaintiff four Hundred and Seven Dollars and $^{50}/_{100}$, with Costs of Suit.

8th June 1813   David Mizele, foreman

Ordered, that the following persons have license to retail Spirituous Liuors, on their Complying with the Law in that Such Cases, to wit.

Allen Thomas, Elizabeth Bailey, Hopkins & Motes, Darius Woodworth, Isaac Lang, and Joseph Semar

Edward Shearman   }
    vs   } Case
James B. Gilman   }

Continued. June Term 1813

John Everingham }
    vs   } Attachment
Asa Hosmer   }

Continued on affidavit of Plff's Atty. June Term 1813

Horatio Lowe   }
    vs   } Attachment
Robert Kershaw   }

Continued by Consent. 8th June 1813

Joseph Reid   }
    vs   } Trover
Elizabeth Arons & }
William Carney   }

Inferior Court Minutes Book 2

Jury N° 1

William Andrews Sworn on the Jury in Lue of Philip Goodbread.

Witnesses Sworn, Mark King, William Neely, Elizabeth Woodland, Gabriel Priest, John Gorman, William Ashley.

The Examination (taken on Interrogatories) of Timothy Hollings Worth and Robert Cowin.

Verdict. We find for the Plaintiff four Thousand Dollars, With Costs of Suit.

June the 8th 1813 David Mizell, foreman

Elizabeth Arons & }
William Andrews }
    ads } Trover
Joseph Reid }

On Motion and Cause being Shewn. It is ordered by the Court, that the Defendants be allowed thirty days to Enter Their appeal or file a Warrant of Attorney for appeal in the above case.

Isaac Crews, Clerk of the Court }
of Ordinary, for the use of }
Elihu Atwater, admor of }
Flavius Waterman }
    vs } Debt
James Hannay, David Lewis }
& James Smith }

Jury N° 1

Verdict. We find for the Plaintiff Six hundred thirty Seven Dollars & twenty One Cents, & Costs of Suit. June 8th 1813

                                                      David Mizele, foreman

The Plaintiffs' Attorney Consents that the Deft^s have twenty days Allowed to Enter an Appeal and pay Costs, in Case the Chose to do so.

Samuel Howard } Claim under
    vs } Attachment
Samuel Parker, Claimant }

Jury N° 1

Inferior Court Minutes Book 2

Verdict. We find the property attached by Virtue of the Within Writ Not liable thereto, but the property of the Claimant.

8th ~~March~~ June 1813 David Mizele, foreman

the Atty for The plaintiff in the Above case is Allowed Sixty Days to Enter an Appeal and file his Warrant of Attorney.

Copp & King }
    vs   } Sci fac
Wiley Thompson & }
Lodewick Ashley }

Jury N° 1

Verdict. We find for the plaintiffs two hundred and thirty five Dollars Eighty One and an half Cents, with Interest from 6th Septr 1804 and Costs. 8th June 1813

David Mizele, foreman

Collen Lincoln }
    vs   } Case
Prince Baxter }

~~Discontinued~~. Dismissed. 8th June 1813

David Lewis }
    vs   } Attachment
Robert Kershaw }

Continued. June 8th 1813

Mickler & Barns }
    vs   } Case
Vincent Taylor }

Judgement by default. June Term 1813

Israel Barber }
    vs   } Case
Hebberion & Young }

Judgement by default against Philip Young. June Term 1813

Aaron Lazarus }
    vs   } Case
John Johnson }

Inferior Court Minutes Book 2

Judgement by default. June Term 1813

Samuel Howard }
    vs   } Attachment
George Parker }

Judgement by default. June Term 1813

Elias Baker   }
    vs   } Sci fac
Silvanus & Matthias }
Crowell   }

Continued. June 1813

It is Ordered, that Dennis Lowe, Francis Sterling, and Isaac Tucker, defaulting Jurors at the last Term, (and having Made Excuses) be Excused.

Ordered, that Defaulting Jurors be fined in the sum of ten Dollars each, unless good and Sufficient Excuse (On Oath) be filed with the Clerk of this Court before the Expiration of Thirty days from the publication hereof.

                                          John Ross
                                          William Scott, J. I. C.
                                          Abra^m Bessent
                                          Wm Ashley

The Court then adjourned Untill Court in Course.

At Chambers, St Mary's, July 6th 1813

Present, John Ross, Abraham Bessent, Esquires, Justices of the Inferior Court.

The following persons ware drawn as Jurors for ~~Janu~~ January Term 1814, to wit.

    1. James Elliott   8. Thomas Clark, Senr
    2. Solomon Osteen   9. Berry Walker
    3. Zacheriah Motes   10. William Hines
    4. John Browne   11. William Cone, Junr
    5. Thomas Tucker   12. Thomas Goodbread
    6. Thomas King   13. Francis Sterling
    7. William Simpson   14. Alexander Elliott

---

    15. Charles Magill   30. Josiah Wilkinson
    16. James Roberts   31. Edward Williams

Inferior Court Minutes Book 2

17. William Marcum
18. James Moore
19. James Whitten
20. John Ennis
21. John Filchett
22. Silas Weeks
23. William Drummond
24. Christopher Grovenstine
25. Duncan Curry
26. John Motes
27. John Holzendorf
28. Danl Brockington, Senr
29. Thomas Settle
32. John D. Young
33. Mills Drury
34. Jacob Rollinson
35. John Prevatt
36. James Williamson
37. Isaac Tucker
38. James Helvingston
39. James Erskins
40. James Stewart

Inferior Court Chambers, 27th October 1813

The Clerk of the Superior Court having communicated an Extract from the Minute of the Superior dated the 25th Inst requiring the aid of this Court to effect a removal of the County Records, as well as the records of the proceedings of the Courts, and also to defray the Expences of Transportation.

Ordered, that the Clerk of the Superior and Inferior Court do cause to be procured Suitable Trunks or boxes to Contain the Records and public papers, and to remove the same, Should any additional alarm take place, to St Mary's, thence to Point Peter, as soon as a Building can be procured to Contain them, and that the Expences Attending the same be allowed out of any County Funds Not otherwise appropriated.

Monday, January 3rd 1814

The Inferior Court was Opened. Present, their Honors John Ross, Abraham Bessent, & William Scott, & Donald Tompkins, Esquires, Justices of Said Court.

The Court then adjourned Untill Tomorrow Morning Nine O'Clock.

             John Ross
             Dol^d Tompkins
             Abra^m Bessent

Tuesday, January 4th 1814

Court was Opened agreeable to adjournment. Present, their Honors John Ross, Abraham Bessent, & Donald Tompkins, Esquires, Justices of Said Court.

Ordered, that Randolph McGillis, Esqr be and is hereby appointed a Commissioner of Roads lieu Timothy Hopkins removed Out of the County.

Inferior Court Minutes Book 2

The Court then adjourned Untill Court in Course.

            Abra^m Bessent
            Dol^d Tompkins
            John Ross

Ordered, that the County Tax & Poor Tax for the Year 1814 be and hereby is Assessed and that the same be Collected agreeably to the full extent of the Powers of this Court Vested in them by the Acts of the legislature of the State of Georgia.

$^1/_8$ & $^1/_{14}$ Abra^m Bessent
               John Ross
               Dol^d Tompkins

At Chambers, in the Town of St Mary's, March 26th 1814

~~the~~ Present, their Honors John Ross, Thomas H. Miller, and Donald Tompkins, Esquires, Justices of Said Court.

The Court proceeded to draw a Jury for June Term 1814, to wit.

1. William Clark	2. Dennis Lowe	3. John Sparksman
4. David Crum	5. Silas Johns	6. Levi Johns
7. John Johnston	8. Allen Thomas	9. William Watson
10. Isham Spalding	11. Samuel Boyd	12. Jacob Clark
13. John Beasley	14. Francis Young	15. Danl McMillin
16. Isaac Greene	17. John Clarke	18. Amos Lindsay
19. Benj. Grubbs	20. Henry Jones	21. John Bailey, Junr
22. Richard Pellum	23. David Mizele	24. John Demott
25. David Lang	26. Cha^r Mizele, J^r	27. James Brooks
28. Nathan Norton	29. Isaac K. Courter	30. Garret Demott
31. Arthur Moore	32. Stephen Gray	33. Adam Cooper
34. Charles N. Drury	35. John Campbell	36. Hardy Laneer
37. Thomas Gardner	38. Danl Brockington, J^r	39. John Cade
40. Ezekiel Smith		

Upon the Petition of Margaret Mickler and Margaret Reddock, praying that Archibald Clark be appointed guardian for Each of them, by & With the Consent of all the parties Concerned.

It is Ordered, that Archibald Clark, Esquire be and he is hereby Appointed Guardian for Margaret Mickler, Daughter of Jacob Mickler, and also that Archibald Clark, Esqr

Inferior Court Minutes Book 2

be and he is hereby Appointed Guardian for Margaret Reddock, agreeably to the Prayer of the petitioners.

On the Petition of John McClure, Stating that he is Confined at the Suit of Nimrod Dye and that he is Unable to pay his debts, but he is Willing to Make a fair Surrender of all his Estate, real and personal, for the benefit of his Creditors, in Terms of the Insolvent Acts of this State.

It is ordered, that the said John McClure be brought up at the Court House in Jefferson On the Sixth day of June Next to be Examined in the premises, and that Notice hereof be Given to Each of his Creditors, and that this Order be published in One of the Gazettes of the City of Savannah weekly for the space of two Months.

On the petition of Levi Sparksman and John Pearce for Tavern License. It is ordered, that they have license to retail Spirituous Liquors for One year from the date here of On his giving bond &c as the law directs.

John Ross
Thos H. Miller
Dol^d Tompkins, J. I. C.

Moday, June 6th 1814

The Court was Opened. Present, their Honors John Ross, Abraham Bessent, Thomas H. Miller, & Donald Tompkins, Esquires, Justices of Said Court.

The Jury Venire Was Called & the following persons attended, to wit.

1. John Bailey, Junr
2. Charlton Mizele, Junr
3. Henry Jones
4. Nathan Norton
5. Chas N. Drury
6. David Crum
7. John Beesley
8. Dennis Lowe
9. David Mizele
10. Jehu Sparkman
11. Arthur Moore
12. Daniel McMillen
13. Allen Thomas
14. Samuel Boyd
15. Stephen Gray
16. Hardy Laneer
17. Isaac Green

Ordered, that Daniel McMillin be Excused.

~~Samuel Howard~~ }
    vs   } ~~Attachment~~
~~George Parker~~ }

Jury N° 1 Sworn, to wit.

1. John Bailey, Junr
2. Cha^r Mizell, Junr
3. Henry Jones
4. Nathan Norton
5. C. N. Drury
6. David Greene

Inferior Court Minutes Book 2

| 7. John Beesley | 8. Dennis Lowe | 9. David Mizele |
| 10. John Sparksman | 11. Arthur Moore | 12. Allen Thomas |

Verdict. ~~We find the property Attached by Virtue of the Within Writ Not liable thereto, but the property of the Claimant. 6th June 1814~~

The Above is an Error.

Micah Stone }
7. vs   } Case
Nathan Bixby }

Discontinued by Consent. June 1814

Josiah Smith }
8. vs   } Trover
John Best   }

Continued. June Term 1814

William Price }
9. vs   } Trespass
Samuel Tayson }

Continued. June 1814

Horatio Lowe   }
10. vs   } Attachment
Robert Kershaw }

Jury N° 1 as

Verdict. We find for the plaintiff Three Hundred and Eight Dollars & Ninety five Cents, With Costs of Suit. Jefferson, 6th June 1814

John Bailey, foreman

Horatio Lowe   }
    vs   } Attachment
Robert Kershaw }

By the return of the Sheriff in the Above Case, It Appears That Micah Stone was Cited as Garnishee, That Said Micah has failed to Make any return. On Motion, It is ordered, that the said Micah render & file a Schedule in the Clerk's Office of Such Affects, on Oath, as may have been in his hands on the Third day of December 1812 belonging to the

Inferior Court Minutes Book 2

defendant, Within Thirty days from the date here of, or that in default an Attachment as for Contempt do issue.

Aaron Lazarus }
17. vs   } Case
John Johnson }

Continued. June 6th 1814

Samuel Howard }
18. vs   } Attachment
George Parker   }

Dismissed. 6th June 1814

Arbana Talles }
2. vs   }
John Fraser   }

Death of Defendant Suggested. June 6th 1814

Vincent Pendegrass }
5. vs   } Attachment
Seymour Pickett   }

No Service. 6th June 1814

Archibald Graham }
7. vs   } Attachment
Colen Graham   }

Judgement by Default. 6th June 1814

Elias Roberts }
8. vs   } Attach[t]
Colen Graham }

Judgement by Default. June 6th 1814

Elihu Atwater }
9. vs   } Attach[t]
Colen Graham }

Judgement by Default. 6th June 1814

Inferior Court Minutes Book 2

Elizabeth Bailey }
10. vs } Attachment
John Armstrong }

Judgement by Default. 6th June 1814

Joseph Reid }
11. vs } Attachment
Colen Graham }

Judgement by Default. 6th June 1814

———

Fitz J. Slocum }
    vs } Attachment
Isaac Sauls }

Settled. June 6th 1814

Aaron Lazarus }
13. vs } Attachment
Joshua Howard }

Judgement by Default. 6th June 1814

Bird Waters }
14. vs } Attach^t
Buckner Harris }

Settled. June 6th 1814

Harmon Courter }
20. vs } case
Hebberson & Young }

Judgement by default. 6th June 1814

James Dell }
22. vs } case
Hebberson & Young }

Judgement by default. 6th June 1814

Levi Sparksman }
24. vs } Case
Wm L. B. Hart }
William Hart }

Inferior Court Minutes Book 2

Settled. 6th June 1814

George Roberts, for the use of }
Elihu Hebbard   }
     vs   } Attach^t
Jehu Underwood   }

Continued for Want of parties. June 1814

The Court then Adjourned Untill Eight O'Clock Tomorrow Morning.

                                              John Ross
                                              D. Tompkins
                                              Thos H. Miller

---

Tuesday, June 7th 1814

The Court was Opened Agreeable to adjournment. Present, their Honors John Ross, Abraham Bessent, and Thomas H. Miller, Esquires, Justices of Said Court. Also, Donald Tompkins, Esqr.

Upon the petitions of Isaac Lang, Zacheriah Motes, and Elizabeth Bailey, for License to Retail Spirituous Liquors.

Ordered, that they have licenses to retail Spirituous Liquors, On their Giving bonds as the law directs.

Daniel Beasley }
7.   vs   } Trover
James Moor   }

Jury N° 1

Stephen Gray on the Jury in Lue of Arthur Moor.

Verdict. We find the Defendant Not Guilty.

June 7th 1814   John Bailey, foreman

Daniel Beasley   }
     vs   } Trover
Philip Goodbread }

Jury N° 1 as above.

Verdict. We find the defendant Not Guilty.

Inferior Court Minutes Book 2

June 7th 1814					John Bailey, foreman

Beasley }					Beasley }
  vs } Trover			 vs } Trover
Moore }					Goodbread }

On Motion of Plaintiff's Att^y in these cases, it is ordered by the Court, that the Plff's Agent Henry

---

Dance have untill the first day of October Next Allowed him for filing a Warrant of AttorneyAuthoring the Entry of Appeals from the Verdicts of the Jury, According to Act in that Case provided, Within the rules of the same, and that the said appeals May be entered Within the four days Allowed.

David Lewis   }
    vs   } Attachment
Robert Kershaw }

It Appearing to the Court, that Micah Stone, a Garnishee, has failed to Make a return in terms of the Act. Ordered, that the said Micah do Make a return agreeably to the exigencies of the Said Writ, Within thirty days, or that Attachment do issue as of Course on Service of this order on the said Garnishee.

George Gates   }
    vs   } Case
James Gilman }

Continued by Plff's Atty. 7th June 1814

Edward Sherman }
    vs   } Case
James Gilman   }

Continued at the Instance Plff. 7th June 1814

John Everingham }
    vs   } attach^{mt}
Asa Hosmer   }

Continued by consent. 7th June 1814

Elihu Atwater   }
    vs   } attach^{mt}
William Price   }

Continued. 7th June 1814

Inferior Court Minutes Book 2

David Lowes }
14. vs } Attach^t
Robert Kershaw }

Continued. 7th June 1814

Mickler & Barns }
15. vs } Case
Vincent Taylor }

Continued. 7th June 1814

Israel Barber }
16. vs } Case
Hebberson & Young }

Continued. 7th June 1814

James Blair & Co }
19. vs } Attach^t
C. B. Shepard }

Continued. 7th June 1814

Catharine Miller, Exix of N. Greene }
vs } Attachment
John McClure }

On Objection ~~Objection~~ taken in this Case, was that No Affidavit was filed in terms of the Attachment law, to ground the Attachment on, and the said Plff's Att^y Suggested on Oath that said affidavit had been Made, and had been lost or Mislaid and Craved time to find the Same.

It is Ordered, that ten days from this date be Allowed to find and file Said affidavit, or on failure thereof, at the expiration of the Said Time, the Said Attachment be dismissed as of Course.

Daniel Nunas }
vs } Attacht.
David Leurry }

It appearing to the Court, that William Ashley, Esqr has been Served as a Garnishee in the Above Case and has failed to Make return in terms of the act.

Inferior Court Minutes Book 2

Ordered, that said William Ashley do Make a return agreeably to the exigency of Said Writ, Within Thirty days, or that Attachment do issue as of Course, and That a Copy of this order be Served on the said William Ashley.

Nimrod Dye }
    vs }
John McClure }

John McClure, Defendant in this Case, having appeared in terms of the order of this Court, with the Intentition to pray the benefits of the insolvent Act, and it Not appearing by a return of the Sheriff that the Noticeses on the Creditors of the said Defendant have been duly Served, Ordered by the Court that the same be post poned to Chambers in the Town of St Mary's on the Seventh day of July Next for the Hearing of the Said Application.

F. M. Aradundo & Son }
    vs } Case
Lodewick Ashley }

Continued. 7th June 1814

Moses Cook }
    vs } Attachment
John McClure }

Dismissed. 7th June 1814

Elihu Atwater, Indorsee }
15. vs } Attachment
James Cashen }

Exceptions taken to the Writ. The Court reserves its Opinion.

William Seal }
16. vs } Slander
Peter Mickler }

Plea filed. 7th June 1814

Hudnall, Paxton, & Weyman }
17. vs } Case
John Sparksman }

Plea filed. 7th June 1814

Inferior Court Minutes Book 2

Ezekiel Hudnall & Co }
18. vs } Case
John Sparksman }

Plea filed. 7th June 1814

Israel Barber }
19. vs } Case
Hardy Laneer }

Plea filed. 7th June 1814

William Gallagher }
21. vs } Cov^t
John Cowan }

Plea filed. 7th June 1814

David Lewis }
25. vs } Case
John Ross }

Want of a Quorum has suspended an Appearance.

Michael Kelly }
26. vs } Case
A. D. Cressent }

Settled. 7th June 1814

———

William Mure, Exor }
Claimant }
    vs } Claim
Moses Cook, Plff in }
Attachment }

Dismissed. 7th June 1814

Isaac K. Courter }
4. vs }
Don Justo Lopez }

to be placed on the Claim docket. 7th June 1814

Exix of N. Greene }
1. vs } Attachment
John McClure }

Sadler & Sands }
vs } Attach^t
John McClure }

Inferior Court Minutes Book 2

In the first of these Cases, the following Exceptions were taken.

1st That the bond was Not executed before the Magistrate issuing the Attachment.

2nd That the bond was Signed by Catharine Miller in her proper person and Not as Executrix of Nathan[l] Greene, Though so Called in the body of the bond.

In the Second Case, the following.

1 that the signature of Sadler and Sands by Henry Sadler to the bond was Not Legal and so Not binding on the two parties for whom it was purported to have been Signed.

2 That the said bond was Not Witnessed by the Officer of the Court issuing the Same, being executed before there parties.

3 that the Original Attachment is Not tested by the issuing Magistrate.

Lawson, Atwater & Her Attornies 7th June 1814

Which Said Exceptions were Over ruled.

The following persons were Appointed Commissioners of the post Road, Viz. Timothy Hopkins, a Commissioner in the Second District; John Atkinson, Hugh Brown, and Robert Paxton, Esquires, Commissioners of the Third district.

Ordered, that the Names of Defaulting Jurors be Published at Jefferson & at St Mary's, and that they be fined in the Sum of ten dollars Each, Unless good Excuse be filed with the Clerk in 30 days from the publication thereof.

John Ross
Thos H. Miller
Dold Tompkins

St Mary's, June 18th 1814

At a Meeting of the Inferior Court at Chambers. Present, John Ross, Thomas H. Miller, & Abraham Bessent, Esquires, Justices of Said Court.

The following Jurors were drawn for January Term 1815, to wit.

1. Levi Sparkman
2. Charles Howell
3. Joseph McCullough
4. Inglehart Cruse, Junr
5. Philip Goodbread

21. John Conner
22. William Drummond
23. Daniel Brockington, Senr
24. Francis Sterling
25. Thomas Goodbread

Inferior Court Minutes Book 2

6. James Vincent
7. Lewis Thomas
8. John Oaks
9. David Hall
10. Nathaniel Beal
11. William F. Kelly
12. William Andrews
13. Nathaniel Stevens
14. Eli Cason
15. Isaac Johns
16. Josiah Winans
17. Daniel Green
18. James Moore
19. James Erskins
20. John Filchett

26. William Hines
27. Berry Walker
28. Thomas Clark
29. Thomas Tucker
30. Thomas King, Senr
31. John Motes
32. Solomon Osteen
33. James Elliott
34. Isaac Tucker
35. William Marcum
36. Charles Magill
37. John Ennis
38. James Roberts
39. Jacob Rolinson
40. Mills Drury

John Ross
Thos H. Miller
Abra^m Bessent

St Mary's, At Chambers, September 15 1814

At an Adjourned Meeting of the Inferior Court. Present, their Honors John Ross, Abraham Bessent, & Thomas H. Miller, Esquires, Justices of Said Court.

Nimrod Dye }
    vs   }
John McClure }

This Case having been Postponed the Seventh day of June Untill the Seventh of July, And from then Untill the fifth[blot] September, And from then Untill the fifteenth of September Instant, by Consent of Parties.

The Said John McClure Appeared and Made a Surrender of his Estate, and a Schedule of his debts & books of Account, and took the Oath as prescribed by Law, Viz.

I, John McClure, do Solemnly Swear, In the presence of Almighty God, that I am Not Possessed of any real or personal Estate, debts, Credits, or effects, Securities or contracts, Whatsoever, My Wearing apparel, bedding for myself and family, and the Working tools or implements of My trade or calling, together with the Necessary Equipments for a Militia Soldier excepted, Other than are Contained in the Schedule Now delivered, and that I have Not, directly or Indirectly, since my imprisonment or before Sold, leased, assigned, or otherwise disposed of, or made Over in trust for My Self, or otherwise disposed of, or made

Inferior Court Minutes Book 2

Over in trust for myself, or otherwise, and part of My Lands, Estates, Goods, Stocks, Money, debts, Securities, or Contracts Whereby any Money May hereafter become payable, or any real or personal Estate, Whereby to have or Expect any benefit or profit to My Self, My wife, or My heir. So help Me God.

Sworn before
John Ross

John McClure

Whereupon, it is Ordered, That The said John McClure be Discharged after he shall have executed a Deed of Assignment of his Said Goods, Chattels, & Effects to Archibald Clark, who is named and is hereby appointed trustee of the said John McClure, for the benefit of Creditors.

Thos H. Miller
Abra^m Bessent
John Ross

Inferior Court Camden County }
Chambers 5th September 1814 }

Present, their Honors John Ross, Thomas H. Miller, & Abraham Bessent, Esquires, Justices of Said Court.

On Motion of Mr Clark, Administrator of the Estate of Joseph H. Stevens, and producing to the Court Satisfactory Evidence

---

of Notice being published according to Law, that Application would be made to this Court for leave to sell part of Lot N^o [blank] in the Town of St Mary's for the benefit of the Creditors of said Estate, the same being the Only real Estate belong to the same, & further that No person had appeared to gain say the same.

It is therefore ordered, that the said part of Lot N^o [blank] be sold, first giving Notice according to Law.

Thos H. Miller, J. I. C.

True Copy of the Org^l order
made at Chambers
Isaac Crews, Clk

Monday, August 7th 1815, At Chambers. Present, their Honors Thomas H. Miller, William Scott, & William Bailey, Esquires, Justices of Said Court.

On the petition of Charles Deshong, Stating that he is Confined in said County for debt, and that he is Unable to pay all his debts, but that he is Willing to Surrender all his property for the use and benefit of his Creditors, in terms of the laws in such Case Made and provided, and praying for the Benefit of the Insolvent Debtors Act.

Inferior Court Minutes Book 2

It is ordered, that the Said Creditors of the petitioner be summoned to be and appear before the said

---

Justices, or Some three or More of them at the Court House in St Mary's & County aforesaid on Monday, the fourth day of September Next, then and there to Shew cause, if any they have, why the benefit of Said Insolvent Debtors Act shall Not be granted to Said Charles Deshon, and likewise that said Charles Deshon be then and there brought before said Court.

Thos H. Miller, J. I. C.
William Scott, J. I. C.
Wm Bailey, J. I. C.

At Chambers in St Mary's }
Wednesday, 13th Septr 1815 }

Present, ther Honors Thomas H. Miller, William Scott, & William Bailey, Esquires, Justices of the Inferior Court.

It is ordered, that the petitioner ~~be brought~~ Charles Deshon be brought up before the Court this Day.

And, the Petitioner, Charles Deshon, Was brought before the Court, a part of the Creditors of Said Petitioner Not having been Notified of this Meeting of this Court.

It is ordered, that the Said Charles be remanded, And that he be brought before the Court at Jefferson on Monday the 18th Ins^t

---

Instant, and that his creditors be notified accordingly.

Upon the Petition of Suzett Duvall, a person of Colour, praying that Samuel Clark be Appointed her Guardian.

And the Said Samuel Clark having signified his consent in Writing to except said appointment.

It is ordered, that be and he is hereby Appointed Guardian for said Suzette Duvall, on his complying with the usual requisits of the Law.

Francis Richard   } In the Superior Court October Term 1815
Exor of Richard Proctor }
    vs   } Case
Andrew Atkinson   }

Inferior Court Minutes Book 2

Upon the petition of Andrew Atkinson, Setting forth that he is under an arrest and in Custody of the Sheriff under a Bail Writ in the Above case, returnable to the Superior Court in October Term Next, that he is unable to Satisfy the said Debt, or to give bail to answer the Same, that he is Willing to deliver up all his Estate, Real & personal, for the Use of his Creditors.

It is Ordered, that the Petitioner Andrew Atkinson be brought before the Court at the Court house in the Town of Jefferson on the first Monday

of January Next, and that the Creditors of the said Andrew Atkinson have legal Notice, to appear by them selves or Attorney at the time and place afore said to shew cause, if any they have, Why the Said Andrew Atkinson should Not be discharged under the Act of the Legislature fo rthe relief of Insolvent Debtors.

Thos H. Miller, J. I. C.
William Scott, J. I. C.
Wm Bailey, J. I. C.

Monday, September 18th 1815

At a Meeting of the Inferior Court at Chambers in the Town of Jefferson for Special Purposes agreeable to Notice.

Present, their Honors William Scott, Thomas H. Miller, & William Bailey, Esquires, Justices of said Court.

Charles Deshon, an Insolvent debtor, was brought before the Court, agreeable to previous order. No person appearing to gain say the discharge of the said Charles Deshon, under the Act of the State of Georgia for the relief of Insolvent debtors.

And the Said Charles Deshon Surrendered the following Schedule of his Estate & Effects, to wit.

2 Pine tables, 1 Pine Slab, 8 Chairs, 2 dozen plates, 5 dishes, 6 Cups & saucers,

6 Knives & forks, 3 pitchers, 3 Milk Jugs, 1 Turean, 1 Sauce boat, 3 decanters. 1 Vinegar cruet, 1 Pr Salts, 1 Pr Pepper boxes, 1 Pr Musterd pots, 1 Coffey Mill, 2 Chests, 3 Trunks, 2 Pots, 2 Kettles, 1 Spider, 1 frying pan, 1 Pr Waffle Irons, 1 Skimmer, 1 Duch oven, 1 Pr Smoothing Irons, 1 Cradle, 1 Bread tray, 1 Wash Tub, 2 Water Pales, 1 five Dollar Bill on State Bank of Pennsylvania, 3 Candlesticks, 5 Tumblers, 4 Wine Glasses, 1 hog, a Open Account against Jacob Worley One Dollar, Open Account against Lewis Levy for One Dollar

18th Septr 1815   Signed   Charles Deshon

Inferior Court Minutes Book 2

And the Said Charles Deshon took the following Oath, to wit.

I, Charles Deshon, do Solemnly Swear in the Presence of Almighty God, that I am Not possessed of any real or personal Estate, debts, Credits, or effects, securities or contracts, Whatsover, My Wareing apparel, bedding for Myself and family, and the Working tools or implements of my trade or calling, to gether with the Necessary Equipments for a Militia Soldier excepted, Other than are Contained in the Schedule Now delivered, and that I have Not, directly or indirectly, since my Imprisonment or before, sold, leased, Assigned, or otherwise dispose, or made over in trust for my self or Other wise any part of my Lands, estates, goods, Stocks, Money, debts, Securities or Contracts, Whereby any money

---

May hereafter become payable, or any real or personal estate, Whereby to have or expect any benefit or Profit to My self, My wife, or My Heirs. So help Me God.

Sworn in Open Court   Chas Deshon
Thos H. Miller, J. I. C.
William Scott, J. I. C.
Wm Bailey, J. I. C.

Whereupon, it id Ordered, that the Said Charles Deshon be discharged from his imprisonment, And that the Sheriff take possession of said Articles in Terms of the Act of Legislature in that case Made & provided.

Ordered, that the County and Poor Tax for the present Year be and is hereby assessed and that the same be Collected Agreeable to the full extent of the Powers of this Court, vested in them by the Acts of the Legislature of this State. say $^2/_6$ & $^1/_{14}$

Ordered, that Maj^r John Hardin have Letters Dismissary as ~~Adminsitrator~~ Executor of the Estate of Mrs Araminta Dilworth, he having proved to the Court his having given due Notice to that effect.

Isaac Crews, Admor of   }
Abraham Bessent, dec^d }
    vs   } Attachment
Henry Younge   }

Upon the petition

---

of the Plaintiff in the above case, and it appearing to the Court that four Negroes has been levied on, and now are in the Possession of the Sheriff.

On Motion, it is ordered, that the Sheriff of this County do proceed to sell the said four Negroes levied on Under the Attachment aforesaid, on giving the Notice required by

Inferior Court Minutes Book 2

Law. and that the proceeds of the sale of said four Negroes be deposited in the Clerk's office of this Court, tp aide the Judgement or further order of Court.

Upon the application of Catharine Lang & Elizabeth Bailey for Tavern License.

It is ordered, that the Petitioners have license, Commencing from the Eighth day of June last, on their giving bond as the law directs.

On the Petition of John Bailey for Tavern License. Ordred that the said John Bailey have License, Commencing from the first of January last, On his giving bond as the law directs.

Thos H. Miller, J. I. C.
Wm Bailey, J. I. C.
William Scott, J. I. C.

Tax on Suits for Justices of the Courts Decr 8th 1806

All Suits Not Exceeding 100$	1$
from 100$ to 300$	1.50
from 300$ to 500	$2.00
above $500	$3.00

Index

___ Francis, 183
___ rowes
  John, 7
Aitcheson
  William, 178
Alexander
  John, 83
Allen
  James, 6, 8
Ancel
  Peter, 66
Anderson
  George, 106
  James, 9
  Jas., 5
Andrews
  William, 99, 100, 171, 172, 178, 183, 184, 186, 205, 206, 211, 226
  Willm., 96, 170
Aneil
  Peter, 95
Aradundo
  F. M., 223
Archer
  Joseph, 5
Aredondo
  F. M., 208
Armstrong
  Jas., 13
  John, 219
Arodundo
  F. M., 203
Arons
  Elizabeth, 204, 210, 211
Ashley, 36, 84, 89, 109, 136
  John, 183
  L., 194
  Lodewick, 172, 188, 203, 208, 212, 223
  Lodwick, 61
  William, 26, 36, 41, 45, 58, 95, 107, 127, 134, 135, 146, 186, 188, 196, 202, 209, 211, 222, 223
  Willm., 37, 42, 48, 60
  Wm., 20, 202, 205, 213
Atkinson, 19
  Andrew, 228, 229
  Burwel, 79
  Burwell, 60, 96, 99, 116
  John, 179, 225
  Nathan, 19, 54, 55, 68, 88, 96, 110, 136
  Nathaniel, 88
  Nathn., 39
Atwater, 88, 91, 111, 163, 169, 177, 179, 185, 188, 190, 194, 204, 209, 225
  E., 64, 107
  Elihu, 70, 152, 166, 201, 202, 208, 211, 218, 221, 223
Austin
  David, 95
  Davis, 156
  Henry, 156
Bachelott

Index

Jan, 187
Bacon
  Daniel, 4
  Danl., 6
Bailey
  David, 11, 39, 45, 48
  Elizabeth, 210, 219, 220, 231
  John, 15, 27, 36, 52, 57, 68, 79, 178, 186, 206, 217, 220, 221, 231
  John, Jr., 81, 149, 175, 206, 215, 216
  William, 227, 228, 229
  Wm., 228, 229, 230, 231
Baily, 24
  Jno., 24
Bain
  Archabald, 121
Bains
  Joseph, 28
Baird
  James, 126, 192, 193
Baker
  Elias, 117, 157, 213
  Josiah, 109, 110, 117, 120, 135, 138, 140, 147, 181
Baldwin
  John, 169, 174
Balee
  John, 73, 75
Baley
  Anna, 90
  Elizabeth, 118
  John, Jr., 111, 205
  John, Sr., 103, 111
  Matthew, 90
Ballard
  Calvin, 169, 174

Banbury
  Michael, 112
Barber
  Israel, 201, 212, 222, 224
Barca
  John, 36, 79
Barco
  John, 103, 149, 183, 196
Barhoff
  Thomas, 36
Barker
  John, 113
Barnard
  Richd., 39
Barns, 212, 222
Barnwell
  Edward, 118, 149
Bashlot
  John, 187, 193
Bashlott
  John, 187
Bassent
  Abraham, 82
Baxter
  Prince, 212
Bayard
  Nicholas S., 116
Beal
  Nathaniel, 184, 206, 226
  Nathanl., 183, 186, 205
  Nathnl., 170
Beasley, 221
  Daniel, 209, 220
  Jno., 13
  John, 215
Beazely
  John, 4
Beazley

Index

Jno., 5
Beazly
  James, 6
Beesley
  Jno., 16, 19, 22
  John, 57, 59, 149, 170, 191, 216, 217
Beesly
  John, 183
Bell
  Joseph, 96, 99, 100, 101, 116
Belvin
  Wiley J., 5, 13, 16
  Wily J., 48
Bemiss
  Eleazer, 25
  Patty, 25
Bennet
  Jas., 13, 19, 21, 24
Bennett
  James, 4, 6
Bennit
  Jas., 13
Bessent
  Abm., 189
  Abraham, 97, 111, 112, 116, 175, 176, 184, 186, 188, 189, 191, 192, 195, 196, 199, 200, 202, 205, 206, 209, 213, 214, 216, 220, 225, 226, 227, 230
  Abram, 119, 176, 183, 186, 187, 189, 190, 191, 192, 195, 202, 205, 206, 209, 213, 214, 215, 226, 227
Best
  David, 48, 68
  John, 208, 217
Bingham

Jno., 9
John, 5
Bishop
  Larse, 44
  Luerelia, 54
  Luuise, 32
  Thomas, 38, 51, 52, 54
  Thos., 43, 53
Bixby
  James, 206
  Nathan, 200, 202, 206, 208, 217
Black
  Jol., 53
Blackmer
  Stephen, 4, 6
Blair
  James, 222
Blue
  Daniel, 85, 97, 100, 168, 178
Blunt
  Reddin, 23
Bogg
  John, 84
Bogge
  John, 85, 87
Bolton
  John, 143
  Robert, 15, 143
Bond
  Micajah, 200
  Thomas, 96, 99, 100, 127, 131, 141, 149
  Thos., 141, 177
Boog
  Jno., 105
  John, 78, 82, 83, 97, 127, 134, 135, 154, 164, 170
Borel

Index

C., 18
Claud, 46, 69, 83
Claud, Sr., 76
Claude, 17, 38
Bown, 142
Boyd, 122
  Saml., 122
  Samuel, 109, 125, 134, 135, 146, 150, 159, 161, 165, 178, 187, 191, 192, 196, 215, 216
  Susannah, 109, 146, 187
Brazell
  Robert, 101
Brazill
  Mathew B., 37
Briar
  Bena., 6
Briggs
  Elkanh., 6
  Eu., 9
Brinkley
  Brelain, 164
  Britain, 183, 196
Bristow
  David, 5
Brockington
  Daniel, 191
  Daniel, Sr., 225
  Danl., 165, 193
  Danl., Jr., 175, 205, 215
  Danl., Sr., 170, 191, 196, 214
Brooks
  James, 176, 205, 215
  Jas., 170
Brown, 43, 89, 97
  David, 201
  Ephrim, 57, 60, 89, 92, 93, 94, 96, 99, 101, 103

H., 58
Hugh, 5, 13, 19, 21, 24, 25, 26, 36, 57, 58, 60, 89, 104, 106, 108, 127, 134, 135, 201, 204, 225
James, 130
Jno., 22
John, 11, 27, 29, 43, 52, 60, 71, 78, 79, 80, 89, 97, 103, 106, 108, 149, 156, 170, 171, 176, 177
Ogden, 81, 111, 127, 149
Robert, 6, 99, 123, 156
Robt., 6, 13, 16, 20, 21, 61, 96, 99, 116, 150
Browne
  John, 161, 176, 178, 213
Brush
  James A., 208
Bryan
  Langley, 4, 5
Bryant
  James, 103, 108
  Jas., 127, 134
  Lang. T., 13
  Langley, 13, 19, 24, 28, 60, 67, 103, 113, 189
Bryon
  Langley, 45
Bryrant
  Langley, 183
Bryson
  Thos., 13
Buckely
  Jehd., 7
Buell
  Benjamin, 95
Bulkely

235

Index

Jehd., 6, 7
Bulkley
  Jehd., 4, 5, 12, 13
Bullard
  Eleazer, 41, 75
Bullen
  John, 47
Bulleneau
  George, 68
Bullineau
  George, 67
Bullock
  A. S., 14
Burah
  Henry, 38
Burnet
  Jas., 70, 105
  John, 36
  R. L., 156
  Robert, 115, 117, 144
  Robert L., 117
  Robt., 89
Burnett
  James, 85, 96
  Jas., 79, 80, 82
  John, 53
  Robert, 92, 94, 147
  Robert L., 148, 168, 178
  Robt., 57
Burrowes
  Jno., 11, 23
  John, 10
Burrows
  J., 13, 16, 17, 19, 20, 22, 23
  Jno., 13, 15, 19, 43
  John, 12, 16, 22, 24, 36
Busby
  John, 25, 36, 196, 197

Butler
  Pierce, 32
Cade
  John, 99, 115, 123, 175, 205, 215
Cadman, 38
  Robert, 38
  Robt., 46
Call
  Thomas W., 71
Cammel
  James, 53, 55
Campbell
  George, 111, 112
  Jacob, 202, 207
  Jas., 61, 103, 111
  John, 24, 37, 43, 48, 50, 52, 79, 80, 184, 185, 186, 187, 188, 205, 215
Candlesh
  Alexr., 22
Cannon
  Smith, 96, 99, 101, 116, 123
Cardlish
  Alexr., 23
Carnehan
  John, 180
Carnes, 15
  R., 9, 10, 11, 12, 15, 16, 18, 19, 20, 21, 22, 24, 25, 27, 29, 31, 33, 34, 36, 37, 41, 43, 44, 48, 51, 52, 55, 56, 57
  Richard, 6, 9, 21, 29, 30, 35, 36, 41, 43, 50, 51, 54, 56, 68, 94
  Richd., 5, 10, 12, 13, 14, 15, 16, 18, 19, 23, 24, 46, 55, 69
  Thos., 21
Carney
  William, 47, 204, 210

Index

Carr
  Thos., 5
Carter
  Matthew, 192
Cartmell
  Wm., 5, 8
Cashen
  James, 182, 223
Cashin
  James, 191
Cason
  Eli, 175, 205, 226
  Ransom, 170, 175, 205
Caulkins
  S., 27
Celusline
  Francis G., 180
Chadwick
  George, 51
Chase
  Paul, 192
Cheavelear
  John, 31
Cheavlear
  John, 30
Cheely
  John, 203
Cheevlear
  John, 30
Chevlear
  John, 31
Christopher
  Spuce, 46
Church, 19
  Silvanus, 165, 170, 171, 182, 189
  Silvinus, 46
Clark, 61, 83, 88, 102, 106, 111, 118, 120, 121, 136, 137, 138, 139, 153, 165, 177, 179, 180, 186, 188, 192, 194, 209
  A., 188
  Archd., 82, 105, 152, 158, 166
  Archibald, 85, 193, 197, 199, 202, 215
  Ethan, 162
  Jacob, 5, 13, 16, 19, 24, 45, 53, 96, 165, 184, 191, 196, 197, 200, 215
  John, 59, 205
  Samuel, 228
  Sarah, 52
  Thomas, 183, 226
  Thomas, Jr., 127
  Thomas, Sr., 213
  Thos., 165
  William, 38, 103, 106, 108, 127, 134, 135, 191, 196, 215
  Willm., 106
  Wm., 17, 19, 20
Clarke
  Archd., 101
  John, 191, 215
Clayton, 19
  Isaac, 6, 16, 19, 37, 43, 48
  Jacob, 13
Cleaton
  Isaac, 22
Club
  William, 164
Clubb
  George, 82, 90
  William, 39
Coalt, 109
Colder, 28
  John, 31, 32
Coleman

Index

Jno., 5
John, 4, 6
Cone
  William, 97, 99, 155, 175, 203
  William, Jr., 119, 127, 134, 144, 155, 193, 199, 213
  William, Sr., 119
  Willm., 76, 96, 101
  Willm., Jr., 119, 135
Coneway
  Charles, 100
Conner
  Jno., 84
  John, 81, 82, 85, 90, 111, 134, 135, 178, 191, 193, 196, 200, 225
Constable
  James, 74
  Jas., 69
  William, 74
  Willm., 69
Cook, 65, 66, 85, 102, 106, 108, 142, 188, 202, 204
  Ephrim, 164
  Geo., 60
  George, 55, 58, 76, 77
  Isaac, 136
  Moses, 223, 224
  William, 54, 77, 158
  Willm., 53, 61, 73, 75
  Wm., 68, 82
Cooke, 65
Cooper
  Adam, 29, 103, 113, 164, 170, 176, 205, 215
Copp, 82, 88, 110, 135, 145, 153, 163, 180, 190, 194, 212

  Daniel, 118, 120, 127, 148, 150, 185, 198, 204
Corbet
  Winslow, 93
Cornelious
  George, 5
Courter
  Harman, 33
  Harmen, 27, 29, 46, 48, 50, 68
  Harmon, 50, 53, 54, 61, 62, 65, 87, 95, 103, 113, 126, 151, 219
  I. K., 123, 175, 180
  Isaac K., 110, 116, 144, 155, 176, 181, 205, 208, 215, 224
  Isaac Kershaw, 81, 155
Courtis
  Harmon, 38
Courts
  Harmen, 42
Cowan
  John, 224
Cowin
  Robert, 211
Cowling, 165
  S., 152
  Slauter, 82, 84, 85, 87, 89, 94, 97, 102, 107, 111, 117, 126, 147, 152, 156, 165
Cox, 153, 157
Craford
  John, 4, 5
Crawford
  Jno., 13
  John, 16
Cressent
  A. D., 224
Crewes
  John, 7

Index

Crews, 72, 112, 119, 145
  I., 66
  Isaac, 22, 23, 25, 27, 28, 29, 30, 31, 32, 33, 34, 35, 36, 37, 38, 40, 41, 42, 43, 44, 45, 46, 48, 51, 52, 53, 55, 56, 57, 59, 63, 70, 71, 75, 78, 79, 82, 84, 86, 88, 90, 93, 94, 96, 97, 98, 100, 101, 103, 104, 105, 108, 112, 113, 114, 119, 121, 124, 127, 129, 130, 133, 134, 137, 142, 146, 153, 154, 155, 156, 158, 159, 161, 164, 167, 171, 172, 175, 176, 183, 189, 196, 201, 202, 211, 227, 230
  Issac, 25, 29
  J., 161, 162
  Jno., 87
  John, 7, 29, 80, 81, 87, 103, 113, 119, 149, 156, 157, 158, 160, 161, 162, 163, 164, 193
  Joseph, 119, 122, 123, 149
Criar
  Benj., 13
  Bnj., 12
Crocker, 8
Crofford
  Jno., 21, 80
Crowel
  Mathias, 117
  Sylvanus, 117
Crowell
  Mathews, 157
  Matthias, 213
  Silvanus, 213
  Sylvanus, 157
Crowford
  Jno., 67

  John, 63, 79, 80, 81
Crum
  David, 184, 196, 215, 216
Cruse
  Ingle Hart, 170
  Inglehart, 191, 205
  Inglehart, Jr., 225
Cryer
  Thomas, 59, 63
  Thos., 24
  Timothy, 57
  Will, 19
  William, 5, 23
  Wm., 13, 16, 17, 25
Culclaser
  Willm., 79
Culclasure
  William, 82
Culclazer
  W., 80
  William, 90
  Willm., 80, 111
Culclazier
  William, 127, 143, 144
  Willm., 134
Culclazur
  William, 135
Cunningham, 145
Cunninham, 69
Cunns
  Jacob, 5, 9
Currey
  Duncan, 170, 176
Curry
  Duncan, 164, 196, 197, 200, 214
Dallas
  William, 37, 38, 48
Damron

Index

George B., 96
Dance
  Henry, 221
Daney
  Daniel, 132
Davidson
  Geo. H., 64
Davies
  David, 196
Davis
  David, 114, 170, 191
Dawson
  William, 6
Deblieux, 124
  Alexander, 124
Delesslen
  Francis G., 175
Dell
  James, 219
Deloney
  William, 77
Delony
  William, 112
Demot
  Garret, 84, 85
Demott
  Garret, 111, 164, 191, 205, 215
  Garrett, 81
  John, 96, 99, 100, 136, 183, 205, 215
Deshon
  Charles, 200, 228, 229, 230
  Chas., 230
Deshong
  Charles, 227
Devugneau
  Leon, 61
Dewherst
  Samuel, 126
Dewhurst
  Samuel, 151
Dickson
  John, 60
Dillingham
  Simeon, 5, 9
Dilworth
  Araminta, 230
  Jno., 13
  John, 5, 9, 11
Dishon
  Charles, 195
Doer
  Joseph, 30, 31, 32, 36, 38
Doherty
  James, 36
  Jas., 48
Dorr
  Joseph, 44, 45, 46, 53, 61, 87, 96, 99, 116, 136, 137, 143, 186
Dorrel
  Saml., 9
  Samuel, 6
Douglass
  Andw., 6, 9
  James, 116, 139
  John, 116, 139
Dove
  Joseph, 27
Dow
  Joseph, 42
Downes
  William, 111
Downs
  William, 81, 87, 116, 198
  Willm., 84, 85, 123
Doyle

Index

Thomas, 118, 148, 150, 169, 173, 175, 178, 179
Drummond
  Waller, 53
  Walter, 23, 39, 51, 96, 115
  William, 183, 196, 214, 225
Drury
  C. N., 191, 216
  Charles N., 205, 215
  Chas. N., 216
  Mills, 57, 79, 103, 106, 108, 165, 174, 178, 181, 184, 186, 196, 197, 214, 226
  N. S., 191
Dudley
  John, 27, 36, 44, 48
Duksa
  John, 79
Duncan
  William, 99
Duvall
  Suzett, 228
  Suzette, 228
Dye
  Nimrod, 216, 223, 226
Dyer, 52
  Joab, 30, 31, 38, 44
Eason
  John, 5
  William, 4
  Wm., 5
Eaton, 56
  John, 29, 45, 48, 50, 52, 53, 54, 56, 79, 80, 84, 89, 92, 93, 94, 97, 199
Eddings
  William E., 59
  Willm., 68

Edes
  Daniel, 202, 208
Edwards
  Jas., 13
  Jno., 13, 14
  John, 14
Elliot
  William, 6
Elliott, 77
  Alexander, 196, 213
  Alexr., 12, 13, 14, 17, 19, 20, 22, 23, 25, 150, 170, 183
  James, 170, 184, 213, 226
  Jas., 127
  R. M. D. J., 12, 15, 16, 18, 19, 20, 21, 42, 43, 67, 68, 72, 76, 77, 90, 92, 94, 105, 127, 135, 136, 146
  Rachel, 102, 106
  Richard, 52
  Richd., 5, 13, 31, 60, 63, 67, 92, 134
  Richd. M. J., 9
  William, 4, 21
  Wm., 13, 16
Ellis
  James, 96
  Jas., 99, 100
  John, 191
  Thos., 39, 79
Elzey
  Berrey, 162
  Berry, 150, 156, 184, 186, 205
Enas
  John, 53
Ennis
  John, 196, 197, 214, 226
Eno

Index

George, 107
Enoe
  George, 102
Erskin
  James, 183, 191
Erskins
  James, 196, 226
  Jas., 149
Eubank
  Stepen, 22
  Stephen, 36, 60
  Stephens, 68
Eubanks, 55
  Stephen, 25
Evans, 70
  Cadwalader, 30
  George, 58
  Samuel, 173
Evens
  Cadwallader, 25
Everingham
  John, 194, 210, 221
Fabren, 74
Fardy
  Domingo, 61
Farless
  Thomas, 203
Ferrea
  Citizen, 14
Filchet
  John, 171, 172
Filchett
  John, 170, 191, 193, 196, 197, 214, 226
Finch
  Jehd., 5
Fitch
  Andw., 4, 6

Fitzgerald
  Catharine, 180
  John G., 180
Fleetwood
  George, 103
Flood
  Isaac, 72
Floyd, 97
  Charles, 53, 68, 71, 78, 103, 113, 127, 161, 165, 170, 193
  Chas., 72, 73, 75
  John, 53, 63, 66, 70, 71, 72, 75, 78, 79, 82, 84, 86, 90, 93, 96, 98, 99, 100, 103, 104, 108, 112, 113, 114, 115, 119, 121, 123, 124, 127, 129, 130, 133, 134, 142, 146, 147, 153, 155, 159, 167, 193, 194
Follard
  Jno., 5
Forbes
  Enoch, 66
Fort
  Drury, 5, 9, 11, 13, 14, 15, 19, 24, 46
Fotheringham
  Isabell, 185
Fowler
  Jno. M., 12, 13
  John, 5
Frank
  John, 149
  Joseph, 112
Fraser
  John, 218
Freeman
  Stephen, 72
  Stephn., 5

Index

Frohock
  Isham, 96, 150
Gales
  George, 164
Gallagher
  William, 224
Gallop
  Prentice, 39
Gardner, 185
  Thomas, 215
  Thos., 14
Garman
  Christn., 5
  John, 58
Garner
  Harper, 103, 106, 108, 115, 144
  Jno. F., 57
  Thomas, 103, 106, 117, 147, 150, 175, 205
Garvey
  Henrey, 64
  Henry, 60, 63, 67, 127
  William, 50
Garvin, 47, 50
  David, 30, 31, 32, 39, 47, 54, 68, 77, 81
  Thos. D., 32
Garvins
  David, 42
Gascoige
  Richd., 18
Gascoign
  Richd., 76
Gascoigne
  R., 19
  Ricd., 6
  Richard, 4, 27, 51, 81
  Richd., 5, 7, 13, 16, 17, 19, 20, 25, 39, 69, 83, 139
Gates
  George, 115, 123, 182, 207, 221
Gerbel
  John Henry, 115, 138
German
  John, 6
Gibson
  William, 18, 32, 34, 39, 42, 48, 50, 53, 54, 72, 86, 89, 95, 103, 106, 127, 134, 135, 138, 144, 145
  William., 75
  Willm., 46, 73, 82, 136, 138, 139, 140, 143, 144, 145, 147, 148, 149, 150, 151, 152
  Wm., 14, 24, 68
Gilbert
  John, 116
Gillet
  William, 43, 127, 135, 176, 177
Gillis
  R. M., 96
  William, 134
Gillit
  William, 37
  Willm., 96
Gilman
  James, 182, 207, 221
  James B., 210
Gilmate
  Francis, 42
Gilmet
  Francis, 42
Godbread
  Thomas, 196
Godfrey

Index

John, 4, 5
Gojon
  John, 55
Gold
  Saml., 110
  Samuel, 108
Goodbread, 47, 221
  P., 191
  Philip, 4, 5, 13, 14, 25, 57, 82, 84, 85, 87, 92, 93, 100, 106, 109, 111, 127, 134, 135, 136, 149, 175, 176, 177, 193, 205, 206, 209, 211, 220, 225
  Philp., 13, 19
  Thomas, 134, 135, 149, 213, 225
Goodwin
  Francis, 14
Gordon
  Elizabeth, 116, 144, 174
Gorman
  Jno., 13, 19, 25
  John, 26, 32, 211
  Willm., 60
  Wm., 28
Gormon
  John, 58, 61, 79, 103, 111, 113, 117, 147, 156
  William, 58, 60, 97, 117, 148
  Willm., 57, 147, 156
  Wm., 22
Gould
  Samuel, 120, 139
Graham
  Archibald, 218
  Colen, 218, 219
Grant
  Daniel, 193, 194
  Danl., 150, 193

Gray
  James, 5
  Jas., 9
  John, 4, 5
  Stephen, 96, 164, 175, 205, 206, 215, 216, 220
  William, 60
Green
  Daniel, 226
  Isaac, 183, 184, 216
  N. R., 150
  Nathaniel, 78
  P. W., 69, 73
  Peter W., 66
Greene
  Daniel, 176, 205, 206
  David, 216
  Eleazer, 62
  Isaac, 150, 185, 205, 206, 215
  McKeen, 203
  N., 71, 222, 224
  Nathaniel, 82
  Nathanl., 78, 225
  Nathl., 111, 115
  Peter W., 62, 67, 68, 75
Griffin, 117, 135, 147
  A., 57
  Owen, 96
  Saml., 111, 116
  Samuel, 82, 90, 123, 125, 148, 149
Grovenstine
  C., 73, 75
  Christ., 149
  Christopher, 73, 87, 113, 183, 196, 214
  Chs., 103
  E., 68

Index

Grubbs
  Benj., 53, 79, 80, 96, 215
  Benjamin, 115, 123, 150, 191, 193, 205, 206
Guilder
  Philip, 4, 6
Guillemette
  F., 43
Guillemutte
  Francis, 42
Gunby
  Leven, 109, 140
  Levin, 175, 178, 198
Ha___
  Ezekiel, 134
Hacket
  Patrick, 202
Hackett
  ___, 5
Haddock
  Zac., 19
  Zach, 5, 12, 13, 16
  Zachariah, 9, 11, 25, 28, 37, 53
Hagan
  John, 155
  Peter, 116
Hair, 109
Hale
  David, 180, 181, 205
Hall
  David, 165, 176, 177, 178, 179, 226
  Jno., 60
  John, 68
  T., 170
  Talmage, 5
  Timothy, 125, 137, 163, 172
Haller
  John, 28
Halon
  Asa, 79
Halvingston
  James, 197
Hamilton
  E., 64
  Edward, 57, 63, 74, 77, 86, 89
  Edwd., 48, 79, 91
Hammond
  A., 14
  Abner, 5, 13, 17, 55, 58
  Abnr., 20
Hampton
  Jno., 5, 11, 12, 13, 16, 22
  John, 9, 25, 28, 29, 36, 45, 48, 53, 89
  Wade, 179, 201
Haning
  Geo., 57, 58, 60
  George, 60, 63, 64, 65, 69, 94
Hannay
  James, 104, 105, 201, 211
Hanney
  James, 127
Haral
  Moses, 126
Hard
  Benjamin F., 207
Hardee
  John, 111, 149, 164, 178, 179, 180
Hardey, 89
  John, 71, 80
Hardin
  John, 230
Hardy, 55, 84

245

Index

John, 53, 55, 80, 82, 84, 85, 87, 88, 89, 120
Harison
  Jessey H., 120
Harper
  William, 72
  Willm., 72
Harrall
  Abner, 115
Harrel
  Abner, 103, 113
  Moses, 76, 78, 88, 90, 126, 157, 171
Harris
  Buckner, 219
  John H., 75
  Robert, 8
  Robt., 6
  Thos., 5
Harrison
  Jessey H., 150
  Moses, 176
Hart
  Benj., 31
  Benjamin, 30, 31, 32
  Henry, 13, 19, 22, 31, 32, 78, 82, 90, 111, 127, 191, 196
  William, 219
  Wm. L. B., 219
Hatcher
  John, 4, 6
Hayes
  James, 28
Haymam
  Richd., 62
Hayman
  Richd., 73
Hays, 27

Adam, 130
  Hugh, 27
Hayse
  John, 39
Hazard
  William, 68, 73
Head
  J., 126
  John, 177
Heart
  Henry, 13
Hebbard
  E., 72
  Elihu, 5, 22, 23, 24, 38, 45, 72, 87, 182, 184, 207, 220
  Eu., 6, 13, 16, 17
Hebberd
  E., 16
Hebberion, 212
Hebberson, 219, 222
Helverston
  Jas., 13, 16, 24
  Jeremiah, 24
  Jerm., 19
  Jerry, 13
  Jno., 13, 16, 22
  John, 14
Helvingston
  Jacob, 156
  James, 135, 156, 171, 184, 196, 214
  Jas., 134, 170, 171
Helvison
  Jeremiah, 22
Hening
  George, 65, 69
Henning
  George, 77

Index

Herron
  Herron, 78
Higgenbotham
  Amos, 68
Higingbotham
  C., 43
  Courtes, 28, 30
  Courtis, 30, 31, 32, 36
  Saml., 39, 48, 50
Higingbothom
  Burrewes, 100
  Burrows, 97
  Samuel, 50, 88, 99
Hines
  William, 99, 100, 116, 134, 135, 183, 184, 186, 213, 226
  Willm., 96, 123
Hitchcock, 170
  A., 170
  Lucius, 104, 113
Hobkirk
  William, 182, 189
Hodge
  Willoughby, 117, 147, 148, 168, 178
Hoge
  John, 50, 53, 54, 82, 84, 85, 87, 102, 108, 111
  Willia, 111
  Willoughby, 117
Hogue
  John, 48
Holcomb
  Justice, 94
Holleway
  Thomas, 90
Hollings Worth
  Timothy, 211

Hollon
  Asa, 36
Holloway
  Thomas, 82
Holmes
  James, 5
  James M., 48, 50
  Jas., 9
  Jas. M., 13, 50, 60
Holsreter
  Willm., 90
Holsrighter
  Wm., 28
Holsroeghter
  Willm., 28
Holswriter
  William, 94
  Willm., 92
Holton
  Asa, 79, 80, 96, 99, 101, 154, 163, 183, 185, 189, 190, 199, 201, 202
Holzendorf
  John, 118, 121, 125, 148, 191, 196, 201, 214
Homer
  Charles, 53, 54, 73, 82, 90, 111, 121, 127
  Chas., 61, 62, 69, 76
Homes
  Churcer, 42
Honeker
  Benj., 170
  Benjamin, 188, 189, 200
Honker
  Benjamin, 36
Hopkins, 47, 210
  B., 47

Index

E. B., 6
F., 79
John, 27, 34, 35, 37
T., 80
Timoth, 48
Timothy, 39, 50, 55, 61, 63, 70, 76, 80, 84, 88, 89, 92, 94, 96, 99, 100, 103, 118, 126, 127, 128, 140, 144, 145, 146, 151, 152, 154, 161, 183, 195, 202, 207, 214, 225
Horns
  Thos., 39
Hosmer
  Asa, 194, 221
Houston, 55
  John C., 118, 149
How
  John, 30, 31, 32
Howard
  Joshua, 219
  Samuel, 211, 213, 216, 218
  William, 7
  Wm., 5
Howel
  Jno., 80
  John, 55, 79
Howell
  Charles, 60, 90, 127, 134, 135, 175, 205, 225
  Jno., 60
  John, 60, 96, 109, 136, 143, 181
Howley
  Sarah, 126, 157
Hubanks
  Stephen, 11
Hubbard
  Elihu, 116

Hudnal
  Ezekel, 103
  Ezekiel, 165
Hudnall, 126, 137, 152, 153, 160, 161, 162, 182, 188, 223
  E., 165, 181, 188
  Ez., 134
  Ezekiel, 126, 127, 135, 144, 152, 153, 160, 162, 165, 174, 177, 181, 186, 224
  Ezekl., 136, 137, 139, 140, 146, 147, 148, 149, 150, 151, 152
Hudson
  James, 36, 104, 108, 116
  Jas., 6, 57, 58, 76, 79, 81, 106, 123
Hughes
  Thos., 116
Hughs, 145
  Tho., 145, 146
  Thomas, 82, 84, 85, 87, 94, 123, 145, 146, 164
  Thos., 146
Hull
  Ezekel, 84, 85, 87
  Ezekiel, 82
  John, 79, 96
Humphreys
  Samuel, 135
Humphris
  Saml., 90
Hunt
  Philip, 48
Hunter, 74, 137, 138, 142, 163, 189
  J. W., 5
Hutchinson
  J., 59

Index

James, 57, 59, 66, 89, 101, 103, 126, 157
Thomas, 57
Inus
  William, 39
Irwin
  Jared, 133
Ives
  Jarey, 126
  Jerry, 152
Jackson
  Jos., 53
  Joseph, 84, 89
  William, 74
Jamieson, 25, 26
  Jno., 13, 16, 17, 18, 20, 22, 23
  John, 4, 5, 6, 9, 10, 11, 12, 14, 15, 18, 20, 21
Jinkins
  Philip, 6
Johns
  Isaac, 176, 205, 226
  Levi, 191, 196, 215
  Levy, 170, 183
  Silas, 191, 196, 215
Johnson
  John, 212, 218
  William, 159
Johnston, 6, 35, 77, 84, 89
  Ben, 5, 13
  Ben J., 13
  David., 39
  John, 150, 191, 196, 215
  Thomas, 51, 59, 76
  Thos., 69
  W., 112
  Will, 19
  William, 4, 5, 15, 22, 24, 29, 40, 47, 50, 58, 60, 61, 63, 66, 67, 70, 71, 72, 75, 78, 79, 82, 84, 86, 90, 91, 93, 96, 98, 104, 108, 112, 113, 121, 122, 123, 124, 127, 129, 130, 131, 132, 133, 134, 142, 146, 153, 154, 155, 156, 159, 164, 166, 167
  Willm., 48, 57, 58, 60, 71, 72, 82, 147, 153, 155
  Wm., 6, 12, 13, 14, 21, 23, 24
Jones, 42, 55, 56, 71, 87, 88, 109, 116, 136, 140, 163
  ___, 5
  Charles, 204, 209
  D., 55
  D. G., 105, 110, 122, 185
  David G., 70, 97, 109, 111, 120, 123, 140, 152, 164, 182, 184
  David. G., 83
  H., 55, 145
  Hamilton, 68, 104, 105, 106, 141
  Henry, 37, 57, 79, 111, 116, 165, 175, 205, 215, 216
  Jno., 13, 17, 24
  John, 5, 19, 28, 48
  William, 39, 42, 53, 58, 59, 60, 65, 68, 152
  William Goodgame, 186
  William, Jr., 45, 186
  William, Sr., 39, 42, 73, 85
  Willm., 58, 60, 71, 110
  Willm., Jr., 73, 75
  Willm., Sr., 72
  Wm., 14, 20
  Wm., Jr., 14, 68
  Wm., Sr., 85
Jordan

Index

James, 7, 29, 30, 34, 35, 36, 43, 45, 46, 50, 60, 103, 113
Jas., 7, 20, 46, 48, 50, 56, 62
Judson, 23, 32
Jos., 20, 58, 77, 91, 136
Joseph, 5, 11, 13, 14, 16, 17, 18, 20, 22, 24, 32, 33, 47, 53, 116, 143
Juson
  Joseph, 14
Kade
  John, 96, 99, 101
Kanard
  John, 47, 54
Kean
  Alexr., 165, 170
  Samuel, 119
Kedal, 58
Keggan
  Allen, 5, 6, 7, 9
Kelley
  Willm. F., 149
Kelly
  Michael, 224
  William, 176
  William F., 176, 177, 205, 226
Kennedy
  Richd., 4, 6
Ker
  Geo., 177
  George, 68, 99, 106, 163
  George, Jr., 185
  George, Sr., 162, 172
Kern
  John Jordn., 145
Kernan
  Patrick, 32
Kershaw
  Robert, 203, 210, 212, 217, 221, 222
King, 15, 55, 82, 110, 116, 135, 140, 145, 153, 163, 180, 190, 194, 212
  James, 57, 60, 86, 96, 149, 156
  Jas., 58, 60, 76, 80
  Jno., 13, 18
  Jno., Jr., 39
  John, 4, 5, 6, 9, 10, 11, 14, 15, 16, 17, 18, 19, 20, 25, 27, 28, 29, 30, 31, 33, 34, 36, 37, 38, 40, 41, 43, 44, 50, 51, 52, 53, 54, 55, 56, 59
  John, Jr., 48, 50
  Mark, 211
  Saml., 73
  Thomas, 4, 29, 39, 41, 43, 50, 51, 52, 53, 57, 59, 63, 67, 71, 72, 79, 82, 84, 87, 91, 92, 93, 99, 101, 114, 115, 119, 121, 124, 127, 131, 132, 133, 134, 135, 136, 139, 142, 147, 153, 156, 159, 164, 167, 176, 180, 190, 213
  Thomas, Sr., 226
  Thos, 3rd, 74
  Thos., 4, 5, 6, 9, 10, 11, 12, 13, 14, 15, 16, 19, 20, 21, 22, 23, 24, 25, 27, 29, 30, 31, 33, 34, 35, 36, 37, 38, 40, 41, 43, 44, 45, 46, 48, 51, 52, 57, 59, 66, 70, 71, 72, 77, 82, 84, 86, 90, 91, 93, 100, 103, 104, 111, 114, 119, 121, 127, 129, 130, 131, 132, 133, 142, 146, 153, 155, 159, 164, 166
  Thos., Jr., 68, 140

Index

Will, 19
William, 4, 14, 22, 28, 36, 38, 103, 113, 192
Willm., 6, 76
Wm., 6, 7, 12, 13, 14, 23, 24
Kingsley
  Zapheniah, 203, 210
Knight
  Peter, 81, 84, 85, 87, 142, 188
Knowl
  George, 103
Köth
  John, 119
  Jon, 119
Lainhart
  Henry, 89, 93
Lamb
  Thomas, 5
  Thos., 9
Lane
  Peter, 82, 110, 111, 135, 140
  Pierce, 36, 38, 45, 53
  William, 68
  Willm., 53
Laneer
  Hardee, 205
  Hardy, 183, 191, 215, 216, 224
Lang, 56, 112
  Catharine, 231
  David, 170, 171, 172, 191, 205, 206, 215
  Isaac, 37, 43, 53, 54, 71, 79, 80, 88, 94, 96, 99, 101, 103, 112, 118, 119, 154, 170, 171, 178, 183, 195, 200, 210, 220
  Richard, 29, 30, 32, 59, 63, 77, 78, 92, 93, 103, 155

Richd., 28, 31, 36, 58, 60, 61, 63, 67
Lange
  Isaac, 112
Langstaff, 6
Lanier
  Hardy, 165
Lasley
  Silas, 45, 53, 103, 106
Latham
  Amos, 149, 162
Lathrop
  A., 126
  Asa, 82, 84, 85, 87, 98, 100, 109, 111, 177, 181, 185, 189, 199
Laurance, 18
Lawson, 225
Lazarus
  Aaron, 212, 218, 219
Le Roi
  Francis, 82
Lechie
  Alexander, 150, 151, 152, 186
Leckie
  Alexander, 163
  Alexr., 125
Lee
  Hugh, 4, 5, 7
  Jesse, 95
  Jessey, 56, 82, 83, 87, 95
  Jesy, 83
Lehare
  Christobal, 47
Lernard
  Hayns, 181
Leroy
  Francis, 84, 85, 87, 111
Leurry

Index

David, 222
Levy
  Lewis, 46, 61, 66, 82, 84, 85, 86, 87, 88, 111, 116, 125, 151, 164
Lewis
  D., 101
  David, 62, 63, 64, 67, 68, 96, 99, 101, 127, 134, 135, 169, 173, 201, 211, 212, 221, 224
  George W., 47
  Jacob, 132
  Robert B., 5
Lews
  David, 158
Lilley, 175, 179, 183, 189
Lincoln
  Collen, 212
Lindsay
  Amos, 79, 184, 205, 215
  James, 111, 123
  James M., 18, 27, 29, 32, 34, 35, 38, 91, 104, 106, 111, 116
  Jas. M., 24, 106
Little
  Thomas, 170
Lloyd
  James, 104, 113
Lockwood
  Luther P., 199
Loftin
  Stephen, 111
Long, 145
  Elizabeth, 84
Longstreet, 135, 147
Lonstreet, 117
Lopez
  Don Justo, 208, 224
Low

Horatio, 82
John, 92
Lowe
  Denis, 104, 106, 108, 170, 171, 177, 181, 182, 188, 191, 193
  Dennis, 191, 196, 213, 215, 216, 217
  Horatio, 84, 85, 87, 111, 203, 210, 217
  Oratio, 76
Lowes
  David, 222
Ludwith
  Garret, 57, 62
Lunsford
  Samuel, 82
Lusby
  Silas, 28
Lynch
  Michael, 177
Mabrey
  Jorden, 96
  Jordon, 53
  Woodford, 53, 54, 71, 72, 76, 78
Mabry
  Charlotte P., 125, 151
  Woodford, 90, 112, 125, 151, 153, 157
Mackay
  Robert, 116
Macleod, 73
MaComb, 61
  James, 28
  Jas., 24
Macoom
  Jas., 12
Macoomb
  Jas., 13

Index

Madden
  P., 173
  Peter, 64, 102, 136, 169
Magill
  Charles, 130, 183, 191, 196, 213, 226
Makay
  Robert, 143
Malcome
  Willm., 89
Marbury
  Hor., 133
March
  Geo., 6, 7, 13
  George, 4, 6, 7, 8
Marcum, 70
  William, 73, 93, 94, 117, 146, 148, 173, 191, 196, 214, 226
  Willm., 70, 73, 75, 76, 92
  Wm., 144
Marcun
  William, 170
Markum
  Wm., 68
Martin
  Thos., 37
Mase, 109
Mason
  John, 5, 7, 9
Mather
  Daniel, 94, 153, 156, 160
  Danl., 13, 16, 19, 25, 28, 39, 60, 67, 90, 92, 93, 150, 153, 156
Mathers
  Daniel, 22
  Danl., 6
Matin
  Thomas, 37

May
  John, 63, 67, 76, 79, 80, 84, 85, 87, 90, 97, 178, 197, 199, 200, 201
Maybrey
  Woodford, 78
Maybry
  Woodford, 51
Mazells
  Joshua, 63
Mc___allan
  Andrew, 164
McCall
  Tho., 75, 76, 77
  Thomas, 78
  Thos., 47, 68, 72, 73, 74, 75
McCarte
  Jeremiah, 48
McCay
  Joseph R., 143
McClain
  Thos., 8
McClary
  Jno., 6, 8
McClean
  Thos., 4, 5
McCleery
  Jno., 6
McClellan
  Andrew, 170
  John, 111
  Samuel, 187
McClellen
  Andrew, 171
McClure
  John, 216, 222, 223, 224, 226, 227
  Wm., 170

Index

McComb
  Jas., 19
McConnel
  Willm., 79, 90
McConnell
  William, 60
  Willm., 95
McCulley
  Nat, 90
McCullough
  Joseph, 170, 176, 205, 225
McCurley
  R., 79, 80
  Roger, 79, 112
McDonald, 95
McFarlane
  Catharine, 108
  R., 94
  Rob, 68
  Robert, 87, 128
  Robt., 83, 89, 92, 116, 123
McFarlin
  Robt., 72, 73, 75
McGillies
  Randf., 5
McGillis
  R., 13, 19, 21, 22, 23, 24, 30, 31, 32, 60, 71, 78, 138, 139, 142, 145
  Randolph, 16, 22, 29, 30, 35, 39, 42, 48, 56, 72, 91, 115, 116, 130, 138, 139, 142, 214
McGirt
  Daniel, 122, 187
  James, 122
  Zachariah, 122, 131
McGirth
  Daniel, 118
  James, 118
  Zachariah, 118
McGirtt
  Danl., 109
  James, 109, 146
  Jas., 82, 92
  Zach, 82
McIntosh, 41
  Henry, 116, 170
  John H., 34, 35, 36, 38, 40, 45, 46, 47, 48, 50, 51, 52, 54, 55, 56, 57, 68
McKinna
  Charles, 95
McKler
  William, 36
McLuer
  William, 197
McLure
  William, 198
McMillen
  Daniel, 216
  Danl., 205
McMillian
  Alexr., 4, 6
McMillin
  Daniel, 183, 184, 206, 216
  Danl., 184, 186, 215
McMurrey
  John, 59
McNeal
  Daniel, 66, 95
McNiel
  Daniel, 102
McNish
  William, 193, 194
McOwen
  Patrick, 197

Index

Means, 81
Measels
  Charleton, Jr., 68
  Charlton, Sr., 68
  Joshua, 64, 68
Measles
  Charlton, 39
Meazell
  Joshua, 57
Meazels
  Charleton, Jr., 48
Meers
  Saml., 5, 72
  Samuel, 36, 38, 43, 81
  Solomon, 51, 93, 109
Meezeles
  John, 57
Mein
  William, 116, 143
Meirs
  Saml., 46
  Solomon, 57
Mellaine
  John, 27
Mercer
  John, 84, 85, 87, 89, 92, 93, 94
Meserve
  Isaac N., 63, 73, 80
Messault
  Francis, 68
Messer
  John, 137
Metcalf
  B., 61
  J., 61
Mezele
  Charleton, 59
Mickler, 212, 222
  Jacob, 4, 6, 7, 13, 16, 21, 22, 23, 24, 48, 50, 51, 52, 55, 79, 80, 96, 215
  Margaret, 215
  P., 19
  Peter, 5, 9, 13, 16, 25, 36, 55, 57, 111, 165, 223
  William, 26, 52, 103, 168, 190, 194, 205
  Willm., 37, 149, 168
Miclker
  Jacob, 170
Miers, 47, 50
Miller, 73
  Catharine, 222, 225
  Daniel, 119, 128, 160
  Danil, 9
  Danl., 5
  David, 161
  Eli, 37, 44, 48, 50
  Jacob, 169, 172
  John, 171
  N. S., 161
  Nimrod Stanhope, 160, 161
  Phenes, 35
  Phineas, 40, 47, 60, 89
  Thomas H., 170, 215, 216, 220, 225, 226, 227, 228, 229
  Thos. H., 127, 134, 135, 144, 216, 220, 225, 226, 227, 228, 229, 230, 231
Mills
  Joseph, 37, 45, 103
  Will, 19
  Will, Jr., 19
  William, Jr., 5, 11
  William, Sr., 11
  Wm., 7, 16

Index

Wm., Jr., 6, 9, 13, 16
Wm., Sr., 5, 7, 9, 13
Mims, 163, 189
Minis, 74, 137, 138, 142
Mintwin, 142
Mirs
  Samul, 45
Miszells
  Charlton, 28
Mitchell
  Abner, 9
  Joseph, 126
Mizele
  Char., Jr., 215
  Charlton, Jr., 176, 177, 205, 206, 216
  David, 45, 170, 171, 205, 206, 207, 209, 210, 211, 212, 215, 216, 217
  John, 170, 171, 172
Mizell
  Char., Jr., 216
  Charleton, 89, 94, 156
  Charleton, Jr., 92
  Charlton, 150, 156
  David, 96, 149, 156, 183, 211
  John, 103, 108
  Joshua, 111
Mizels
  Charlton, 23
Moles
  John, 191
  Matthew, 57
  Zachariah, 183
Monbray
  Will, 18
  William, 5, 16
  Wm., 9, 13

Monfort
  John, 45
Monson
  Lemuel, 102
Montbray
  William, 6
Moor
  Arthur, 134, 149, 220
  James, 220
Moore, 221
  Arther, 90
  Arthur, 126, 127, 135, 146, 151, 183, 205, 206, 215, 216, 217
  James, 5, 9, 11, 23, 68, 90, 93, 94, 191, 193, 196, 197, 209, 214, 226
  Jas., 13, 16, 25, 53, 62, 92, 95, 170, 171, 172
  Step W., 168, 171, 175, 187, 189, 190, 206
  Stephen W., 111, 165, 167, 171, 186, 189, 195
  Stephen West, 82, 175, 191
More
  Jos., 21, 22
Morgan
  Joseph, 28
Morisson
  George, 55
Morris
  Robert, 25, 30, 32
Motes, 210
  Jas., 60
  John, 170, 191, 193, 196, 197, 214, 226
  Mat, 46
  Mat, Jr., 36
  Mathew, 45

Index

Mathew, Jr., 28
Matthew, Jr., 53
  William, 28, 39
  Willm., 79, 80
  Zach, 186
  Zachariah, 184, 220
  Zacheriah, 213
  Zack, 164
Mott
  Simon L., 175
Mottbray
  Will, 9
Mottes
  John, 53
Moubray
  Will, 19, 20, 21, 22
  William, 18, 21, 22, 24, 38, 39
  Wm., 19, 24
Mudy, 70
  Peter F., 70, 76
Munson
  Lemuel, 107
Mure
  William, 224
Mursault
  Francis, 145
Musles
  Joseph, 39
Mussault, 191
  F., 182
  Francis, 87, 95, 103, 110, 180, 181
Muter
  Robert, 104
Myrick
  Littleton, 201
Naylor
  William, 145

Neely, 87
  William, 85, 99, 127, 140, 164, 172, 211
  Willm., 96
Neilson
  James, 5
Nelson
  James, 51
Newton
  Francis, 82
Niblack
  William, 4, 72, 103, 106, 108, 112, 158, 160, 161, 171, 188
  Willm., 73, 75, 106, 107, 109, 170, 172, 173
  Wm., 5, 13, 16, 17, 22, 25, 68, 106, 107, 108, 109, 172, 173, 174
Nicoll
  A. Y., 47
Niger
  Alexander, 193
Nightingale
  John C., 53, 90, 92, 93, 94
Nix
  James, 36, 48
  Jas., 13
Nixon
  Edward, 85
Nobles, 128
  James, 128, 129, 130, 176, 205
Norris, 39
  Tho., 7
  Thomas, 39, 59, 60
  Thos., 5, 8, 39
  William, 62
  Willm., 69
Norton

Index

Nathan, 96, 99, 100, 101, 116, 123, 164, 177, 184, 186, 197, 205, 206, 215, 216
Nunas
  Daniel, 222
O'Kelly
  L., 16, 19, 21
  Laurance, 5
  Laurence, 9, 11, 13
Oaks
  John, 36, 48, 60, 149, 165, 176, 205, 206, 226
Ogden
  Alexander, 125, 151
Ogier, 110, 120, 138
  Thomas, 117, 147
Oliver
  Francis, 5, 13
  William, 5
  Wm., 8
Oneale, 145
Ordonaux
  Pierre, 144
Ordronaux
  Pierre, 110
Oscar
  Benj., 16, 17
  Benjamin, 16
  Bens, 4
Ostean
  Sol, 150
  Solomon, 175
Osteen
  Solomon, 156, 213, 226
Oswould
  Joseph, Jr., 61
Palmer
  Nathl., 5, 7

Paris
  Jno., 13
  John, 4, 6, 103, 108
Parish
  Ezekel, 96, 99, 101
  Ezekiel, 127
Parker
  George, 213, 216, 218
  Jacob C., 82, 84, 85, 87, 111
  Jno., 6, 9
  Samuel, 211
  Wm., 9
Parris
  Ezekel, 57, 58
  Ezekiel, 134
  J., 55
  Jno., 13
  John, 101
Parrish
  Ezekel, 100
Patterson
  Jno., 83
  John, 23, 42, 45, 46
Paxton, 126, 153, 160, 161, 162, 182, 188, 223
  Henry W., 178
  Robert, 225
Pearce
  John, 216
Pearis
  Ezekiel, 135
  Richard, 106
Pelham
  Richard, 164
Pellum
  Richard, 149, 175, 205, 215
Pelot
  John F., 102

Index

Pelott
  John F., 136
Pendegrass
  Vincent, 218
Pendergrass
  Vincent, 203
Pendleton
  Nathaniel, 106, 185
Penkie
  Augt. F., 91
Pevatt
  James, Sr., 92
Phaup, 89
  John, 94
Philips
  John, 132
Picket, 74
  Seymour, 203
Pickett
  Seymour, 218
Pidge
  Nathaniel R., 178
  Nathl., 169
Plowden
  Wm., 14
Ponder
  Hezekiah, 165, 170
Pool
  Iza, 90
Poole
  Isaac, 116
Pottle
  John, 195
Powell
  George, 82
Powers
  Joseph, 92, 93, 94
  Timo., 5

Timothy, 4
Pratt, 145
  Abram, 140, 145, 162
  Cary, 67, 74
  John, 149
Prevall
  Jas., Jr., 60
  John, 149
  Peter, 53
  Thos., 53
Prevat
  James, 48
Prevatt
  James, 81
  James D., 90, 183, 191, 196
  James, Sr., 89, 111
  Jas., 79
  Jas. D., 92, 94, 127
  John, 37, 48, 50, 57, 58, 60, 68, 96, 116, 123, 156, 183, 184, 186, 196, 214
  Joseph, 90, 92, 94
  Peter, 92, 94, 116, 150
  Petter, 90
  Thos., 68
Price
  William, 194, 202, 208, 217, 221
Priest
  Gabriel, 203, 211
Privall
  John, 60
Procter
  Richd., 58
Proctor, 38
  Richard, 38, 228
Puryear, 89
  Ellis, 94
Ragland

Index

Hudson, 137, 163
Raglen
  Hudson, 189
Rain
  Joseph, 25, 53, 127, 170, 171, 204, 209
Randal
  Archibald, 50
  Peter, 98, 100
Randall
  Archd., 23
Randolph
  Jno. F., 12, 13, 19
  John, 9, 200
  John F., 5, 11, 15, 39
  Thos., 13
Rane
  Joseph, 96
Rea
  Patrick, 66, 73
Ready
  Will, 19
  Wm., 16
Reddick
  David, 46
  William R., 45
  Wm., 6, 9
  Wm. R., 11
Reddock
  David, 46
  Margaret, 215, 216
  William, 54
  William R., 39
  Willm. R., 53, 79
Reddy
  William, 5
  Wm., 13
Reid
  Joseph, 176, 177, 181, 203, 204, 210, 211, 219
Reily
  Thos., 17
Reynolds, 198, 199
Reys
  Patrick, 61
Rhune
  Lewis Conrod, 35
Richard
  Francis, 228
Richards, 66
Richardson
  Edward, 207
Richmond
  Silas, 100, 110, 135
Ridgeway
  Saml., 89
Rigby
  Thomas R., 101
  Thos. R., 101, 120
Right
  John, 130
Ripley
  Robert, 158
Roberson, 145
Roberts
  Elias, 218
  G., 126
  George, 126, 169, 172, 173, 177, 182, 198, 207, 220
  James, 191, 196, 213, 226
Robertson
  Jacob, 165
Robinson
  S., 120
  Silvester, 110, 139
  William, 110, 120, 139

Index

Roceter
  White, 115
Rockwood
  Luther P., 189
Rogers
  Edward, 90
  Edwd., 57
  Neddy, 26
  Thos., 170
Rolinson
  Jacob, 184, 226
Rollinson
  Jacob, 196, 214
Ross
  Jno., 105, 168, 171, 175, 176, 183
  John, 59, 63, 73, 80, 83, 86, 89, 94, 95, 96, 99, 102, 120, 133, 142, 166, 167, 171, 175, 176, 184, 186, 187, 188, 189, 190, 191, 192, 195, 196, 200, 202, 204, 205, 206, 209, 213, 214, 215, 216, 220, 224, 225, 226, 227
  Robert, 99
Rosseter
  White, 138
Rudolph
  Michl., 4, 5
  Thos., 5, 21
Rudulf
  Thomas, 89
Rudulph
  Elizabeth, 27, 47, 55
  Robert, 61, 64, 72, 80, 192, 203, 210
  Robt., 46, 53, 62, 74, 76
  Thomas, 34, 39, 59, 63, 78

  Thos., 10, 16, 19, 20, 24, 46, 93, 116
Sadler, 137, 204, 207, 224, 225
  Henry, 53, 96, 165, 225
  Heny., 202
Sand
  Ray, 84
Sands, 137, 204, 207, 224, 225
  Ray, 39, 57, 68, 89, 90, 125, 150
  W. Wm. P., 92
  William P., 94
  Willm. P., 92
  Willm. Pitt, 90
Sauls
  Isaac, 219
  Saml., 60
  Samuel, 36
Sayre
  Francis, 107
Schueltz
  John George, 59
Scott, 116, 143
  William, 82, 90, 167, 171, 176, 183, 184, 186, 191, 192, 196, 206, 209, 213, 214, 227, 228, 229, 230, 231
  William, Jr., 170
  Willm., 111
  Wm., 168, 171, 175, 186, 189, 192, 195
Seagrove, 41
  J., 132, 133
  James, 9, 11, 15, 28, 29, 30, 33, 34, 35, 36, 37, 38, 39, 41, 45, 50, 52, 56, 57, 59, 67, 91, 93, 96, 99, 101, 104, 108, 112, 114, 116, 121, 124, 125, 127, 129, 131, 132, 133, 134, 138,

Index

142, 145, 147, 150, 153, 156, 159, 163, 164, 174, 188, 189
  Jas., 5, 13, 16, 19, 20, 24, 28, 29, 30, 31, 33, 34, 35, 36, 37, 38, 45, 46, 48, 51, 52, 57, 59, 63, 66, 69, 70, 71, 72, 74, 75, 79, 91, 92, 93, 96, 98, 100, 103, 104, 108, 112, 113, 114, 122, 123, 124, 127, 130, 131, 132, 142, 146, 153, 155, 159, 163, 164, 166, 167
  Robert, 5
  Robt., 69, 74
Seagroves
  Jas., 129
Seal
  William, 223
Semar
  Joseph, 210
Sephens
  Nathaniel, 170
Seton
  Charles, 188, 200
Settle
  Fr., 158
  Francis, 127, 134, 139, 157
  Thomas, 214
Settles
  Francis, 36, 48, 90
  Thomas, 196
Shaffer
  Bethaser, 85
Shearer
  M., 162
Shearman
  Edward, 165, 182, 210
Sheffel
  West, 80
Sheffeld
  West, 67
Sheffield
  Shared, 150
  Sherrard, 156, 170
Sheftel
  West, 64, 79
Sheftell
  West, 60, 80
Shepard
  C. B., 199, 222
  Chancy B., 193
Sherman
  Edward, 221
Shields
  Archibald, 45
Shipweth
  Payton, 79
Shuffel
  West, 63
Sibley, 175, 179, 183, 189
Silber
  John, 53
Silbert
  John, 103, 106, 108
Silcock
  John, 68
Simpson
  John, 90, 92, 94
  Mathew, 79
  Mathw., 11
  Matt, 92
  Matthew, 54, 94
  Matthw, 53
  Matts., 92
  Matw., 90
  Walter, 175, 178
  Wiliam, 22

Index

Will, 19
William, 36, 38, 57, 58, 170, 171, 172, 191, 193, 213
Willm., 43, 58, 60, 90, 92, 93, 94
Wm., 5, 9, 11, 13, 14, 17, 19, 20, 21, 23, 24

Simson
  Wm., 13

Skipwith
  P., 71
  Payton, 56, 60, 72, 73, 75, 77, 78, 91, 92, 93, 96
  Peyton, 98, 114, 115, 119, 121, 122, 123, 124, 166
  William, 122

Skrine
  Thos., 7

Slade
  Fredrick, 199
  Frelhrick, 103

Slaves
  Dick, 118, 122
  Philip, 194

Sleigh
  John, 42, 53, 54, 96, 99, 183, 190

Sliegh
  John, 54

Slocum
  Fitz. J., 219

Smart
  James, 68
  Jas., 60

Smith
  Charl., 13
  Charles, 13, 19, 22
  Ezekel, 36, 53, 54
  Ezekiel, 5, 13, 170, 175, 205, 215
  James, 31, 42, 45, 46, 94, 125, 137, 142, 163, 170, 201, 211
  Jas., 46, 61, 90, 92, 100
  John, 169, 174
  Josiah, 203, 208, 209, 217
  Saml., 5, 11, 13, 16, 20
  Samuel, 9, 11, 30, 31
  William, 81, 90, 127
  William B., 138, 145
  Willm., 79
  Wm., 28

Spalding
  Isham, 5, 12, 13, 81, 90, 111, 116, 170, 183, 197, 215
  Isham, Jr., 196, 197
  Isom, 19

Sparkman
  Jehu, 216
  John, 33, 34, 170
  Levi, 225
  Levy, 33
  Levy, Sr., 34

Sparksman
  Jehu, 184
  John, 196, 215, 217, 223, 224
  Levi, 176, 205, 206, 216, 219
  Levy, 33, 206
  Levy, Jr., 34
  Stephen, 175, 176, 177, 205, 206

Spaulding
  Isham, 25

Speer
  Benjamin, 55, 60

Speers
  Benjamin, 51

S^ت Clair, 89
  John, 94

Stafford

Index

James, 200
Robert, 4, 68, 149
Robt., 5, 13, 16, 19, 22, 48, 90
Thos., 5, 29
Stahl, 137, 141, 142, 150, 177, 180
  Charles, 88, 105, 141, 154, 177
Starrat
  George, 157
Stephens
  M., 189
  Nathaniel, 176
  Nathl., 205
  Richard, 79
  Richd., 12, 13, 14, 16, 17, 19, 20, 24, 60
Sterling
  F., 58
  Francis, 36, 43, 45, 57, 58, 60, 82, 84, 85, 87, 111, 127, 134, 135, 153, 178, 191, 196, 213, 225
Sterrat
  George, 175, 180
  John, 159
Sterret
  George, 90
Stevens, 67
  Joseph H., 227
  Nathaniel, 226
  Richd., 5, 9, 11, 79, 80
Stewart
  George, 198, 199
  James, 191, 196, 197, 214
Stheel
  Charles, 59
Stillwell
  Wm. T., 5
Stoddard, 173

Elijah, 169, 173
Stodert, 169
Stone
  Micah, 208, 217, 221
Stover, 198
Street
  John, 132
Strother, 70
  John, 53, 65
  Rufus, 57
Strover, 199
Stuart
  James, 170
  James C. W., 134
  James Charles William, 134
Studstile
  Thomas, 64
Studstill
  Thomas, 63, 82, 84, 87
  Thos., 60, 67, 85
Sturges
  Danl., 65
Sturgis, 8
Styers
  Michael, 4
  Michl., 5
Suares, 72
  A., 20, 48, 72
  Antoin, 23
  Antoine, 22, 23, 38, 42, 44, 50, 55, 60, 72
  Antonia, 13, 14, 16, 17
  Antonie, 18, 20
Suaris
  Antoine, 36
  Antonia, 7, 8
  Antony, 6
Talles

Index

Arbana, 218
Talley
  William, 36, 57
  Wm., 27
Tate
  Jeramy, 13
  Jere., 5
  Jeremh., 13
  Jeremiah, 11
  Jerm., 16
Taylor
  Charlotte P., 51
  Ephrem, 176, 177, 184
  Jno., 6, 13
  John, 51
  Robert, 68
  Robt., 39, 48
  Selby, 82
  Vincent, 212, 222
  William J., 51
  Wm., 5
Tayson
  Samuel, 194, 208, 217
Teasdel, 58
  Isaac, 75
Terrel, 52
  E. C., 61, 62, 64
  Edward C., 80
Thomas
  Alen, 16
  Allen, 5, 21, 39, 48, 60, 68, 82, 90, 111, 178, 183, 191, 195, 196, 197, 200, 210, 215, 216, 217
  Alvin, 12, 13
  Joseph, 48, 53, 86, 90, 92, 93, 94, 127, 170

Lewis, 81, 90, 111, 170, 183, 186, 205, 226
Thompkins, 155
  Donald, 39, 45, 82, 84, 164
  Donold, 53
  Jno., 57, 80
  John, 72, 79, 82, 164
  Willm., 80
Thompson
  Edward, 51
  Hughs, 95
  John, 165, 183, 185, 186
  Peter, 116
  Ralph, 8
  Wiley, 153, 212
  Wyley, 163, 194
Tinker
  Allanning, 5
Tompkins
  D., 165, 220
  Dold., 214, 215, 216, 225
  Donald, 84, 85, 87, 89, 119, 134, 135, 197, 214, 215, 216, 220
  Donold, 127
  John, 111, 119, 165, 170, 198
Townsend, 69, 72
  James, 77
  Jas., 72, 74, 77
Travank
  John, 28
Travant
  Elizabeth, 32
  John, 32, 33
Trevant
  John, 82
Tucker
  David, 206
  Ezekiah, 44

Index

Ezekiel, 36
Hezekiah, 79
Isaac, 60, 183, 191, 193, 196, 213, 214, 226
Thomas, 45, 79, 111, 175, 176, 177, 213, 226
Thos., 36, 53
Tufts, 185
  G., 181
Tunno, 153, 157
Turner
  Benjamin, 36, 44, 48, 96
  Peter, 95
Tyson
  George, 47
Underwood
  Jahu, 182
  Jehu, 118, 121, 148, 184, 207, 220
Upton
  Nathan, 102, 107
Verry
  Nathaniel, 132
Vickary, 27
Vickery
  Hugh, 32
Vickorey
  Hugh, 42
Vincent
  James, 5, 11, 31, 32, 175, 205, 226
  Jas., 9, 12, 19, 24, 28
  Thomas, 185, 204
Wagner
  Samuel S., 200, 206
Walker
  Berry, 175, 213, 226
  Littleberry, 176, 177
  Robert, 204, 207
Walsby
  Adam, 168, 177
Walter
  John, 57
Walters
  John, 84, 85, 87
  Samuel, 111
Warner
  Philip, 28
Washburn
  Joseph, 5, 9
Waterman
  Eleazar, 76
  Eleazer, 4, 6, 67, 69, 77, 183, 203, 209
  Flavius, 90, 211
  Francis, 201
  Stephen, 33, 179, 208
Waters
  Bird, 219
  John, 82
  Samuel, 81
Watson
  Robert, 82
  Robt., 84, 85, 87
  William, 115, 162, 163, 172, 183, 191, 196, 215
  Willm., 123
Webber
  George, 132
Weeks
  Silas, 165, 191, 193, 196, 214
Weyman, 126, 152, 153, 160, 161, 162, 188, 223
  Edward, 197
  Edward W., 197
  Edwd. W., 149, 160

Index

Wheeler
  Isaac, 59
Whelwell
  Thomas, 200
White
  John, 126, 151
Whitgrove
  John, 32
Whitten
  James, 165, 191, 196, 214
Wilder
  Thomas, 182, 184
Wiles
  Nathanl., 61
  Nathnl., 37
Wilkinson
  Josiah, 165, 191, 196, 213
Williams, 98
  Edward, 158, 191, 196, 213
  Edwd., 156
  J., 64, 65, 66
  James, 37, 56, 63, 64, 68, 71, 84, 89, 98, 100
  Jas., 53, 64, 67, 72, 73, 75, 76, 78, 80, 96, 99, 101
  Ned, 149
  Wilson, 5, 9, 11, 13, 16, 21, 22, 23, 25, 38
Williamson
  James, 164, 172, 183, 196, 199, 214
Williford, 65, 85, 102, 106, 108, 142, 188, 202, 204
  David, 53, 90, 158
Willm.
  John, 69
Willy
  James, 116, 140
Wilson
  Thomas H., 112
Winans
  Josiah, 96, 99, 101, 176, 205, 226
Winslow
  William, 130
Wood, 169, 173
Woodland, 180
  Elizabeth, 211
  James, 4, 36
  James, Sr., 5, 7, 30
  Jas., 13, 16, 19, 21
  Jas., Jr., 22
  Jas., Sr., 7, 13, 14, 21
  Jno., Jr., 5
Woodruff
  Geo., 73
  George, 68, 73, 75, 82, 84, 85, 86, 87
Woodworth
  Darius, 60, 86, 154, 183, 195, 210
  George, 178
Worth
  Thomas, 96
Wright
  Claborn, 50, 103, 149
  Clabourn, 50
  Clay Borne, 45
  Clayborn, 48
  Eave, 18
  Eve, 11, 27, 44, 51, 55, 84
  Habakkuh, 64, 109
  Habakkuk, 19
  Habakuk, 15
  Habk., 22, 37, 43, 48, 60, 67
  Henry, 5, 9, 11
  Hobk., 28

Index

J. N., 20
James, 5, 11
James N., 30, 31
Jas., 13, 22, 25
Jas. N., 12, 16, 20, 22, 23, 47
Susannah, 109
Thomas, 21, 27, 38, 47, 77
Thos., 5, 13, 16, 22, 25, 36, 39, 43
William, 4
Wm., 5, 11
Wylly
  Jas., 163
Young, 212, 219, 222
  Alexander, 4, 5, 101
  Alexr., 7, 9
  F., 31
  Francis, 30, 31, 45, 46, 53, 68, 94, 102, 107, 116, 165, 176, 187, 205, 215
  Francis, Jr., 65
  Franes, 28
  J. D., 193
  John, 6, 9, 79, 80
  John D., 96, 191, 196, 214
  Philip, 212
Youngblood
  Wm., 7
Younge
  Henry, 230